DAVY CROCKETT
AND OTHER PLAYS

AMERICA'S LOST PLAYS

VOLUME IV

A series in twenty volumes of hitherto unpublished
plays collected with the aid of the Rockefeller
Foundation, under the auspices of the Dramatists'
Guild of the Authors' League of America, edited
with historical and bibliographical notes.

BARRETT H. CLARK
GENERAL EDITOR

Advisory Board

A complete list of volumes, with the names of
plays contained in each, will be found on pages
232-3 of this volume.

Davy Crockett

& Other Plays

BY

LEONARD GROVER · FRANK MURDOCK
LESTER WALLACK
G. H. JESSOP · J. J. McCLOSKEY

EDITED BY ISAAC GOLDBERG
AND HUBERT HEFFNER

WILDSIDE PRESS

PREFACE

THIS volume of miscellaneous plays was originally assigned to the editorship of Dr. Isaac Goldberg. Dr. Goldberg had just begun work on the volume at the time of his death. Barrett H. Clark, the general editor of *America's Lost Plays,* then prepared the scripts of these plays for the press and asked the present editor to take over the remainder of the task. Dr. Goldberg had succeeded in assembling photostats of programs of the New York production for each of these plays. Though these productions in some cases did not represent the original productions, they did represent in each instance important productions, and they aided in dating the plays. Dr. Goldberg had also collected a single note on each of the authors whose plays now appear in this volume. Under instructions from the general editor I have not attempted, beyond correcting a few errors, to do more than he has done with the texts reprinted here. As with many of the manuscripts used as texts in the entire series, those in this volume are left largely as they were found, no attempt being made by the editors to establish exact uniformity of spelling or punctuation. I have examined some other typescripts of these same plays but have avoided confusing the purpose of this volume by attempting to note variants. Much yet remains to be done in tracing down productions of these plays, in preparing biographies of their authors and the actors that appeared in them, in studies of sources, techniques, vogue, subject-matter of the plots, characters and characterization. Time, space, and limited materials now available to the editor do not permit such extensive studies for this specific volume, nor was it our purpose to provide such definitive editing. Our purpose has been to make available to future students who would undertake such studies a text of the plays in printed form, with some of the major facts of authorship and production indicated.

HUBERT HEFFNER
Stanford University

CONTENTS

INTRODUCTION

THE five plays which go to make up this volume—*Rosedale, or the Rifle Ball*; *Across the Continent, or Scenes from New York Life and the Pacific Railroad*; *Davy Crockett, or Be Sure You're Right, Then Go Ahead*; *Our Boarding House*; and *Sam'l of Posen, the Commercial Drummer*—are representative of certain popular types of plays that were being written by American playwrights for the American stage during the period that falls roughly between 1850 and 1890. The first of these had its original performance on the stage in 1863, and the last in 1881. Each was a decided popular success when it was first performed in New York City and each continued to be performed season after season. I believe it can be said without contradiction that each of these plays is utterly without literary value or literary pretension. They were each written as stage pieces and conceived entirely in terms of their immediate theatric values. Thus they are excellent examples of that cleavage between literature and theatre that had arisen in the eighteenth century and continued down through the nineteenth to the renascence of the modern drama.

In technique these plays definitely follow the pattern established by refined or "gentlemanly" melodrama. The primary objective of each of the authors is to tell a thrilling and effective theatrical story that will elicit from the audience the most immediate emotional responses; hence in each play the author places his chief reliance upon suspense, continued or enhanced, and upon pathos. The characterizations are very slightly and roughly sketched. They are usually mere examples of the types to be found in all melodrama: the hero, the heroine, the villain, and the comic. Again, as is usual in melodrama, these authors employ a form of immediate surface realism in their compositions which undoubtedly served to give these works verisimilitude to their contemporary audiences. The use of music and the employment of elaborate pantomimic scenes are characteristic of this type of drama and of the technique of the period.

Though the plays are not and make no pretense of being either high comedy or great tragedy, they do have a definite significance for the student of American drama. That significance is in the first place historical. In these popular plays are to be found a record of the theatrical interests and taste of an age, a record of the progress and development of dramatic structure, and an indication of the theater techniques of the period. They are significant as examples of the development of realism on the American stage and in the American drama. They are significant because, with the exception of *Rosedale*, they illustrate the interest in American material, American characters, settings, themes, and idiom. They are a part of that development towards a distinctively, though not a self-consciously, American drama which marks the writings of our playwrights of today.

The texts of all these plays are based on typescripts collected and prepared for the press by the general editor of *America's Lost Plays*, Barrett H. Clark. Only one of them, *Rosedale*, has previously appeared in printed form. *Rosedale; or, The Rifle Ball, A romantic Drama, in Five Acts, by Lester Wallack, Esq.* was privately printed, but not published, in 1890. The typescripts from which the texts have been printed represent stage or acting versions. In no instance was the original script prepared as the basis for a printed or literary edition of the play, though Mr. Clark has collated the typescript of *Rosedale* with the privately printed version, and with a holograph manuscript formerly owned by Clarence Bennett, the author of *The Royal Slave*. The attempt in this volume has been to preserve for the student printed versions of the plays as used by stage managers in their presentation.

In the period represented by the plays in the present volume and up to the contemporary period, authors and owners of play scripts usually did all in their power to keep their plays out of print and out of circulation. This attitude and condition was current because authors and owners had as a rule no control over their plays or protection of their rights once a copy of a play was in circulation. Dion Boucicault had often suffered from the theft and unauthorized use of his plays and consequently had thrown his weight behind the passage of the Copyright Law of 1856. This law was too weak and ineffective, however, to offer playwrights any real protection. Moreover, under the conditions that then obtained among publishers and play agents, there was no method of keeping a real record of the use of a play made by the many local stock companies and the multitude of independent producers throughout the nation. It was not until Bronson Howard had founded the American Dramatists' Club in 1891 and taken the initiative as its first president in pushing through amendments to the copyright laws making piracy of a play a misdemeanor, that American dramatists could print their plays and still control their rights in them. Prior to this, producers and stock companies were usually dependent upon various play agents for scripts if they were not able to secure new scripts directly from the playwrights. These agents obtained their scripts in various ways and many of them frequently had no legal rights to them whatever. A few collections of these unauthorized or "bootleg" scripts are still in existence, and in some instances contain the only available copy or copies of certain American plays. Two of the scripts of plays in this volume, *Our Boarding House* and *Sam'l of Posen,* bear every indication of having come from one of the large stock of such manuscripts that were so widely used up until recent times.

Under these circumstances it is to be expected that various unauthorized scripts of the same play would show wide divergences in text. In many cases the unauthorized version was taken directly from the best and most commonly used version. Each producer would in turn revise, bring up to date, and adapt the script to the specific needs of his company. In general, as Barrett H. Clark says, the unauthorized or "bootleg" versions are easier in style, less "literary," less "English" throughout (in the case of American plays), insofar as the style of the dialogue is concerned; of over a hundred manuscripts so examined by him the majority are in all probability much closer approximations to the play as actually seen by the public than what the author wrote in the first instance. Such alterations frequently led to changes in the form of the play and sometimes even in the cast of characters, as well as revisions in the dialogue. In the process incongruities often crept into the script—incongruities which, like those in the Elizabethan drama, are more noticeable to the reader than they were to the spectator. For example, in the text of *Across the Continent,* which is based upon a transcript of a version loaned to Mr. Clark by the actor and agent, Royal S. Stout, there occurs in the third act a reference to the panic of 1873. The play was first produced July 28, 1870, and presumably represents contemporary action. This reference to the panic obviously indicates a revision of the prior version.

Because the scripts of these plays are definitely the products of successive revisions, it is well-nigh impossible to state accurately the facts of authorship or to apportion shares in the authorship. It is well known that eminent actors in this period frequently bought outright the author's rights in a script and then proceeded to readapt it to suit his needs and those of his production or company. Frank Mayo, who played Davy Crockett in Frank Hitchcock Murdoch's play of that name, had without question a considerable share in the revision of the version used in this volume. *Across the Continent,* which the actor, Oliver Doud Byron, played with eminent success through the United States for many years, was originally written by James McCloskey. Byron bought the play and rewrote it to suit his needs. His son, Arthur Byron, informs me that the version reprinted here is largely the work of his father.

With these general facts in mind, we now turn to the available facts concerning the specific plays.

ROSEDALE,

OR THE RIFLE BALL

Lester Wallack's play, *Rosedale, or The Rifle Ball,* was first presented at Wallack's Theatre in New York on September 30, 1863, with the following cast:

Elliot Grey	Mr. Lester Wallack
Miles McKenna, a returned convict	Mr. John Gilbert
Matthew Leigh, a village doctor	Mr. Charles Fisher
Bunberry Kobb	Mr. George Holland
Colonel Cavendish May	Mr. H. Daly
Sir Arthur May	Miss Emma Le Brun
Romany Rob, a Gipsy	Mr. John Sefton
Farmer Green	Mr. Browne
Corporal Daw, of the Lancers	Mr. Pope
Docksy	Mr. Parkes
Robert	Mr. Palmo
Lady May, mother to Sir Arthur	Mrs. Hoey
Rosa Leigh	Miss Mary Gannon
Tabitha Stork, housekeeper to Matthew	Mrs. Vernon
Lady Adela Grey, mother to Elliot	Miss Fanny Morant
Sarah Sykes, Matthew's servant	Mrs. John Sefton
Primrose, Lady's maid	Miss Mary Barrett
Mother Mix	Miss Carman

The play was announced with new scenery, consisting of the following: Act I.—Rosedale Manor House, with Park and Grounds adjoining; Act II.—Gothic Apartment in the Manor House; Act III.—Interior of Matthew Leigh's Cottage in the Village; ACT IV.—Scene 1, Reception Room in Rosedale Manor House; Scene 2, The Gipsy Dell by Starlight; Act V.—Scene 1, Matthew Leigh's Cottage; Scene 2, Ante-room adjoining the Conservatory; Scene 3, The Conservatory at Rosedale, festooned and lighted for a Ball. The program gave credit to Mr. H. Isherwood and Mr. C. Ingalls for the scenery, and to Mr. J. Timony for the stage appointments. Costumes by Messrs. Flannery and Benschoten were announced as follows: "The Costumes in this play have been selected with the strictest regard to correctness of detail. The Rifle Volunteers, Artillery Volunteers and Lancer uniforms being from paintings imported for the purpose." The incidental music was performed by an orchestra under the direction of Mr. Edward Mollenhauer.

The play was an immediate popular success. It was given one hundred and twenty-five performances during this first season of its run, 1863-1864, and thereafter was repeated season after season for nearly a quarter of a century, with occasional revivals thereafter, some of them taking place as late as the early years of the present century. It was one of the best-known features of Lester Wallack's repertoire, and he continued to play it as long as the Wallack company held together. George C. D. Odell (*Annals of the New York Stage,* Vol. VII, pp. 542-3), in commenting on the original production of this play, describes it as "one of the greatest successes known to our history." The text of the version printed in this volume is based on a typescript obtained by Mr. Clark and collated by him with the privately printed version before-mentioned.

The play is based on a novel, *Lady Lee's Widowhood,* which was first printed in *Blackwood's Magazine.* Though Lester Wallack is generally recognized as the author of the dramatized version, some dispute has arisen over the original authorship. T. Allston Brown (*History of the New York Stage,* Vol. II, p. 252) states that in 1890 Charles Gayler said that *Rosedale* was first written by Fitz-James O'Brien, who was killed in the Civil War. William Winter (*Vagrant Memories,* pp. 88-93) completely and vehemently refutes Brown's statement, saying, "It is *possible,* though *not likely,* that Wallack may have paid O'Brien for doing some slight hack work on an early draft of the play."

Lester Wallack, born in New York City December 31, 1819, and christened John Johnstone, came from one of America's foremost theater families and helped to establish more firmly the enduring reputation of the Wallacks in the annals of our theater. The facts and events of his life and career are so well known and have been repeated so often that it is not necessary to rehearse them here. A brief outline of the salient facts of his life may be found in the *Dictionary of American Biography,* but the most delightful account is to be found in Wallack's autobiography, *Memories of Fifty Years,* published in New York in 1889.

ACROSS THE CONTINENT,
OR SCENES FROM NEW YORK LIFE AND THE PACIFIC RAILROAD

The highly sensational and widely popular melodrama, *Across the Continent,* was originally written by the actor, manager, and author, James McCloskey; but, according to Arthur Byron, the version here reproduced is largely the work of Byron's father, Oliver Doud Byron. I am indebted to Arthur Byron for the following account of *Across the Continent.* This account aids in clearing up questions of authorship and original production.

Mr. Byron became a star and his repertoire consisted of *Don Caesar de Bazan, Ruy Blas* and *Richard the Third*. While on tour in those plays, *Across the Continent* by J. J. McCloskey was produced in New York and was a failure. Later on McCloskey offered the play to Mr. Byron for a cash transaction; to do with as he saw fit. Mr. Byron read the play and told McCloskey he would rewrite it, and bought the play. In its original form Mr. Byron played it in Toronto, Montreal and Quebec, and it failed. By that time the season was over and Mr. Byron went to Long Branch, N.J., for the summer vacation. He rewrote *Across the Continent*, produced it in September, and it was an instant success. He played it for ten consecutive seasons.

According to Odell (*Annals of the New York Stage*, Vol. IX, p. 101) the first metropolitan production of the play occurred at Mrs. Conway's Park Theatre on November 28, 1870, with the following cast:

Joe Ferris	O. D. Byron
John Adderly	J. W. Carroll
George Constant	Mark Bates
Thomas Goodwin	F. Chippendale
Dennis O'Dwyer	W. Lamb
Master Adderly	Willie Shepperd
Ambrose Walsh	J. W. Shannon
James Sallin	Mark Hughes
Thomas Goodwin, Jr.	Mark Bates
Giovanni	W. H. Cooper
Caesar Augustus	A. Queen
Black Cloud	W. J. Ferguson
John O'Dwyer	E. Lamb
Louise Goodwin	Jennie Carrol
Giga	Fanny Reeves
Bridget O'Dwyer	Mrs. Barker
Dolores	Edith Crolius
Susie Lillis	Fanny Reeves

After a successful run at Mrs. Conway's Park Theatre, Byron took the play to Wood's Museum where it was likewise successful. Its sensational New York success occurred at Niblo's Garden. The play opened at Niblo's on July 17, 1871, and despite the summer weather, continued to play until August 11. The following program announcement of the cast of characters and the various scenic and dramatic effects of that production is transcribed from a copy of the Niblo's Garden program for July 29, 1871, now in the Harvard College Library:

ACT I. PROLOGUE

John Adderly, keeper of a barroom, Five Points

         Mr. Charles Waverley

George Constant, a victim of delirium tremens

        Mr. Charles A. McManus

Thomas Goodwin, a merchant prince	Mr. J. H. Jack
Dennis O'Dwyer, the kind-hearted Irishman	Mr. Harry Clifford
Leatherhead, a watchman	Mr. S. B. Duffield
Master Jack Adderly, aged ten years	Mr: S. K. Stroke
Ambrose Walsh ⎱ friends of Adderley	⎰ Mr. E. K. Collier
James Callin ⎰	⎱ Mr. W. Enos
Agnes Constant, the broken-hearted	Miss Lizzie Safford
Mrs. Bridget O'Dwyer, Dennis' wife	Mrs. Brutone

THE WOLF AND HIS CUB.—Fearful Snowstorm.—The Broken-Hearted.
—The Curse of Drink.—Dying in the Streets.—The Orphan Twins
and the Good Samaritan.—The Morning of Life and the Evening of
Death!

*A supposed lapse of twenty years takes place between the Prologue
and Act II.*

ACT II.

Joe Ferris, known as the "Ferret"	Oliver Doud Byron
John Adderly	Mr. Charles Waverley
Knuckle Bone Johnny	Mr. H. Clifford

Thomas Goodwin, Jr., adopted son of the merchant

        Mr. Charles A. McManus

Giovanni, an Italian organ grinder	Mr. Matt W. Snyder
Pablo ⎱ —same sort, with song	⎰ Mr. Mackey
Pietro ⎰	⎱ Mr. Russell
Bilky, keeper of the "Underground Parlor"	Mr. E. C. Kean
Dolore, an Italian Street Arab	Miss Alice Newman
Giga ⎱	⎰ Miss Kate Byron
Francesca ⎰ Italian Street Arabs, with song	⎰ Miss Bessie Sudlow
Beppina ⎰	⎱ Miss Chandler

Scene 1.—VIEW FROM THE STREET, OF PIER 30, NORTH RIVER.—New
Life!—The "Ferret."—The Wealthy Son and the Outcast Gambler.
—*Scene 2.*—THE UNDERGROUND PARLOR.—The following songs and
dances during this scene:

Crossing the Ferry	Miss Kate Byron
Bella Napoli	Miss Bessie Sudlow
Medley of Popular Airs	Mr. M. Russell
Irish Eccentricities	Mr. John O'Neil

Little Dolore, the Street Arab.—Fearful Murder by the Italian.—

Fear of Betrayal.—"Kill Her."—The "Ferret" and "Knuckle Bone Johnny."—Ferret Rescues Dolore from her Brutal Master.—"I Will, Most Effectually."—Dolore's Sad History.—"Knuckle Bone Johnny" Spoils His Best Patent Leathers.—Joe Will Provide for the Innocent Little One.—"Put Me Down for a Front Seat."—Meeting of the Tempter and His Dupe.—"I Feel So Much Better when I Do an Act of Charity at Another Man's Expense."—The Conspirators and the Listener.—"I Have Heard Enough."—The Kiss of Innocence.— The Lights Put Out.—The Italian Kills his Brother by Mistake.— The "Ferret" Still Alive.—"I See the Plot."—"Leave the Instigator to Me."—Animated Tableaux!

ACT III.

Joe Ferris	Oliver Doud Byron
John Adderly, under the assumed name of Ellerton	
	Mr. Charles Waverley
Thomas Goodwin, Sr., a retired merchant	Mr. J. H. Jack
Thomas Goodwin, Jr.	Mr. C. A. McManus
Caesar Augustus, a Shakespearean cullud gent	Mr. Sam Hemple
Bollin, an M.P.	Mr. Enos
Louise Goodwin, twin sister to Tom, and adopted daughter of the merchant	Miss L. Safford
Clara Goodwin, daughter of the merchant	Miss Hattie O'Neil
Susie Lillis	Miss Marian Mordaunt

Thomas Goodwin, Sr.'s House in Lexington Avenue.—The Twins United Again.—The Shakespearean Colored Gentleman.—The "Ferret" Visits His New-Found Friends.—Meeting of the Waifs.— Adderley Under False Colors.—The "Ferret" Will Rid the House of the Reptile.—The Plan of Operation.—Woman's Cunning.—The Mock Faint a Success.—The Despairing Merchant.—The Forged Check.—"I Didn't Tell Him of the Other."—Ellerton's Proposal of Marriage Declined.—One Check Destroyed.—"Now Sign."—"Not Yet."—Sudden Appearance of the "Ferret."—The Son of Adderly, of the Points.—Adderly Attempts to Take the "Ferret's" Life.— Both Checks Destroyed.—Arrest That Man.—Thrilling Picture.

ACT IV.

Joe Ferris, keeper of station 47 P.R.R.	Oliver Doud Byron
John Adderly, disguised as Piegan Indian	Mr. Charles Waverley
Black Cloud, Piegan chief	Mr. W. L. Street
Pretty Bird, Piegan brave	Mr. J. Hammond
Yellow Feather, Cheyenne brave	Mr. Brutone
Thomas Goodwin, Sr., settler of the plain	Mr. J. H. Jack
Caesar Augustus	Mr. S. Hemple

Thomas Goodwin, Jr.   Mr. C. A. McManus
Knuckle Bone Johnny   Harry Clifford
Louise Goodwin, noble-hearted as ever   Miss L. Safford
Clara Goodwin   Miss Hattie O'Neil

Emigrants, Settlers and Indians

ACROSS THE CONTINENT.—Rocky Mountains.—Snowy Peaks and Verdant Valleys.—Station 47 Pacific Railroad.
DEPARTURE OF THE TRAIN.—Joe in His New Home.—Meeting with Old Friends.—Whar's de Cullud Population Gwine to Sleep.—The Tiger at Large.—Black Cloud and Tribe.—Adderly in a New Character.—Yellow Feather, "The White Man's Friend."—Cutting the Telegraph Wires.—Opium in the Indian's Whiskey.—Great Telegraphic Feat.—The Attack.—Thrilling Fight.—Tom's Leap for Life.—Caesar's Fright.—Knuckle Bone Johnny Perfectly at Home in Such a Fight.—"Ferret" Saves Louise.—Danger to the "Ferret."—Terrific Hand-to-Hand Fight Between Adderly and Ferret.—Joe Shot in the Shoulder by a Stray Shot.—Ferret and His Party Overpowered.—The Drowsy Indians.—Opium Has the Desired Effect.—Pretended Insensibility.—"Show Me Your Treasures."—"They Are Here."—The Scream of Joy.

ARRIVAL OF THE EXPRESS TRAIN

Pacific R.R. Train Makes Twelve Miles in Eleven Minutes.—The United States Guard.—Death of Adderly and Destruction of Black Cloud and His Tribe.—TABLEAUX!

For the following facts concerning the life of Oliver Doud Byron I am again indebted to his son, Arthur Byron. Oliver Doud was born in Fredericksburg, Md., in 1843. He made his first stage appearance at the age of fourteen at the Holliday Street Theatre in Baltimore. Then began an association with the Booth family, especially with Edwin and John Wilkes Booth, that lasted throughout their lives. Byron was associated with his best friend, John Wilkes Booth, in the Stock Company of Richmond during the season of 1859-1860 and during later seasons. His acceptance of an engagement in Pittsburgh, Pa., finally terminated his association with John Wilkes Booth.

In Pittsburgh, Byron became leading man of the company. From Pittsburgh he went to New Orleans. At a later date he played with Wallack's Stock Company in New York. During the long course of his career he acted with Adah Isaacs Menken and played Iago to Edwin Booth's Othello. These actors frequently alternated the rôles, Byron playing Othello to Booth's Iago.

In 1869, Byron married an actress, Kate Crehan, whose sister, Ada Rehan, eventually became one of America's greatest actresses. Mrs. Byron's stage name was Kate O'Neil. Ada Rehan made her first appearance in *Across the Continent!* with Mr. and Mrs. Byron. William Gillette and Arthur Byron, Oliver Doud Byron's only son, also made their first stage appearances in that play. In addition to the ten years' run of *Across the Continent!*, Byron produced with his company many other successful plays. He revived *Across the Continent!* around 1888, and continued to play it until about 1895. He discontinued his own company shortly after the successful organization of the Theatrical Syndicate. He retired from the stage in 1912 and died October 22, 1920.

The manuscript from which this version of *Across the Continent!* is taken was owned by the actor and agent Royal S. Stout. He permitted Mr. Clark to transcribe his copy for inclusion in this volume.

DAVY CROCKETT,
OR BE SURE YOU'RE RIGHT, THEN GO AHEAD

Davy Crockett, by Frank Hitchcock Murdoch, is probably the best-known of the American frontier melodramas, a popular type to which *Across the Continent!* may also be said to belong, by virtue of its last act. Apparently the play was written by Murdoch specifically for the well-known actor, Frank Mayo. The manuscript on which this version is based was supplied to Mr. Clark by Professor Arthur Hobson Quinn, who secured it from a member of the Mayo family. Both Professor Quinn and Mr. Clark had access to another manuscript of the same play, which was shorter and otherwise less satisfactory than the one here printed.

Murdoch, who was acting in Philadelphia at the time, did not see the original production of his play by Mayo at the Opera House in Rochester on September 23, 1872. This original production was by no means a success, but Mayo believed in the play and continued to work over the script. From time to time he tried it out on other audiences as he toured from place to place. On February 24, 1873, Mayo brought the piece to the Park Theatre in Brooklyn, and played it with the regular Park Theatre company. In this production Blanche Mortimer played the rôle of the heroine, Eleanor Vaughn, opposite Mayo in the title rôle; J. Z. Little played the villain.

Mayo's faith in the play was gradually being justified, but the real success of the piece and its long run began with the first Manhattan production at Wood's Museum on June 2, 1873, starring Frank Mayo and Rosa Rand in the leading rôles. The following is a transcript of the cast of characters and the program of the presentation at Wood's:

Davy Crockett, aged twenty-five	Mr. Frank Mayo
Eleanor Vaughn, aged sixteen	Miss Rosa Rand
Major Hector Royston, aged forty	Mr. T. W. Keene
Oscar Crampton, aged fifty	Mr. J. J. Wallace
Neil Crampton, his nephew, aged twenty	Mr. Harry Stewart
Yonkers ⎫	⎧ Mr. Charles Sturges
Big Dan ⎬ hunters (his first appearance)	⎨ Mr. C. M. Manley
Briggs ⎭	⎩ Mr. R. J. Lewis
Quickwitch, a lawyer	Mr. L. R. Willard
Watson, an old steward	Mr. G. C. Charles
Parson Ainsworth (his first appearance)	Mr. Welsh Edwards
Little Bob Crockett, aged nine	Miss Aggie Keene
Little Sally, aged six	Miss Mary Page
Dame Crockett, Davy's mother	Mrs. D. B. Van Deren
Little Nelly, aged four	Little Kittie

Act 1—The Pine Clearing,
    "Sunshine under the Trees."

Act 2—The Trapper's Hut,
    "Wolves at the Door."

Act 3—The Trapper's Hut,
    "The Living Barrier."

Act 4—Squire Royston's House,
    "Lochinvar's Ride."

Act 5—Dame Crockett's House,
    "Quickest Marriage on Record."

After the successful production at Wood's Museum and after having played it in various other cities, Mayo again brought *Davy Crockett* to New York City. On March 9, 1874, he opened a successful run at Niblo's with himself and Rosa Rand still in the leading rôles. The other rôles were played by the regular members of Niblo's company. This production, which ran continuously to April 18, further established the success of the play and justified Mayo's faith in it. From this time on until his death on June 8, 1896, Mayo continued to play *Davy Crockett* throughout the United States with continuous popular success and acclaim. One June 9, 1879, he began an English tour with the play at the Alexandra Theatre in Liverpool. Mayo kept count of the number of times he appeared in the play up to his two thousandth appearance, but after that he states that he lost count. He gave his last performance of the play at the Broadway Theatre in Denver on June 6, 1896, just two days prior to his death from heart disease.

SAM'L OF POSEN, THE COMMERCIAL DRUMMER

Sam'l of Posen, by George H. Jessop, is another example of popular farce with definite melodramatic features. Facts concerning the author, the play, and M. B. Curtis, the leading actor in the successive productions, are few and obscure. A play entitled *Sam'l of Posen; or, the Commercial Drummer, a comedy-drama in 3 acts*, by G. H. Jessop, was copyrighted by Jessop in October 1880. In June 1883, M. B. Curtis copyrighted a play entitled *Sam'l of Posen* as the *Drummer on the Road; a comedy in 4 acts*, by M. B. Curtis and Ed. Marble. Prior to this, on May 16, 1881, he had presented the play, *Sam'l of Posen, The Commercial Drummer*, in New York at Haverly's Fourteenth Street Theatre, with success. The program announcement for that production reads as follows: "Limited Engagement of that popular young Comedian, Mr. M. B. Curtis, Who will present, for the first time in New York, a new Comedy-Drama, in Three Acts, by George H. Jessop, entitled SAM'L OF POSEN THE COMMERCIAL DRUMMER [,] Supported by a Company of Superior Excellence." Strangely enough, after this statement and after the cast of characters, the program proceeds to list four acts, as follows:

ACT I.—Winslow & Co.'s Jewelry Store.
ACT II.—Winslow & Co.'s Private Office.
ACT III.—Celeste's Private Club House.
ACT IV.—Uncle Goldstein's Pawnbroker's Shop.

The cast of characters is given as follows:

Sam'l Plastrick	Mr. M. B. Curtis
Mr. Winslow	Mr. Welsh Edwards
Frank Kilday	Mr. Frank Losee
Jack Cheviot	Mr. Nelson Decker
West Point	Mr. Ed. Marble
Con Quinn	Mr. Chas. Rosene
Mr. Fitzurse	Mr. Gerald Elmar
Uncle Goldstein	Mr. R. O. Charles
Folliot Footlight	Mr. Walter Eytinge
Celeste	Miss Albina De Mer
Rebecca Dreyfus	Miss Gertie Granville
Ellen	Miss Carrie Wyatt
Mrs. Mulcahay	Miss Fanny Rouse

Odell (*Annals of the New York Stage*, Vol. XI, p. 257) gives the following account of this performance:

Then, on May 16th, what I venture to call a summer season began with M. B. Curtis, launched into stellardom, in a piece that lasted him for years—*Sam'l of Posen.* . . . According to Allston Brown, Albina De Mer was Mrs. Curtis; Gertie Granville became Mrs. Tony Hart. Allston Brown also assigns Con Quinn and Uncle Goldstein to Charles Rosene; perhaps R. O. Charles is a sort of metathesis of his letters. Sam'l of Posen was a Jewish commercial traveler, with most of the brass required by his profession, and the play involving his activities went into the group of pieces that had carried to fortune such performers as W. J. Florence, John T. Raymond, Lotta and others—pieces that had but little merit as drama, but a happy knack of hitting off national traits in their leading characters. Curtis was able to keep his lucky hit at the Fourteenth Street Theatre until August 6, when the theatre closed for a very few nights preparatory to the operations of 1881-1882.

According to a note left by the late Dr. Goldberg, but without indication of source, the play was apparently first produced in Detroit. Prior to opening in this play, M. B. Curtis had played a number of parts in other New York productions, but all of those were of a seemingly rather minor and unimportant nature. *Sam'l of Posen* was not Jessop's first play to be presented in New York. On April 27, 1879, his *A Gentleman from Nevada,* starring J. B. Polk, opened at the Fifth Avenue Theatre for a successful run. His farce, *All At Sea,* was produced by I. C. Clayton on June 3, 1881.

Concerning the authorship of *Sam'l of Posen,* the following conjectures may be permitted. The play was originally written by George Jessop in three acts and copyrighted by him. M. B. Curtis saw the opportunities that the play offered him as an actor, and bought it outright from Jessop. Either before or after trying out the play in production, he secured the aid of the comedian, Ed. Marble, in revising it. This revision probably entailed the rewriting of the second scene of the third act as a complete fourth act. Since the manuscript on which the text of this version is based came originally from a collection which includes several hundred prompt scripts of plays as they were seen in their most finished form in the larger cities, it is not unlikely that the text here printed is that substantially of the Curtis-Marble revision.

OUR BOARDING HOUSE

Our Boarding House, by Leonard Grover, though it incorporates many of the tricks and devices that characterize the melodrama of its time, is more specifically written as a light comedy or farce than is any one of the preceding plays in this volume. Leonard Grover was for some years, with his brother-in-law, manager of Grover's Theatre in Washington. After a disastrous fire in his theater, Grover gave up the management there and began writing the plays and undertaking the management of various road companies. He succeeded Mrs. John Wood in the management of the Olympic Theatre, New York, in June of 1865. Odell (*Annals of the New York Stage,* Vol. VIII, p. 17) says: "On September 3d, began his first fall and winter season by presenting Joseph Jefferson, for the first time in New York, in his great London success—Boucicault's version of *Rip Van Winkle*." During the following spring, Grover was managing a company engaged in presenting German opera in German. Grover's venture into opera production was evidently none too successful. Though he tried later to return to the production of "regular" drama, he finally gave up control of the Olympic in August, 1867. When the new Tammany Hall was opened in 1869, the Society retained Grover as director of entertainments. Later, after the success of his best-known play, *Our Boarding House,* he appeared frequently in various rôles in productions of that drama.

Grover probably wrote *Our Boarding House* in 1876; at least he copyrighted it on August 19 of that year. It was in the production of this play at the Park Theatre in New York that the two eminent American comedians, Stuart Robson and William H. Crane, first played together and began an association that continued to the time of Robson's death. It was their acting in this production which in large part began and assured the success of the play. Prior to this Grover had, it would seem, tried out the play in various places, including San Francisco, Chicago, and Philadelphia, but without much success. Henry E. Abbey, manager of the Park, evidently perceived the merits of the piece and decided to produce it. The play was at last launched upon its successful career with the production at the Park Theatre on January 29, 1877, with Robson in the rôle of Professor Gregarious Gillypod and William H. Crane in that of Colonel M. T. Elevator.

William H. Crane (in his *Footprints and Echoes,* pp. 85ff.) gives a most interesting account of the arrangements for this production and of his joining forces with Robson:

> It was Grover's comedy, then, that brought Robson and Crane together. In fact, we were, strangely enough engaged for the same part. While I was playing in Rice and Goodwin's extravaganza, *Evangeline,* at the Boston Museum, I received a letter from Henry E. Abbey, of the Park Theatre, in New York, asking me if I would play the leading comedy part, Professor Gillypod, in *Our Boarding House.* The terms were satisfactory and I accepted. A few weeks later I received another letter from Mr. Abbey saying that without his knowledge his partners, A. M. Palmer and T. Henry French,

had engaged Stuart Robson, formerly of the Union Square Theatre, to play the principal comedy part, and he suggested that I accept twenty-five dollars more a week and play the part of Colonel M. T. Elevator in *Our Boarding House*.

I was naturally greatly disappointed, as I wished to make an appearance in New York and I wanted to do so in a part that would be helpful to my reputation and career. Gillipod, I felt sure, would have done this, but I didn't feel I could do much with the part of Elevator. When the play had been done in San Francisco, Joseph Polk, who was afterwards comedian at the Union Square Theatre, had played Gillipod, and A. D. Billings, who was a first old man, had played Colonel Elevator. In Philadelphia the first old man had been cast for the colonel. I felt it was too early in my career for me to become identified with old men parts. . . .

During the rehearsals, I had not been particularly friendly with Stuart Robson, because I felt that he knew that he had supplanted me in the leading comedy part, but that Friday before the opening night, he came to me and said: "Crane, I just heard this morning that you had been engaged for this part that I am rehearsing. Is that a fact?"

"Yes," I said, "didn't you know it?"

"No; and had I known, I would of course have refused to take anyone else's place. If you say so now, I won't play it."

I saw that he was perfectly innocent of any complicity in the matter, and I told him: "I'm going to do the best I can with Elevator, and you and I will get together and do our best to put this **play** over." We shook hands.

Thus started a friendship which lasted to Robson's death, and a partnership which lasted for twelve years with great success.

The cast which performed the play at the Park Theatre was as follows:

Professor Gregarious Gillypod, inventor of the
    great Flying Machine   Mr. Stuart Robson
Colonel M. T. Elevator, a Corn Exchange operator
    (engaged especially for this part)   Mr. W. H. Crane
Joseph Fioretti, a Piedmontese, our last
    new boarder   Mr. W. E. Sheridan
Dr. Amariah Shouter, manufacturer of a
    superior patent medicine   Mr. T. E. Morris
Clarence Dexter, our "Swell" boarder   Mr. Harry Little
Walter Dalrymple, possessed of means,
    desirous to speculate   Mr. H. Stuart

Matthew Eligible, dealer in corner lots, and given
  to occasional flirtation   Mr. J. W. Carroll
Jack Hardy, a detective who "pipes" our
  boarding house   Mr. J. W. Cogswell
Tim, a positive hackman   Mr. John P. Cooke
Alonzo, a colored servant   Mr. J. P. Wilkes
The New Letter Man, on his evening delivery   Mr. F. E. Lamb
Eugenio, a street musician   Master Bogardus
Mrs. Maria Colville, proprietress of our
  boarding house   Mrs. Alexina Fishér Baker
Beatrice Manheim, the teacher at the Conservatory;
  our interesting boarder   Miss Maud Harrison
Florence Manheim, her little child, our
  pet boarder   Miss Allie Dorrington
Mrs. Walter Dalrymple, a sterling woman, wealthy
  and charitable; a new boarder   Miss Virginia Buchanan
Mrs. Violet Eligible, our society boarder   Miss Minnie Doyle
Miss Annie Colville, daughter of her mother;
  just from boarding school   Miss Meta Bartlett
Miss Nash, our amiable boarder   Miss Ella Hunt
Betty, our maid of all work   Miss Roberta Norwood

THE SCENE is laid in Chicago. Time—Midsummer.

ACT I.—WE BECOME ACQUAINTED WITH EVERYBODY AND EVERYBODY
WITH US.

Evening round of the letter man—letters for everybody—Answers
to our Advertisers—Walter and Mrs. Dalrymple engage board—
Our dining room—Our last new boarder—Mr. Joseph Fioretti.

ACT II.—WE FLIRT AND SCHEME.

Matthew Eligible trifles with the heart of little Annie Colville—
Fioretti becomes impassioned over Mrs. Eligible—All the other
gentlemen are enamored with Beatrice—The episode of the diamond
ring—A practical joke played upon Colonel Elevator and Professor
Gillypod, which nearly results in a real duel.

ACT III.—WE ENJOY A PLEASANT EVENING IN THE GARDEN.

Beatrice returns triumphant from the examination at the Conservatory—Many of us saunter to the lake—Gillypod practices his
scene of love-making with Betty—Fioretti tells Mrs. Colville his version of the story of Beatrice's past life, and Mrs. Colville resolves that
the character of our house is endangered by her longer remaining
with us—Poor Beatrice, in the moment of her professional triumph,
is forced to leave us.

ACT IV.—WE COME IN FOR A GAME OF WHIST.

Beatrice recovering, and before her departure, receives a proposal from Walter—She leaves him to impart to Mrs. Dalrymple, his mother, the story of her bitter past—Mr. Dexter tells the story of his love for Beatrice to Mrs. Dalrymple, and entreats her good offices in his behalf—A complication ensues.

But now comes our good friend Mr. Jack Hardy, a detective, all the Pay [*sic*] from New York, and what he does, and how cleverly he gets us into a calm and contented assemblage of boarders, is left for the performance of the comedy to determine.

After the run at the Park Theatre, Grover took *Our Boarding House* on tour, with Crane and Robson in his new company. At a later date, Crane and Robson bought the play from Grover. Despite the sale, Grover tried to use it on the West Coast, but was finally stopped by Crane and Robson.

The text of this version is based upon a manuscript formerly in the possession of Mr. Robert L. Sherman of Chicago, and is a copy of what was used by the stage manager of one of the road productions.

ROSEDALE; Or, THE RIFLE BALL

By Lester Wallack

CAST OF CHARACTERS

ELLIOT GREY

MATTHEW LEIGH

MILES McKENNA

MR. BUNBERRY KOBB

COLONEL CAVENDISH MAY

CORPORAL DAW

FARMER GREEN

ROMANY

DOCKSEY

ROBERT

ARTHUR MAY

GARNER (*no lines*)

LADY FLORENCE MAY

ROSA LEIGH

LADY ADELA GREY

PRIMROSE

MISS TABITHA STARK

MOTHER MIX

SARAH

SOLDIERS, GYPSIES, DANCERS, VILLAGERS, SERVANTS, ETC.

ACT I.

PROPERTIES: *Carpet down in house, white oval top table, three in house 5—6—7. Vases with flowers on table. Branches to cut off tree L.1.E. Garden seat built around tree L.C.3. Garden chairs L.2.F. Note book and pencils, basket, book and blank check, riding whip, silver coin, parasol, jack knife, table and lights under stage, branch on tree L. Music: Eight bars before rise, blank receipt, band up after rise.*

SCENE: *Rosedale Manor with portion of park on R.H.E., an old-fashioned brick mansion. Large, latticed window facing audience, open down to ground, bay window over it. Two similar windows over it in upper side wall. Roses and honeysuckles growing over the house. Large tree L.C. with green bench around it; the foliage very luxuriant and reaching over house. Full tree L.1.E., with branch to cut off. Garden cloths, grass plots and gravel walk. At back a small brick buttress surmounted with stone wall. Lively music at rise. Enter Primrose and Farmer Green L.U.E.*

PRIM. [*Speaking as she enters*]   And do, if you please, Mr. Bean.

GREEN. Green, ma'am.

PRIM. I beg pardon, Green—you're to sit down, and my lady will send you the receipt in a few minutes [*going into house R.*]

GREEN. [*Taking chair C.*] Stop a bit, if you please, Mrs. ———?

PRIM. Primrose—

GREEN. Mrs. Primrose?

PRIM. *Miss* Primrose!

GREEN. Miss Primrose; I wanted to explain to my lady that it was an attack of rheumatism as prevented me from waiting on the steward yesterday, so I comed up the first thing this morning.

PRIM. Very well, Mr. Dean.

GREEN. Green, ma'am, Farmer Green.

PRIM. Ah, well, Green—but we—a—really we see so many farmers and people of that sort, that it's quite impossible to remember names. [*Exits into house R.*]

GREEN. Likely! Likely! Well, for certain, yonder lass do seem to have a tydish opinion of herself. Ecod! if I ever lived to see a daughter of mine wi' such fanciful airs I'd—

PRIM. [*Re-enters with papers*] I've brought your receipt, farmer, and as breakfast is nearly ready—

GREEN. [*Advancing to her*] And I'm peckish—it's very kind of your ladyship's—

PRIM. You had better go!

GREEN. Oh! Very well. Good day, Mrs. Shamrose. [*Going*]

PRIM. Shamrose! Primrose, sir.

GREEN. Ah! well, Primrose. H'it—ah—really, we see so many chambermaids and people of that sort that it's quite impossible to remember names. [*Exit L.U.S.*]

PRIM. Such impudence—

COL. [*Enters down steps R.*] Primrose, your lady up yet?

PRIM. Just dressing, sir.

COL. Does she know that Mr. Kobb and Lady Adela Grey have just arrived?

PRIM. No, sir, but I'll go and tell her. She desired me to inform her the moment they came. [*Exit R. into house*]

COL. When a man is in a position like mine, and is about to play a desperately planned game to get out of it, it behooves him to the last thing, before commencing and without shrinking a single point, however unpleasant, to look calmly at his chance, and place himself boldly, not where he *would* be, but where he is, and coolly and calmly meet his position face to face. So courage, *mon Colonel! En garde!* for the game begins.

LADY F. [*Enters from window R.C. She has a parasol. Down L.H.*] Good morning, Colonel.

COL. Ah, my dear niece, here you are looking as fresh and as blooming as one of the flowers you have doubtless come out to gather.

LADY F. Ah, Colonel, your compliments are always so *apropos.*

COL. Compliments? Oh, nonsense. But, Florence, I have a few words to say to you, which I think you will regard in their true light, for they are simply dictated by good feeling. Why do you shut yourself up, and lead the moping life you do? The mere casting aside of widow's weeds is not everything—you owe it to your health—you owe it to your friends—you owe it to your dear child, to emerge from this dull atmosphere of eternal seclusion—to come once more into the world, to—to—in short, to live!

LADY F. My health? Why only just now you were remarking on my fresh and blooming appearance?

COL. True, true, but—

LADY F. Well, well, Uncle, do not waste any more arguments on the subject, for—

COL. I'm sorry, very sorry, if my solicitation on this point annoys you, but I must insist—

LADY F. Insist?

COL. You do not like the word?

LADY F. Indeed I do not.

COL. And yet you might permit it when it is used merely to press a kindly suit. The time may arrive when I shall use it with some show of right.

LADY F. The time has come, Colonel, when we should thoroughly understand one another, and painful though the subject be, I will now remind you of a few facts of which you are well aware, but which it is requisite you should know *I* do not forget. My late husband, your nephew, Sir Charles May, left all his property, real and personal, to me, his widow—and after me, to his son, Arthur, providing always that I did not marry again without your consent. If I do so marry, you and the child become joint heirs to the estate— you being the guardian of my son.

COL. A wise and excellent provision! His motives were clear enough. He knew perfectly well the disinterestedness of my character, and he took this effectual method of preventing your becoming the prey of some needy adventurer, to whom your beauty and fortune might offer a strong temptation.

LADY F. Be that as it may, you see I thoroughly remember and understand our relative positions and as your words and manner just now implied a threat—

COL. Oh, not at all!

LADY F. Pardon me, they did; therefore I deem it proper to remind you that, although as a near relative of my late husband I shall always be happy to tender you the hospitalities of this house, I deprecate the slightest exertion of authority on your part! [*Crosses*] You have called to my mind that in case of certain action on my part, you have certain rights. I beg to call to *yours* that until that certain action takes place you have *none,* and I venture to hope that in future you will measure your language to me accordingly. [*Exit L.2.E.*]

COL. Humph! A family difference of opinion! So, so, my gentle lady, you have a spirit of your own! All the better guarantee of my eventual triumph! But in the meantime—money! money! By Heavens! I *must* have money, and that directly. Well, well, have I not at least one unfailing resource for is not that the squire coming down the walk?

KOBB. [*Outside, L.H.*] Hall-o-o-o, Colonel, ahooy!

COL. Here I am, squire. Hang it all, man, don't make such a noise. You'll destroy the nerves of all the late risers. [*Enter Kobb, L.U.E.*] Ah, here you are, Kobb, still in the antediluvian style of get up, eh?

KOBB. Stuff! Nonsense! As if a man wanted a better or more becoming costume than that of his father, or grandfather before him. By Jove, sir, the good old county aristocrat is dying out, oozing away, and when he's gone, the country's gone—mind that.

COL. Well, but education—

KOBB. Education? Fiddle faddle! Look at me—I had the education of a gentleman, sir, none of your Eton School and Oxford College trash. No, sir! My father stuck me on a pony, at six years old, and into topboots at twelve, and at seventeen I could shoot better, ride farther and drink deeper than any man for thirty miles around, and as for the girls—

COL. Ah, there I know you were a tremendous fellow.

KOBB. Well, well, that ain't for me to say. Tell you, though, 'tain't always pleasant to be a dasher in that respect. Here, sit down; I'll tell you all about it. [*Points to bench around tree and brings chair forward*] Better to keep things quiet, don't you see a certain person might have heard of it.

COL. A certain person?

KOBB. Yes.

COL. I don't quite—

KOBB. Someone you and I know. Your lady niece, my dear Colonel.

COL. Oh! ah! yes. By the bye, you have certain aspirations in that quarter?

KOBB. Aspirations? Yes, by Jove, I think I have. Don't I show it enough? Didn't I buy this handkerchief because she said she liked blue? Didn't I have the library at the Hall filled with new books because she said she liked learning?

COL. Books? You? And who selected your library? Your head groom?

KOBB. Groom? No, sir. I left it to the bookseller—gave him the size of the shelves to an inch; wait till you see them—quite full—all bound alike—devilish expensive, too.

COL. Ah, bound in Russia, I suppose?

KOBB. Russia? No! damn it! bound in London, every one of them. But I say, old fellow, I know you have great influence over her.

COL. More than influence, I have *power,* my dear friend! If she marries without my consent she forfeits her income and this estate.

KOBB. But it won't do any good to say "no."

COL. Won't it, really? Why, part of what she would forfeit comes to me, and you don't think me quite such a fool as to give this all away to any but a tried friend? [*Rises and takes stage in a meditative manner to R.*] She's a devilish exclusive, highbred superior sort of person.

KOBB. [*L.*] Oh, very.

COL. Her presence always produces a certain effect.

KOBB. Makes me perspire.

COL. Such a woman is not easily to be won.

KOBB. My dear fellow, use your influence for me—do now; I tell you what, I've an odd two hundred by me. [*Takes out pocketbook*]

COL. Two hundred! pooh! my dear friend, five hundred would hardly stand me much.

KOBB. Phew! [*Puts up the book*]

COL. Fact—no—I'm infernally crippled. Lost like the devil on the last Derby—however, we'll say no more on the subject.

KOBB. Hem! Yes, yes, we will. Do what you can for me, and we'll say five hundred. [*Takes out book*]

COL. Five. Humph! I don't know why I should trouble *you* about the matter. My young friend Whittacker, of Fainencourt, would cheerfully—

KOBB. [*Puts up book again*] Why of course he would! A capital fellow! Go to Whittacker by all means!

COL. Certainly. She's been casting sheep's eyes in a certain direction, too. Well, well, her ladyship could hardly do better than to marry a fine gentlemanly young fellow—

KOBB. [*Dragging out book*] Oh, hang it! There, there's a check for a thousand, filled and signed. You shall give me your note by-and-bye.

COL. I'm afraid I'm inconveniencing you?

KOBB. Yes—no—that is—no—not much—not at all. But you'll do what you can?

COL. My dear Bunberry, I'll do all I can and that's not a little, I can tell you; but see, isn't that her ladyship in the geranium walk yonder? [*Off L.U.E.*]

KOBB. Eh? I don't know. Oh [*wipes forehead*], yes it is she.

COL. Well, go and pay your respects.

KOBB. What, by myself? [*They change sides and come down again*]

COL. Of course; offer her your arm.

KOBB. Oh! Come now, Colonel, that's going it for a beginning. No, no, let me alone, Colonel. I shall come out strong at last but quiet and respectable at starting, eh, Colonel? I know 'em. You go leave us alone. All right—eh? Phew!

COL. Good luck attend you! [*Exit through window R.*]

LADY F. [*Enters with parasol L.U.E.*]

KOBB. Good morning, my lady. Phew! I beg pardon, my lady, but isn't it hot?

LADY F. I confess I do not feel it. There's a lovely breee; but your cousin, Lady Adela, arrived with you, I believe. Is she well?

KOBB. Pretty well, thank you, but rather mopy. Seems always to have something heavy on her mind.

LADY F. I don't think she ever quite recovered from the loss of her husband and her son. How is Mr. Grey?

KOBB. Mr. Grey? Pretty well, thank you. He is with his regiment. [*Rosa and Arthur heard outside R.C. window*]

ROSA. [*Outside*] Oh, you naughty little boy. [*Arthur laughs*]

KOBB. Ah, here's that noisy little devil, Rosa Leigh, just when I was getting along so finely.

ROSA. [*Outside*] See if I don't tell your mamma.

ARTHUR. [*Outside*] Do! I don't care.

ROSA. [*At R.C. window*] You don't care! Very well now I'll just—[*Enters through the window*] Ah, Florey, good morning. [*Kisses her*] Good morning, Mr. Kobb.

KOBB. Good morning, miss.

ROSA. Ah, Florey dear, I've got such news for you! Who do you think is coming?

LADY F. But what has Arthur been doing?

ROSA. Oh, nothing of importance; he would insist on putting one of his shoes in the milk, that's all, the darling. But only think, the Gray's Lancers, Elliot's regiment are going to pass through the village. They are visible now from the upper windows about a mile off with the band, all splendid isn't it? They'll pass the park gates presently. One troop is to be left in detachment and quartered in the village. You can invite them to the ball you are going to give to the volunteers. All the servants have scampered off to see them pass. And I had to dress Arthur—and he was so naughty, so good I mean. He only squeezed the sponge down my back and I'm quite out of breath! [*Music. Distant march heard*]

KOBB. [*Aside*] I should think so! Half o' that would have winded me.

LADY F. Is that all your news?

ROSA. Not quite! There's that nasty, great, rough-looking man been asking for you again, but they wouldn't let him in and he's gone away.

LADY F. He here again?

ROSA. Yes, but only for a moment. Oh, he's gone. Don't look so pale, darling, I saw him go. [*Music nearer*]

ARTHUR. [*Enters R.H. from bay window*] Oh! mamma, dear mamma! The soldiers! The soldiers! Do come up to the window! Such flags at the ends of their spears, and such pretty blue coats. Oh, do come!

LADY F. I don't know that I will. You've been a naughty boy, I hear.

ARTHUR. Oh, but dearest mamma, I will be good. [*Music ceases*]

LADY F. And you won't throw water on Rosa any more?

KOBB. And you'll keep your shoes out of the milk?

ARTHUR. You be off, old man Kobb!

LADY F. Arthur! Arthur!

ARTHUR. Well, I beg your pardon, Mr. Kobb. There now come—do come —do come.

LADY F. [*Crosses to window*] Well, come along then, but you don't de-serve it.

KOBB. Not a bit.

ROSA. Mr. Kobb, I wish you would not interfere! [*Crosses to C.*]

KOBB. Not again. [*They are going toward the house when Miles Mc-Kenna coolly walks out from window R.*]

MILES. Good morning, my lady.

LADY F. I thought I told you when last you were here that I forbade you from coming again?

MILES. You certainly did, my lady. It would be a great pleasure to obey your commands but certain reasons make it quite impossible for me to in-dulge in it. Going to breakfast, eh? I've just left the breakfast room. Don't be alarmed! You'll find the tea and coffee where the flunkeys left them. The brandy on the sideboard was more to my taste.

KOBB. Who is this fellow?

MILES. Fellow yourself, old gentleman! Just you keep cool and don't in-terfere with what don't concern you. [*Kobb goes up and gets to R. of Miles*]

LADY F. It is time to put an end to this persecution. I'll not endure it longer! Miles McKenna if that be your name, begone! And never dare to enter these grounds again!

MILES. Grounds! I'll enter the *house*, madam, *how, when,* and *where* I choose! Faith, I know more of it than any of you—which you'll find out some of these days.

ROSA. Ah, do please go, there's a good man. Here, take this. [*Offers coin*]

LADY F. Rosa, I forbid you to give him one penny. Begone at once, fellow, or my patience will give way.

MILES. Will it? Really, mine won't. [*Sits*]

KOBB. Why—you—impudent—

MILES. I've told you not to interfere. If you speak to me again, I'll smash your head!

ROSA. Oh dear! I'll run for the servants.

KOBB. No, miss, that's a man's duty. Remain. I'll go for the servants. [*Hurries off up steps R. into house*]

ARTHUR. Look at old Kobb—but I ain't frightened of him.

LADY F. Arthur!

ARTHUR. [*Rolls up cuffs and goes to Miles*] How dare you insult my mamma! You nasty, dirty brute!

LADY F. [*Takes child away*] Arthur, be quiet, darling, I beg. [*Miles deliberately gets up and with his knife, cuts branch from tree L.H.*]

MILES. Let me see—the servants can't be here yet? No! I've just nice time for it! [*Trimming branch*]

LADY F. Once for all, will you be gone? [*Rosa goes upstage, looking for assistance*]

MILES. Do you think I will take an insult from a toad like that without leaving my marks on his dainty hide? So now, my young friend, I'll just—

LADY F. If you approach him it must be over his mother's body. [*Crosses to Miles*]

ARTHUR. Mamma, dear mamma! [*Miles tears Lady Florence away from Arthur, and lays hold of him. Enter Elliot Grey at same moment from L.U.E.*]

ELL. Hello! I say, my friend, I'll trouble you for that child.

MILES. Will you though, my pigeon? You won't have him, though. [*Music. Elliot makes a movement with his right hand to settle his cap. Miles, thinking he is going to be struck, throws himself into a position of defense. The child runs to Rosa*]

ELL. Did you think you were going to get it?

MILES. No, but damn me—you shall get it! [*Music. He makes two blows R. and L., which Elliot parries, and returns with a terrible facer. Miles staggers, but recovers, and endeavors to renew the fight. Arthur runs to R., looks off, then back to L.1.E.; beckons on servants, who enter just in time to catch Miles as he falls. Colonel May appears at window R. Ladies, etc. enter. Gardener enters from R.1.E. and looks on in amazement*]

ELL. Take away that parcel of damaged goods! And now, ladies, let's go into breakfast. [*Music. Elliot takes lady on each arm, and exits into house R. through window*]

TABLEAU. CURTAIN

ACT II.

SCENE: *An antique room in Rosedale Manor. Sideboard under the window, with pens, ink, and paper on it. Table C. with hand-bell on it. Chairs, etc.*

COL. [*Discovered seated R. of table R.C.*] Upon my honor, this is all very strange. So strange that I'm really glad to find myself in this most retired room of the house, to think it over. This impudent scoundrel appears to know every hole and corner in the building! Why, the servants never seem to know when they may or may not see his exceedingly unprepossessing person pop up before them; there's some mystery here that it might serve my purpose to unravel. [*Rings bell*] I've a great mind to—I'm inclined to think my friend Kobb is rabid enough toward my niece to be worth a few more hundreds to me yet. [*Enter Robert L.1.E.*] Did you find the man?

ROB. Yes, sir.

COL. Very good! It is necessary I should examine him, as I have seen the magistrate and they are ready, if I think it necessary, to send him to jail. Bring him here.

ROB. Yes, sir. [*Going*]

COL. And hark ye! by the servant's staircase. I should not like her ladyship to be annoyed by the sight of him again.

ROB. Yes, sir. [*Exit L.1.E.*]

COL. Yes, there is certainly some game that fellow is playing, which I must ferret out. [*Lady Adela enters down steps L.C.*] Lady Adela, I'm charmed to see you; how uncommonly well you are looking.

LADY A. Ah, Colonel, even you cannot escape using the commonplace nothings with which the world greets the world, regardless of their truth or falsehood.

COL. [*Gives chair. They sit*] You are inclined to be cynical, fair lady.

LADY A. No; but when you tell me I am looking well it almost seems a sneer, knowing as I do, anxieties like mine must leave their traces. But I am glad that I have found you alone; I have faith in your judgment, your coolness, and your knowledge of the world, and I wish to consult you with regard to Elliot.

COL. [*R.*] What, still a bad boy, eh?

LADY A. Believe me, my dear friend, I am serious. You know how anxious his poor father and myself were that he should marry Florence, and it cannot be denied that she gave him encouragement. But the immense wealth and influence of your nephew, Sir Charles May, made him so formidable a rival—especially when her father, to whom she gave implicit obedience, cast his command into the scales, so Florence became Lady May.

COL. And Elliot a misanthrope!

LADY A. No—not exactly that; he became cold—careless of his health, seeking in unwonted, and sometimes objectionable amusements, forgetfulness of the past, and encouraging indifference to the future.

COL. But his profession—he used to be fond of that, and really had the promise of a first-rate soldier in him.

LADY A. He cares for it no longer. The purchase money lodged for his captaincy—

COL. Lost at play?

LADY A. No. Presented to the manager of the Brambledon Theatre, to help him through a bad season.

COL. Why, how did he ever become acquainted?

LADY A. Bless you, didn't you hear of it? He got six months' leave of absence on private business, and went to play an amateur engagement. Turned out a capital actor.

COL. Well, but surely this freak gave you some power over him, were it known at headquarters?

LADY A. Good gracious, it *is* known, but he's such a favorite, they hushed it up. Power over him? Power over *me*, you mean. Why, he says if I bore him about his promotion any more he'll give up the army and go on the stage.

COL. Oh, pshaw! He'd never keep his word.

LADY A. Ah, Colonel, you don't know him. The other night at the Duke of Kinstown's, just because I pressed him to sing when he didn't feel in the humor, he told me to take the consequences, and actually gave a slang comic song he got from a Mr. Sam Cowell of Canterbury Hall. I thought I should have fainted.

COL. And the duke?

LADY A. Made him sing it again.

COL. Well, this is a terrible state of things, certainly, but what can I do, my dear Lady Adela?

LADY A. Oh! Colonel, if you would only exert yourself—[*Robert enters R.1.E.*]

COL. Hush! Well, what is it? [*Rises*]

ROB. We've found the man, sir; he's coming up. [*Exit L.1.E.*]

LADY A. [*Getting towards foot of stairs*] You have business, Colonel— well, another time—

COL. At any time I shall be at your ladyship's service. [*Enter Miles and Robert L.1.E. Robert exits. Miles keeps his hat on all this scene, and when alone with the Colonel is coarse and insolent in his manner*]

LADY A. Well, tomorrow, if you'll allow me, I'll—[*Sees Miles, when a glance of recognition takes place between them, and she utters a suppressed scream*] I'll see you on that subject. Good day, Colonel. [*Exits up steps, L.C.*]

COL. [*Sits R. of table*] Au revoir, Lady Adela. Now my man—

MILES. Now, Colonel!

COL. You know me?

MILES. Well, that's as it may be. I know who you *are*.

Col. Very well distinguished. Sit down.

Miles. No, thank you.

Col. I beg you will.

Miles. Well, if you insist upon it—[*Sits L. of table*] though I give you warning—extreme politeness always puts me on my guard.

Col. Indeed!

Miles. Always. I know my personal appearance don't invite it, so if it's offered there must be some reason for it.

Col. Logic.

Miles. Gammon!

Col. Well, common sense.

Miles. Ah, that's more like it. And now what do you want of me?

Col. Listen—you are now in custody for an assault.

Miles. Well, who got the worst of it?

Col. Why, to be frank with you—

Miles. Frank! Look at my eye!

Col. It certainly was a hard knock. Mr. Grey's hand was a good deal hurt.

Miles. Ah, ha! Good! That's some comfort, at any rate.

Col. Now you have been prowling about the place for some time, and I am told you are a grandson to the former steward here, John McKenna, whose son, your father, ran away and went to the bad.

Miles. Yes, he didn't leave a good reputation behind him when he kicked the bucket; but he left better than that.

Col. Ah, ha!

Miles. Yes; a secret or two concerning this family and another one, which I hold possession of.

Col. I thought so!

Miles. Did you? Ah, Colonel, you're a knowing card, you are! But you've your mate this time.

Col. Have I? Then only think how strong a team we would make if we *worked together!*

Miles. Umph!

Col. Your secrets—are they for sale? Two, you said—two families, I think? Um! Singular that a member of one of these families should have inflicted such severe punishment on you.

Miles. Who said his family was one of them?

Col. You did, just now.

Miles. I did?

Col. Certainly you did, when you saw his mother here just now. Looks, my fine fellow, *looks* can sometimes speak.

MILES. Aye, you're right; you know *so* much, and that's all you're going to know, so you'd better let me go to jail at once! [*Rises*]

COL. Not so fast! I wish to serve you. [*Motions him to sit*]

MILES. Well, answer me a question or two, then, and that'll serve me. Didn't old Mr. Leigh, the parson as died a year or two ago—didn't he leave two sons?

COL. He did.

MILES. Wasn't one of 'em, the youngest, stolen when a baby by gypsies, and never heard of since?

COL. He was.

MILES. And isn't the other living in the village yonder?

COL. He is.

MILES. He's a doctor, ain't he?

COL. Quite right.

MILES. And he's got a sister, ain't he?

COL. Yes.

MILES. And old Mr. Leigh had three children, mate?

COL. Just so.

MILES. Thank you, that'll do. [*Rises*] I say, Colonel, what a blessing a gypsy might be to you just now, eh? [*Leaning with folded arms on the back of his own chair*]

COL. I don't understand you!

MILES. Yes, you do! Lord bless you, only think what a fortune might be made out of that young brat as got me this gash under the eye.

COL. Oh! Ah! By stealing him!

MILES. Exactly.

COL. You mean the reward for returning him?

MILES. Not a bit of it—I mean the reward for *not* returning him.

COL. Why, you scoundrel! Would you dare insinuate—

MILES. Pull up, Colonel, pull up! Don't you come the virtuous game with me. You ain't got it in you. I see'd that in your face afore I'd been ten minutes in your company. [*Goes to door L.1.E.*] Don't be alarmed. I'm not going out. [*Returns*] If Lady Florence May takes a fancy—she's just the woman to marry whether you like it or not—then you and the young 'un share the property; but if there's *no young 'un, you gets it all!* Now you ain't a-going to ask anyone to make way with the—child—*not you,* you wouldn't think of such a thing; but there's a wicked, bad man as would do it without being asked, if he thought he'd get five hundred pounds for it. And—stop—don't you speak—and this bad man wouldn't hurt the child either, but—but he'd take precious good care that no one of his folks ever heard of him again;—

and hush! don't commit yourself. If this same bad man should some day find a certain gentleman's initials cut into the trunk of the old willow near the Black Pond, why he'll think there's five hundred pounds coming this way pretty soon, and he'll feel himself bound to see that boy don't bother a certain liberal gentleman no more.

COL. And what does all this rubbish mean?

MILES. That's it! That's it! That's right! You don't understand none of it, not a bit. Stick to that—but—*don't forget it!*

COL. [*Rises*] There, there, fellow! I've had enough of you. So!

MILES. To jail?

COL. No. You may go where you please, but don't show your face here again. [*Rings bell R.*]

MILES. [*L.*] Excuse me, Colonel, here's a scar [*Touches his wounded face*] I must settle before I leave these parts, and as the settlement may make it necessary for me to leave *dear* old England—why, I should like to take five hundred pounds with me—mum! [*Robert enters L.1 E.*]

COL. Show this man out. I will explain to your lady—[*Going, gets foot on bottom stair*]

ROB. Very good, sir. [*Colonel goes slowly up stairs, pauses at door to see Miles off*]

MILES. I wish you a very respectable good day, sir! I shouldn't forget what you told me, and I hope you'll believe what I promised you, sir. [*To Robert, going*] Going to usher me down, eh? Um! That's very kind. This is such a fine big place, with so many halls and entries—and I'm such a stranger, I might lose my way, eh? Mightn't I? Thank you—after you, sir. [*Music. Exits after Robert, L.1 E.*]

COL. [*At door, looking off. Speaks through music*] Ah, Matthew Leigh and his sister. Umph! I will avoid them for the present. [*Exit door L.C. and off R.H. After a momentary pause, enter Rosa and Matthew, L.C. Rosa has Elliot's dressing-gown on her arm*]

ROSA. [*At door L.C.*] Nobody here! Matthew, dear, you may come.

MATT. [*Enters and descends stairs*] Why, Rosa, this is the old room in the East wing. There used to be *all* sorts of stories about this room, I never believed the half of them. To me it always appeared one of the most comfortable in the house.

ROSA. [*R.*] Well, so it is, with its cosy little bedroom attached. It's a lodging for a prince—and it's going to have a prince for a lodger. But now tell me, how did you get away from the village with so much richness about? [*Puts dressing-gown on arm-chair, near fireplace*]

MATT. Oh, there's nothing more pressing just now at the surgery than an assistant can attend to—and I wanted so much to tell you about Tabitha Stork. She gets worse and worse every day. Nag, nag! row, row! scold, scold! There was never anything like her. I almost wish you were at home again, for she has some regard for you, and the place would be more pleasant with you there.

ROSA. And for you, too, dear Matthew. It's only her queer way. She loves us both dearly, I'm certain.

MATT. Well, I wish she'd find some more agreeable way of showing it, that's all. And how is Florence—Lady May?

ROSA. "Lady May?" What nonsense that is, Matthew! Haven't we known her since we were children together? And didn't you always call each other "Florence" and "Matthew" until lately, when all of a sudden you have become so extremely polite that it's awful to behold? "Lady May"—why, what's the matter with you, dear?

MATT. What's the matter with me, Rosa? You mean to say that you don't know?

ROSA. Upon my word, I don't.

MATT. And you call yourself a woman?

ROSA. I do take that liberty.

MATT. I had always heard that woman's perceptions were so much quicker than ours in matters of the heart.

ROSA. Heart! What heart? Whose heart? Matthew, what do you mean? [*Matthew buries his face in his hands*] Matthew, darling, my own dear brother! I—I do know—I see it all now. [*Falls into his arms weeping*]

MATT. There, there, we must talk no more of this. Enough! We understand each other as brother and sister should. A weary, sad, hapless listless path should be mine, dear Rosa. No—no—not listless, while Heaven gives me strength and knowledge to lessen the sufferings, and perhaps, perhaps prolong the lives of many of my fellow creatures.

ROSA. My own dear, noble brother! But, after all, what nonsense all this is! You are a gentleman born and educated, why should you not—?

MATT. No—no—not for worlds! Even if she could return my love, which I feel and know she could not—do you think her uncle [*Enter Colonel unobserved L.C.*]—the Colonel would give his consent and—, if he refuses, you know the penalty. My mind is made up.

ROSA. And so is mine! The Colonel, indeed! Who's the Colonel? What's the Colonel compared to your happiness and hers? Yes, hers, for who could help loving you, my darling brother! And she *will,* if she does not already. So I'll just go to her at once, and—

MATT. Rosa, if you say one word to betray the confidence I reposed in you, we shall know the misery of the first quarrel in our lives.

ROSA. But, Matthew—

MATT. Not another word on the subject; henceforth a forbidden one between us. In future my energies, my youth, my heart shall be in my profession.

COL. [R.] And a very nice resolve, my friend.

MATT. [C.] Colonel May! I had no idea we had so distinguished a listener.

COL. Listener! My good sir, if people in their energy will express their virtuous resolutions so emphatically, other people may chance to hear them without being actually listening. [*Lady Florence enters unperceived by the other side. Lady Florence and Elliot Grey L.C. down a few steps only*] I did hear, because it sets my mind at rest upon a point, of which I confess I had some misgiving. Stick to your resolution, Mr. Leigh, you may come to eminence after all; and though not quite on a *par* with the pulpit, the army, or navy, still it is an occupation inferior only—

MATT. Inferior to none! As noble an art, sir, as any that taxes the intellect of man. At all times, in all seasons, under every variety of circumstances are our ministrations sought. The summer's heat and winter's cold; storm and sunshine, night and day, alike witness our labors, and attest our fidelity. Among the vehicles which throng your cities' crowded streets, at midday, you may mark the roll of the physician's wheel, and in the still small hours of the night you may hear the sound of his footfall as he traverses the deserted pavement on some errand of mercy. The navy? Is there a blood-stained deck on which he is not found? The army? Is there a battlefield without him? Nay, is he not often the last to leave the scene of slaughter, remaining a voluntary prisoner to the enemy, whose columns find him at his post, ministering to friend or foe alike? The pulpit? Our duties to the human race begin with the first feeble breath of the new-born infant, and we are watchful sentries to the building until its due expansion shall enable it to receive those treasurers with which the minister is prepared to store it. Henceforth our duties lie side by side, body and soul within our united keeping until a greater and a mightier minister than either shall dismiss the guard. [*Elliot and Florence come forward*]

COL. Eloquence, my dear sir, is a very fine gift, but it don't coin money.

LADY F. [*Advancing L.C.*] No! but it coins respect when vindicating his profession and as nobly as you have done, Matthew.

MATT. [R.C.] Bless my soul! Were you there? And—and—who is that? Is it—?

ELL. [*L.*] Of course it is; your old schoolfellow, your everlasting plague—your true friend, Elliot Grey.

MATT. Good gracious, Elliot, my dear fellow, I'm delighted! Why, how you've grown! Pshaw! What a fool I am! Of course you have—Why shouldn't you? And what have you been doing these seven years? Have you seen a great deal of the world? How has it prospered with you?

ELL. So, so, Matthew, so, so, the usual equipoise, good health, some luck, and some disappointments. An Indian campaign, a medal, and—no wounds.

MATT. No wounds! Why, look at your hands!

ELL. Oh! that? I got in that house skirmish; it's of no consequence.

MATT. No consequence? Let me see it. Humph! Cut, inflamed, and swollen. Rosa, come here. [*Speaks aside to Rosa, who exits D.L.E.*]

LADY F. [*To Colonel*] I wish to return you my sincere thanks.

COL. [*R.*] Indeed, Florence, and why?

LADY F. Because you have been the means of developing in one whom I have already esteemed, powers that have my admiration.

COL. [*Aside*] Esteem and admiration! Good, we are progressing. [*Crosses to C.*]

LADY F. [*Takes stage to R.H.*] And now, good people, I must very inhospitably turn you out of the premises, in which I have for the present installed Mr. Elliot Grey. This and the next room adjoining are yours whilst you favor us by remaining at Rosedale.

ELL. Capital quarters, indeed.

COL. [*L., going up stairs about three steps when he turns and addresses Matthew, who is leaning elbow on lower corner of mantelpiece, back to audience*] Oh, well, we'll not intrude! Mr. Leigh, if you will spend an hour with me I have some particularly fine claret in my room, which her ladyship's kindly consideration of a bachelor's whim allows me to keep a small store for solitary imbibing.

MATT. You're very good, Colonel! don't think me churlish, I seldom drink wine. I have a little business with my sister. I shall smoke a quiet pipe on the lawn, and end by driving the old horse home and enjoying the lovely moonlight which I observe approaching. [*Advancing a little to L.*]

COL. Well, each man to his taste. Au revoir. [*Exits L.C.D.*]

MATT. I shall see you again, Flor—Lady May. Elliot, keep particularly quiet, attend to the directions I shall send you, and your hand will be nearly well in the morning. Good night!

ELL. Good night, old boy! I think I shall come down to the village tomorrow. So be ready for a long chat over old times.

MATT. Very well, I shall expect you. [*Exit L.C.D. Put moonlight effect full so that effect may come when lights are checked*]

LADY F. Now, Elliot, install yourself "monarch of all you survey." There's your arm-chair near the fire; you won't find it a bit too warm, for the early summer nights are cold in these parts. And now I'll light the candle—so that's all right. If you wish for anything ring that bell; and now adieu. [*Going up stairs, exits L.C.D.*]

ELL. Good night. And I once thought myself in love with that woman! [*Takes off coat and puts on dressing-gown*] What wretched judges we are of our own hearts; the meeting which was to have revived such recollections has after all passed off in a quiet, rational and almost business-like way! What a monstrous humbug life is. Men talk of healthful excitements. Bah: the true philosophy is to take our luck as it is doled out to us, if not contentedly, at least easily. But love—truth—poetry—happiness—fudge: [*Knock L.C.D.*] Dear Matthew, how his voice brought back old times! [*Knock*] He's not looking well, though; aye, works too hard at the surgery, I suppose. [*Rosa peeps in L.C.D.*] And his sister, I remember seeing her once when her father was living; Rosa, I think her name was. She is grown up pretty. A nice round bit of humanity.

ROSA. [*Aside*] Oh dear! [*Disappears, then knocks loudly at L.C.D.*]

ELL. Come in! [*Rosa enters L.C.D. She has a bandage and a bottle of lotion*] By Jove! Here she is.

ROSA. Captain Grey.

ELL. Thank you, Miss Leigh, for my promotion—but, Mr. Grey for the present.

ROSA. [*Getting down R.H.*] Oh, I beg pardon. I'm sure my brother told me to say that this cloth is to be kept around your wrist—you are to wet it with the lotion every half-hour unless you are asleep, and then you needn't. [*She has placed basin on the table, poured lotion in it, and wets bandage*]

ELL. Thank you! You are very kind to bring it yourself.

ROSA. I thought it better to bring it because—because if you'll allow me, I think I understand how to bind it on, Mr. Grey.

ELL. Oh, I really don't like to give you the trouble.

ROSA. Not the least trouble in the world, I assure you; if you'll just hold out your arm—thank you. [*She proceeds to dress wound*] Now, then, a little this way. Thank you—there.

ELL. Is it done?

ROSA. Yes! no—there's a wrong twist in it.

ELL. [*Aside*] I rather like this.

ROSA. Now then, we are all right.

Ell. Stop! there's something hurts me.

Rosa. Where?

Ell. I don't know—but it hurts deucedly. You had better take it off again.

Rosa. We'll have it right this time. I won't tie it. I'll pin it.

Ell. Do—ah!

Rosa. What's the matter?

Ell. The pin!

Rosa. Oh, it's not in your hand?

Ell. Only about half an inch.

Rosa. Oh, I'm so sorry.

Ell. You'd better take it off again.

Rosa. Oh dear! oh dear! how awkward I am. There, where is it? I don't see the wound.

Ell. Closed up. I've a wonderful skin for healing. Now, we'll try once more.

Rosa. Yes. There so; is that right?

Ell. I'm afraid it is—I mean yes—oh, quite. Thank you.

Rosa. Good night. [*Crossing to steps*]

Ell. You didn't look at the other hand—

Rosa. [*Down*] Why, is that hurt, too? [*Down L.H.*]

Ell. Not at all. But—it may be some day. However—never mind.

Rosa. Good night, Mr. Grey. [*Going up stairs*]

Ell. I beg your pardon, one word: your brother always called me Elliot.

Rosa. Good night, Elliot. [*Exit L.C.D.*]

Ell. Good night, Miss Leigh! [*Knock at L.C.D.*] Come in.

Rosa. [*Looks in*] I beg your pardon; my brother always calls me Rosa.

Ell. Good night, Rosa.

Rosa. Good night, Elliot. [*Disappears, mind lights*]

Ell. What an excessively nice little thing she has become! Now, if I had a sister like that it would be something worth living for. Lucky fellow, that Matthew. [*Goes to window R.*] What a heavenly night—dim firelight, bright moonlight—and [*Blows out the candle*] no wax light, I thank you! Charming indeed! I have a great mind to join Matthew in a cigar on the lawn; but no, I had my orders and promised obedience. [*Sits in armchair*] Well, this is really cozy; nice hand, Rosa, and a lovely arm. I always had a weakness for handsome arms. [*Yawns*] I wonder if she can play the harp. [*Yawns*] Graceful thing when nicely done. Who the deuce wants to go to bed, with such a chair as this to—to—to—go—to—sleep—[*Music. He sleeps in chair. Panel of secret door R.C., slowly opens and Miles appears in opening, with moonlight shining through window, full upon him. He comes quietly forward*]

MILES. Confound the place! The old fellow must have been half seas over when he mapped it out, I think. Let's see—"through the trap on the left of the landing, feel the wall all the way with your left hand, till you're stopped; then for an iron clamp on your right. Press that down and a secret door will bring you into an old room in the east wing." Well so far, so good. If it wasn't so dark I would swear this was the same room I left half an hour ago. [*Feels way to table R.H.*] Umph, candle! The very thing—where's my match-box? All right, now we shall see. [*Lights candle. Lights partially up*] What was t'other directions? [*Takes paper out of pocket, holds it back of candle, and reads*] Um-um-ah: here it is: "Press to the left the leaf ornament cut in the mantelpiece, the one nearest the corridor. A recess will reveal itself, and in that is your fortune, the proof that will be the making of you." All right. But first, I'll lock the door. [*Locks door L.1.E.*] If the old cavalier ancestors of this family had known the use their secret contrivance would some day be put to, my eyes—how they would stare! So—so—here we are, all right. [*Presses ornament on mantelpiece, an opening is revealed, into which he puts his hand and draws forth a small leathern bag and box*] By Jove, the old chap was a man of his word, and I'm a made man for life! [*He has pocketed the bag and box, and turning round, for the first time, sees Elliot who, awakened by a slight noise, is staring at him*]

ELL. Well, if I'm asleep, that's about the ugliest dream I ever had.

MILES. You'll find it the worst reality, young man. Why, this is glorious! I'm up to my neck in luck tonight.

ELL. What do you want, fellow?

MILES. I want you to sit and listen to me for one minute. You are alone—unarmed—with a disabled hand. Look at this. [*Takes hammer from his pocket*] If you make a movement to escape, or raise a cry for help, I'll brain you like a mad dog. If not, I'll content myself with giving you just such a mark as you have left on me, with this difference—that yours shall last for life—just to teach you not to meddle again where you have no concern; the fire's convenient, here's the iron [*Sticks hammer into fire*] and now by your leave—[*Takes rope from pocket and is about to bind him*] well, you're a plucky one! Damn me if you don't take it cool. [*Binds him to chair with slip-knot; then gets R. of Elliot, holding extremity of rope*]

ELL. I shall take it warmly enough presently if you carry out your amiable intentions, my friend. [*Miles takes hammer out of fire, crosses before Elliot*] Well, I value the present arrangement of my countenance enough to pay lib-erally for its preservation. Reconsider your intention, and you may escape two hundred pounds the richer.

MILES. [*After a pause*] How am I to get the money?

ELL. Loosen my arm, and I'll write you a check.

MILES. What guarantee have I that it will be genuine?

ELL. The word of an officer and a gentleman! If you keep faith with me, I will, with you.

MILES. [Aside] I know them! They daren't break that—it's a kind of religion with the fools.

ELL. Well?

MILES. I'll take it. [Unbinds him] There, go to the table. There's a light, pens, ink, and paper. [Elliot goes to table R., which is near the open window. Sits and writes] And whilst you write, I'll take care that you can't be interrupted. [Goes to fire, replaces hammer in it, then goes up stairs, locks door L.C.; comes down, crosses to R. and cuts down the bell-pull. As he is doing this, Elliot has written one slip of paper, wrapped it around paperweight, and thrown it out of open window. He is writing on a second slip when Miles speaks—after looking around room, gets C.] Well, have you written the check?

ELL. I've written two.

MILES. Two?

ELL. Yes, as well as a left-handed man can do. Come here! Look out of the window—bright moonlight, isn't it?

MILES. Yes, but that won't prevent my escape.

ELL. I don't suppose it will. See anybody on the lawn?

MILES. Yes! a man smoking his pipe; he stoops to pick something up—looks like paper.

ELL. It is a paper. Shall I tell you what it is?

MILES. Well—

ELL. A duplicate of this. Read!

MILES. [Reads] "A ruffian is in my room, the man I struck this morning. He is armed! If I am murdered, he is my assassin! He came by a secret passage; watch the grounds, as well as the house, and you must have him! Elliot Grey."

ELL. True copy.

MILES. Ah! [Noise without, back of stage] And they are around already.

ELL. Yes, Matthew Leigh is an energetic man.

MILES. Damnation! Give me the money you promised me—a check!

ELL. Well, you've got one! Run, man, while you've a chance to escape. [Music pp.]

MILES. You pledged your word as a gentleman.

ELL. Yes, if you kept faith with me.

MILES. Well?

ELL. You never meant to do so.

MILES. How would you know?

ELL. [*Noise without, which has been increasing all this time, has now approached the door, at which there is a loud knocking*] The iron is in the fire! —Go— or they'll have you as sure as you are born.

MILES. Hell's curses on you! But I'll pay you yet! [*Rushes through secret panel, the other doors are burst open and Matthew, Florence, Colonel May, Lady Adela, Rosa and servants rush on. Servants R. and L. with candles. Lights up full*]

LADY A. Safe, safe! Thank Heaven!

COL. What has happened?

MATT. Where's the scoundrel? ⎫

ROB. The fellow's gone!   ⎬ [*All said together*]

LADY F. My dear Elliot!   ⎭

ROSA. Oh dear—oh dear—are you hurt? Your hand—the bandage?

ELL. Very bad! You had better take it off again!

TABLEAU. QUICK CURTAIN

ACT III.

SCENE 1: *A room in Matthew Leigh's Cottage in the village. Windows in flat L., opening on landscape. Door in flat N. closet door L.3. Table, chairs, etc., cupboard R. Enter Tabitha Stork.*

TAB. [*Goes and looks out of window*] Nothing of the sort! Not a sign of him yet, upon my word! A pretty pass things have come to. Out all night— ah, no consideration for the poor hard-working creature left at home. I've looked at the desks. No urgent calls on either. [*Rings surgery bell*]

[1] SARAH. [*Enters R.1.E.*] Did you ring for me, mum?

TAB. Nothing of the sort. I rang the surgery bell.

SARAH. E'es, I know 'e did, but t' assistant told me to attend to physic shop while he be gone fishing.

TAB. Fishing!

SARAH. E'es but l'or bless'e he won't catch anything.

---

[1] All through this act Sarah acts as if she had just left the washtub; she wipes her hands and rubs her elbows with her apron. Every time she opens the door to go out she does it with a violent swing, which would seem to take it off the hinges. All the announcements are made in a very excited manner, gesticulating, pointing, violently swinging her arms about in a most agitated manner. The more awkward, violent and abrupt Sarah is in her manner the better it will be for herself and Matthew's imitation.

Tab. That'll do. You may go.

Sarah. E'es, where shall I go?

Tab. Oh, go to the kitchen! [*Sarah exits R.U.E.*] Very well, very well, Mrs. Leigh..

Col. [*Enters R.H.D.F.*] Good morning, madam, Mr. Leigh at home?

Tab. Nothing of the sort. He's out.

Col. [*Aside*] Perhaps I may obtain some information.

Tab. [*Aside*] Oily sort of person. What does he want, I wonder?

Col. I'm very well acquainted with Mr. Leigh. Have I the honor of addressing a relative of his?

Tab. Nothing of the sort. Housekeeper.

Col. Oh! To be sure! Miss Stork, I've heard him speak of you very often! You've been a long time with the family.

Tab. About thirty years.

Col. Bless me! A long time indeed. And in all that time had you no news of the missing child?

Tab. What child?

Col. Why, the boy that was stolen. Stolen, it was supposed, by gypsies. Had you no tidings of him?

Tab. No, we hadn't.

Col. Pardon my curiosity. I am an old acquaintance of Mr. Leigh's but John McKenna, the former steward's son, wasn't he a very bad character?

Tab. Very!

Col. And, ahem—an [*Aside*] I'm getting along very slowly—[*Aloud*] mightn't he perhaps—

Tab. No he mightn't. Nothing of the sort.

Col. Now for good reasons, I'm in want of information.

Tab. I see that.

Col. Which it is very necessary I should possess.

Tab. I *don't* see that.

Col. Can you give it?

Tab. I don't know.

Col. Would you if you could?

Tab. No!

Col. Well, that's to the point at any rate.

Tab. I flatter myself it is. Good morning, Colonel.

Col. Good morning, my good lady.

Tab. Nothing of the sort. Housekeeper. [*Exit R.1.E.*]

Col. Bad pumping, Colonel. It does seem as if the fates conspired to foil me at every turn. My situation now is little less than desperate. Nothing more can be got from Kobb. Arrest! Expulsion from my club! Dishonor staring me in the face! [*Sarah enters with letter between her lips. R.D.*]

SARAH. Be you Colonel May, zur?

COL. Yes.

SARAH. Messenger from Manor House told I to give'ee this letter. [*Shakes it from between her lips. And as the Colonel is about to take it she withdraws it to wipe the soapsuds off. He opens it slowly. She stares hard at him. Pauses, then says*] You're welcome! [*She exits with a jerk and an awkward manner*]

COL. Umph! From London, urgent. [*Reads*] "Dear Colonel: It can't be done at any price. Were there not a male heir to the property in the way, money might be raised on the probability of her ladyship's marriage, which would give you the whole estate. But for the mere chance of your coming in for half we cannot raise you fifty guineas." And there goes my last—umph! Last? Last chance? Come, Colonel Cavendish May, no trepidation, no hurry, no fluster—cool and calm. A quiet walk in the meadow. [*Taking out book*] A last summing up for and against it and—then we'll think it over, we'll think it over. [*Exits R.D.F., passes window*]

TAB. [*Enters R.1.D.*] Yes, you may go your ways for an inquisitive meddling customer, if you *are* a colonel, if you are a colonel. What could he want to pump me for, I wonder?

MATT. [*Enters R.1.E. Aside*] Now for it! Good morning, Tabitha.

TAB. Oh, indeed! You are here, sir, are you?

MATT. Yes, I came in by the back gate, and through the surgery.

TAB. Oh! Did you, sir! A pretty good proof you didn't wish to be seen returning home! A dignified way for Mr. Matthew Leigh to come into his own house.

MATT. No, Tabitha, only listen, I was detained by—

TAB. Nothing of the sort! I don't believe a word of it—a patient, I suppose?

MATT. Exactly. An accidental one.

TAB. There! didn't I say so? I *knew that* would be the story. Oh! oh! Mr. Matthew, I promised your poor father to watch you like a mother, and I have done it to the best of my poor ability, and now—

MATT. But ask my sister—ask Rosa—she knows.

TAB. Knows?—nothing of the sort! I should hope, but once for all—[*Gate bell. Sarah enters R.1.E., pulls open D.R.F. with an ill-tempered swing, and flounces about to answer bell*]

MATT. Thank Heaven! There's someone at the gate.

TAB. I don't care! But mark this—I have borne much from you for your fathers' sake; have been a patient victim to unwiped shoes in muddy weather;

to dripping umbrellas in the hall, and clean stockings every day, with other outrages to numerous to mention, without referring to my memorandum book, but the last calamity—[*Sarah enters D.R.F.*]

SARAH. A gentleman to see 'e, zur. [*Matthew is startled at first by her abruptness and loud tone—then laughing and imitating her*]

MATT. Well, show him in. [*Sarah goes out with long strides, flinging the door after her, and is seen through window, gesticulating violently. Matthew close to flat, back to audience, imitates her*] That is the most impressive female I ever saw. She's got an arm like a windmill. [*Crosses to L.*]

TAB. Of course, there's another pleasure; one of those clanking free and easy dragoon officers. Fine sort of acquaintance for a decent, respectable medical man.

ELL. [*Enters R.D.F.*] Well, Matt, I have come pretty hard upon your heels. However, my fellows are comfortable in quarters, and now—

TAB. [*At back of table*] I beg pardon, Mr. Leigh, but your lunch is ready.

MATT. Yes, yes, Tabitha, thank you; but I—you see—this is an old friend of mine, an old friend, and—

ELL. A hungry friend, Miss Tabitha, who purposes to share his chop.

MATT. [*Aside*] His chop! He little knows.

TAB. Excuse me, sir. Chops! Nothing of the sort. Bread and cheese is ready exactly at twelve, and—

ELL. [*R.*] We are ready for the bread and cheese, Miss Tabitha, and shall eat it with more appetite if we have your cheerful, smiling face to look at. [*Aside*] Underdone meat and raw potatoes in every feature.

TAB. Umph! Well, sir, I really—

ELL. Come now, you must pardon the rough and ready manner of the soldier but to a fellow just arrived from India, the presence of a lady is so inspiring.

TAB. [*Mollified*] Oh, sir!

MATT. [*Aside L.*] Lord, what a man he is!

TAB. [*Gets to R. of Elliot*] We have some very fine ale and if you would like—

ELL. Of course we would, my dear Miss Tabitha, the better to drink your health.

TAB. I'll go for it myself, sir. [*Going*]

ELL. You are too kind! Matthew, what a devilish fine looking woman that is!

TAB. [*At door*] Cook two chops and a kidney, Sarah! [*Exit R. Matthew shakes head and raises hands in mock deprecation*]

ELL. That was a good shot!

Matt. [*L. of table*] Elliot, what a splendid humbug you are.

Ell. I should hope so. You don't suppose I have been knocking about the world for the last two years for nothing, do you? [*Re-enter Tabitha with ale and glasses, R.1.E.*] Nonsense, my dear Matthew, she can't be more than two and thirty.

Tab. I might find an old bottle of wine, sir, if the ale—[*Puts key in closet L.H.*]

Ell. By no means, Miss Tabitha, by no means. [*Sings*]

"For a foaming glass of ale,
    Not too new nor yet too stale,
With its frothy face all smiling from the jug so brown,
    Toss the liquor with an air
To the lassie standing there,
    And look in her eyes, while the malt goes down!"

Tab. [*In ecstasy*] Now that is pretty. [*Ladies pass window*]

Matt. [*Turning aside, laughing*] Lord! What a man!

Ell. But I'm afraid I am giving you a great deal of trouble, indeed I am.

Tab. No sir, not at all. I know pretty well, I think, when I meet a real gentleman and shall wait upon you myself. [*Enter Lady Adela and Lady Florence R.F.D.*]

Lady F. [*H.C.*] Yes, he's at home. Matthew we have taken your cottage on the way home, that I might show Lady Adela your beautiful garden.

Matt. Delighted to welcome you, Lady Adela, though I'm afraid Lady Florence has slightly exaggerated my merits in the botanical line.

Lady F. Of that she shall be the judge herself, presently. Those noisy ones, Rosa and Arthur, have gone out on an independent ramble by themselves so we shall have a little peace and a quiet chat in their absence. You shall give us some lunch. [*Tabitha draws herself up in dignity*]

Matt. [*Looks alarmed*] Oh! Yes, to be sure, a double pleasure.

Tab. [*Near door R.*] Nothing of the—

Matt. Hem! [*Rosa passes window*]

Tab. I beg pardon, Mr. Leigh, but you know—

Ell. Of course [*Advances*] he does, Miss Tabitha; he knows you have chops and kidneys, bread and cheese and ale; you remember you said so just now.

Tab. Well but—

Lady A. Why, Mr. Leigh, your fare is sumptuous. That's a lunch for an emperor. [*Enter Rosa and Arthur R.D.F.*]

Rosa. Ah! Ah! We've caught you, have we?

Lady F. Why, you rogues! Where did you spring from?

Arthur. From the top of the hill among the trees.

Lady F. The top of the hill?

Rosa. Yes, from that point we have such capital views and we could see you along the road for about a mile.

Arthur. So we watched and followed you, and we shan't go home till *you* do; and I'm very hungry and I want some lunch. [*N.B. Another blow for Tabitha and fright for Matthew. Lady Florence and Lady Adela retire and sit in the alcove. Matthew walks up with them, then comes down L.H.*]

Ell. Well, be a good boy and you shall have some of Miss Tabitha's nice preserves.

Arthur. Oh! How jolly.

Tab. Indeed, sir, I've got nothing of the—

Ell. Ah, Miss Tabitha, I never saw a truly handsome face without a certain amount of modesty in the possessor. Why, your pastry and preserves are the talk of the whole neighborhood.

Tab. Well, sir, I *do* flatter myself I can—

Ell. Of course you can. Oh, ladies, you don't know the treat that's in store for you all!

Matt. [*Aside*] Lord! what a man he is.

Arthur. [*R. of Rosa*] Well, her jelly may be good, but her face ain't handsome a bit.

All the Ladies. Arthur!

Ell. Now you have done it, youngster!

Tab. [*With much asperity*] Indeed, young gentleman! Upon my word, ladies, I—

Kobb. [*Enters D.F.*] Oh! Here you are, eh? Glad of it. Couldn't find anybody at home at the manor house, so I wandered back in hope of finding you at home, Doctor. And I thought mayhap when you've seen my leg as it's [*Looks at his watch*] just one o'clock—you'd give me a bit of lunch.

Matt. [*Aside*] My cup of misery runs over!

Tab. [*Advancing to Matthew*] Excuse me, ladies and gentlemen, but Mr. Leigh, sir, for thirty years, I believe, I have proved to you that your table was tolerably well supplied, but when you ask people to your house by the dozen at a time—

Matt. My good Tabitha—

Rosa. Tabitha dear! [*They close on her and try to coax her*]

Tab. Nothing of the sort! It's Tabitha cheap—Tabitha nowhere—Tabitha nobody—that's what it is! But if you'll ring your bell, Mr. Leigh, and order your servant to do her duty by informing you what provisions are in the house, I shall be quite ready in appropriating the same; and so, your most obedient, ladies and gentlemen. [*Exits R.D.*]

MATT. 'Pon my word, a pleasant situation!

LADY A. [*Speaks from seat in alcove*] Oh, don't be annoyed, Mr. Leigh. You have pounced upon Mrs. Tabitha a little too suddenly, and too numerous. Like all good housekeepers she is tenacious of being taken at disadvantage.

MATT. Well, I'll ring for Sarah—though I don't think she'll be of much use.

ELL. Oh, she's not celebrated for her preserves.

ROSA. No—she's celebrated for red arms and scrubby caps.

KOBB. [*Near surgery door*] I smell something cooking!

LADY F. The chops, I'll be bound.

KOBB. [*Sniffs*] I think it's cabbage.

ROSA. Oh, Matthew, if we dared!

MATT. Dared what?

ROSA. The closet—

MATT. What! The sacred cupboard? Across the threshold of which I have never dared to set foot!

ROSA. I looked once—some years ago. The store was bountiful then. It must be sumptuous now. And—and—*the key is in the door!*

ELL. [*At back of table*] The commissary general has departed and left the army to its own resources. I propose a siege.

KOBB. [*R.*] I second the proposal.

MATT. Rash man, you know not what you are venturing! Florence—I mean Lady May—warn them!

LADY F. [*Advances with Lady Adela*] I? No, indeed, I will crown the hero who first enters *the lion's den!*

KOBB. And as the lion's not there *I'll be the man!*

ARTHUR. Hooray for old Kobb!

ROSA. Be quiet, you naughty boy. [*Crossing to closet*]

MATT. This is a terrible epoch in my personal history.

ROSA. [*Looking in on shelf*] Jams—jellies—tongues—hams—preserved ginger—wine, etc.

KOBB. Say no more—here goes! [*Goes into closet*]

MATT. I wish you safe through it.

LADY A. Hush! Is not that her step returning?

ELL. If it is, all the more glory for Kobb! Get your crown ready, Florence.

LADY F. I—I don't feel so courageous as I did.

LADY A. I confess I'm frightened.

Rosa. I shall run! [*Makes a bolt. Florence stops her*]

Matt. I'm extinguished.

Ell. What a valiant army!

Tab. [*Enters R.H.D.*] I don't want to intrude, but I left a key in my closet. [*Rosa makes a bolt—Matthew stops her*]

Ell. Ah, to be sure—it must have fallen out. [*Gives key he has taken out of the table drawer*] Here it is.

Tab. Nothing of the sort, sir, it's—

Arthur. I'll tell you where it is—it's in the door.

Tab. So it is. [*Locks closet and comes forward L.C. As Tabitha crosses to cupboard Elliot crosses to Arthur, stoops to bring his face level with his and gives with mock ferocity*]

Ell. Oh, you wicked child!

Lady F. [*Getting around to Arthur, aside*] I'll whip you, sir.

Tab. And now, Mr. Leigh, if you want Sarah, you'll find her—

Kobb. [*In closet*] All right!

Tab. What's that?

Kobb. Lots of good things.

Tab. Somebody in my closet? They must have a deal of—

Kobb. [*In closet*] Pig's feet!

Tab. Very fine indeed, Mr. Leigh! You number among your acquaintances some nice—

Kobb. Pickles!

Tab. But whatever he is I'll give him—

Kobb. Ginger!

Tab. For the present he may remain where he is, I shan't open the door.

Kobb. [*In closet*] I'm up on the second shelf. [*Loud crash in closet followed by shrieks and yells of pain from Kobb*]

Lady F. Oh, dear!

Tab. Ah! Ah!

Lady A. What has happened?   } [*All said together*]

Rosa. [*Runs to R.*] Open the door.

Matt. Poor lost man!

Ell. There's a shell exploded in the fort. [*Tabitha opens door revealing scene of destruction. A shelf has given way. Kobb's face is covered with jam, hat torn by nail, right hand grasps shelf, left thumb in a mouse trap, right leg in a rat trap. Elliot, Lady Adela and Matthew assist in bringing him forward. Matthew sees stains on shirt front, puts hand to them and finds molasses and wipes it on Kobb's hair*]

Lady A. Are you hurt, Mr. Kobb?

Kobb. This comes of being a volunteer.

Matt. Take him to the surgery and I will soon doctor his wounds.

Tab. Oh, don't be alarmed, Mr. Leigh. I'm not going to triumph over a fallen enemy. I'll do what I can. You'll want to take off those traps and I'm the only person that understands them.

Ell. Come along then. Ah, Miss Tabitha, this is the largest rat you ever caught. [*Exit Elliot, Lady Adela, Matthew, Tabitha and Kobb, R.H. Rosa comes between Florence and Arthur*]

Lady F. Oh, you naughty, mischievous little boy, what have you to say for yourself? [*Arthur clings to Rosa with his face buried in her dress*]

Lady F. [*L.*] If he's truly sorry—

Rosa. Oh, he is, he is, see how he's crying. [*Kneels and pulls her dress away from Arthur, who is convulsed with laughter. Aside to him*] Why don't you cry?

Lady F. That's what you call crying, is it? But he caused all the mischief and—

Arthur. Very well, mamma, I know I did. I know I've been a bad boy— so punish me, dear mamma, but don't be cross to Rosa.

Rosa. There, how can you punish him after that?

Lady F. Oh, take him away, do—

Rosa. Come along, darling, mamma says you're to go home. [*Lifts him up and comes gradually to the back of Florence*] Of course, we must do as mamma tells us. [*By this time she suddenly puts the child up close to his mother's face; she clasps him to her and kisses him*]

Lady F. There—go—go—you pair of plagues.

Rosa. Come, Arthur, there's a good boy. We'll go home now before there's any more mischief. [*Exit with Arthur R.D.F.*]

Lady F. I really must take strong measures with that boy—

Arthur. [*Re-enters R.D.F.*] Mamma! Rosa says you're a "stern parient."

Rosa. [*Re-enters R.D.F.*] Oh, you little story-teller! Come home directly.

Lady F. Upon my word, I'll—You're one just as bad as the other. [*Both exit R.D.F.*]

Matt. [*Re-enters R.D.*] What's the matter, Florence? You seem angry.

Lady F. I must have a serious talk with Rosa or the child will be ruined.

Matt. Well, she certainly does spoil him terribly. But is she alone to blame? Will you pardon an old friend if he speaks a little more freely to you than any right he has to warrant?

Lady F. Ah, I know you're going to scold me about Arthur. Well, perhaps I deserve it but first how is your patient?

MATT. Well, he is in the hands of his victorious foe and doing well enough; but this boy—think, Florence, it is not now while he is yet a child that you will perceive the full consequences of an overindulgent system. But when grown to manhood he will assert an independence of thought and action, which despite his affectionate nature, he will. How can you answer to yourself for allowing weeds to grow and flourish where nothing should bloom but what is pure and lovely?

LADY F. Oh, I have little fear for the result. His natural love of truth—his generous impulse—

MATT. A garden confided by Providence to your hands. Heaven prepared the ground; see you the cultivation be worthy of the soil.

LADY F. Indeed, Matthew—

MATT. I have been too free. I have offended you with my preaching.

LADY F. The sermon shall not be thrown away, believe me. But remember my position, amid all my wealth, amid friends—how lonely. I am not afraid you misunderstand me, when I say that amongst the many with whom I may associate—some may be found willing to seek the rich widow for her position, to bribe my worthy uncle to consent to good guidance and protection to that fatherless child for his sake—

MATT. For his sake, Florence? If among them there should be one whom you could respect and love, whose character and honor was beyond a doubt or reproach, whose means were equal to your own—why then—then—

LADY F. Then?

MATT. Then no rich or titled one of all your friends would pray more fervently for your happiness than the poor village doctor.

LADY F. And you, the upright, truth-loving Matthew Leigh would counsel me to wed for money?

MATT. Yes! For no one could suspect your motives. But if he were poor—

LADY F. Well?

MATT. Well, do you think any man of pure honor would allow the world to say—

LADY F. Pure honor? Allow the world to say? Oh, good heavens! How headstrong and how selfish, even in your best inclinations. You would then have given your own, and won a woman's heart—consign her to a life of long wretchedness from fear that the world, whose opinion the consciousness of your own rectitude should enable you to despise.

MATT. Florence, Florence, you try me too far. Were I but a thought nearer victory in this struggle for something more than mere existence, I even I, humble as I am, would then enter the list with those gayer champions, and fight my best to win, not your dowry, but your beauty and your true woman's heart.

LADY F. Then you—

MATT. I love you, Florence May. To my own misery be it spoken; and that love is part of my life; but true and pure as it is hopeless.

LADY F. Then blame yourself, if I am over-bold in saying that it—it—need not be hopeless, Matthew Leigh.

MATT. Oh, how have I deserved this happiness? And you believe I love you?

LADY F. I *will*, if you promise to let me have no more of your high-flown scruples.

MATT. Guide me! Direct me! Do with me as you will.

LADY F. And do you remember [*crosses*] I have too large a stake in the honor of the man I love to urge him to one action that should bring a blush into his face.

MATT. But your uncle will never—

LADY F. Leave him to me. I know more of his affairs than he thinks.

MATT. And my profession—

LADY F. You shall not leave it until—[*Matthew is about to kiss Lady Florence's hand when Sarah bolts in R.H.D. rubbing her elbows and her arms as if fresh from the washtub. He turns about suddenly on his heel and tries to look unconcerned. Florence smiles and turns away. Sarah blurts out her message as an excuse for her sudden appearance*]

SARAH. There be a man at the gate wants to speak to 'ee, zur.

MATT. I don't want to see any man. Tell him I can't see him now. Why do you hesitate?

SARAH. He be old and poor, zur, and them's the zort you never turn away.

LADY F. Nor shall he now! Admit the man, my good girl. [*Exit Sarah R.D.F.*] And while you see him, I'll go and inquire about our poor wounded knight. [*Gives her hand to Matthew, he holds it a moment in his*] Oh, 'tis your own, *do as you like.* [*He kisses it. Music. Exit Florence R.*]

MATT. I can hardly believe my happiness! What will Rosa say? And Tabitha? [*Enter Miles McKenna, disguised, R.H.D., unseen*] No matter, we'll leave that for—[*Crosses, sees Miles*] Now, my friend, say what you have to say and say it quickly. How can I serve you?

MILES. Not with your drugs. I want your attention and *that* only for a short time.

MATT. Well, shut the door and take a seat.

MILES. I will! And *near* you if you please; for it won't do for our conversation to be overheard.

MATT. Well, I'm all attention.

MILES. [*At gesture from Matthew sits in chair R.H.*] Is it true that of the little property your father left, you hold the half still in trust, in case the brother you mourn as lost should ever appear to claim it?

MATT. [*Seated L.*] I do not admit strangers to—

MILES. Strangers! Well, I'll take it for granted that you have done what the world gives you credit for. Now, what proofs do you require to convince you of your brother's existence?

MATT. First, his presence before me!

MILES. You have it! These gray locks are merely worn for a purpose. What! No hand for me?

MATT. I'm not convinced by mere assertion.

MILES. Well?

MATT. My brother at the time of his abduction wore a mysterious antique locket filled with his mother's hair.

MILES. [*Producing it*] You have it. What! No hand yet?

MATT. Great heavens!

MILES. Does it resemble the one you have heard described?

MATT. The same in every particular. I'm bewildered. Give me some explanation—some clue!

MILES. Easily done. The old steward of Rosedale had a son, John McKenna, whom I have always considered my father. He died some months since. Remorse, I suppose, or fright, induced him to reveal to me that I was no son of his; that I had been stolen by the gypsies for the sake of reward, with his connivance. No reward being offered, I remained a captive. As some atonement he confessed his crime, and gave me the trinket and letters with the proof of my birth and parentage. The letter I have safe. The locket you now hold in your hand.

MATT. And you are—

MILES. William Leigh! The branded felon, thief—forger—but none the less your brother.

MATT. Oh! Shame and misery!

MILES. Well, that's just the welcome I expected. However, I'm not particular on that score; the money is all I care for.

MATT. Yet, this may be an imposition, after all.

MILES. Well, then, withhold the money. Become a robber like myself—denounce me to some magistrate—take the consequences if you dare.

MATT. [*Rises in agitation*] I dare not! Hark ye! You shall have this money —more—all I have that is not my—oh, Heaven! *our* sister's—on one condition!

MILES. Condition! Condition to a man who demands his own! [*Rises, coolly*]

MATT. No matter! I shall exact—. Hark, they are returning—go now! Leave me at once.

MILES. Shan't we meet again, brother?

MATT. Yes, but I'll meet you—or no—come here at ten tonight. But go! Go now.

MILES. Very well! The locket?

MATT. May I not retain it?

MILES. Retain it? Oh, no!—no. You're a very honest man I dare say, but I think I'd rather—[*Takes it and exits R.D.*]

MATT. And so beams the sunlight of happiness upon the heart, and in our hour of triumph so gathers the cloud of blackest woe; to burst in storm and tell us we are human. Well, well—have my father's teachings, all my own reflections, gone for nothing? No! I'll bear it! Face it like a man! Oh, Florence! Florence! Florence! [*Sinks into chair*]

LADY F. [*Enters R.D.*] I saw your visitor depart, and have come to—. Why, Matthew, are you ill? What's the matter?

MATT. No, I'm not ill—I'm simply thinking.

LADY F. Well?

MATT. How shall I bear your anger and contempt?

LADY F. What do you mean?

MATT. Florence, you never can be my wife.

LADY F. In the name of—

MATT. Ask me no cause. Have mercy on me; if you would have me state my reasons—suffice it that a disgrace, a foul disgrace, has fallen on the name you should have borne.

LADY F. [*Reflects a moment*] Oh! That man, your visitor; his strange, mysterious manner of coming. Oh, women's eyes are quick, the quicker where she loves. Some tidings of your brother?

MATT. No!

LADY F. And would you deceive me? You cannot if you would. You have heard things that have again called up those very scruples against the indulgence of which I warned you, Matthew Leigh. I am your affianced wife, you are my promised husband—would grief or shame to *me* induce you to break the troth?

MATT. Oh! Never, never!

LADY F. And will you deny me a share of that devotion to the hearts' choice which you yourself profess? Keep a good heart, Matthew, keep a good heart. We'll see this man together, his words and his pretensions, whatever they may be, shall be thoroughly sifted, and if the worst or best result, it shall be the worst—or best—to both.

MATT. Florence, you're an angel. [*Noise outside*]

ROSA. [*Without L.U.E.*] Oh, Florence, Florence!

LADY F. What has happened?

MATT. Rosa's voice! [*Rosa enters in great alarm and grief, passing window from L.U.E. She leans against sill of door, faint with grief and terror*]

LADY F. Do not fear, Matthew, I am quite calm—quite calm. Quick, Rosa, explain this.

ROSA. Oh, dear Florence, I can hardly collect my thoughts. We took the park on our way home, and when we came to the Fern Copse, Arthur insisted on playing hide-and-seek. Two or three times he disappeared and I found him; at last he—he—ran off toward the pond and was so long gone I became frightened, 'looked everywhere, I ran to the side of the pond—

LADY F. [*With a shudder*] The pond? [*Robert enters R.F.D., down R.*]

ROSA. Yes, the Black Pond! I called, I sought in vain! I met several of the village people, they are seeking now. Oh, Robert, have you found him?

LADY F. Rosa, be calm. Well, Robert?

ROBERT. [*R.*] It be very curious—I've looked all around for half a mile, and I can't find him.

LADY F. Well, well, we shall find him, never fear. Why, Matthew! Why, Rosa, you silly child, you're both more frightened than I am.

GREEN. [*Without L.U.E.*] Where is my lady?

ROSA. Oh, thank Heaven, they have found him.

GREEN. [*Farmer Green and villagers at R.D.F.*] Oh, madam. My lady!

LADY F. Here? Arthur, my child?

GREEN. No, madam, I was coming from the house. I joined them searching near the Black Pond for my young master.

LADY F. Ah! [*Farmer Green produces Arthur's straw hat, which he has held behind him. Florence clutches it in her hands, holding it before her and stands gazing at it. Elliott, Tabitha and Lady Adela enter R.D.F. Adela and Tabitha go to Matthew*]

MATT. Oh, heavens! [*Falls into chair. Elliot goes to Florence*]

ROSA. Forgive me! Forgive me!

ELL. Florence! Florence! What is this?

ROSA. [*Falling on her knees and embracing Florence*] Speak to us, dearest—only one word! [*Florence stands as if stricken into stone, her eyes still fixed on hat. Music as drop descends*]

TABLEAU. SLOW CURTAIN

ACT IV.

SCENE 1: *Chamber at Rosedale Manor. Window R.2.E. Another door R.F. Easy chair R.C. Stool on stage R.C. Lady Adela discovered R.C. Music at rise of curtain.*

LADY A. [*Laying down letter she has been reading*] Still no tidings! It is now—stay, let me think—yes, it is now a full year since the death of that poor child, and, oh, how deeply I feel for the desolation of the mother; widowed and childless! In one bereavement I am her fellow sufferer. The other—I dare not dwell on that. Dare not? Why? Let conscience ask, and oh, how quick will memory and repentance answer. What has become of that man, McKenna? And why did he leave our neighborhood a year ago, to visit this? Could *he* know that *one* event? And yet, if not, why that interview with me before he came here, and whence his threats in case I would not bribe him? I must not think! [*Rises*] Reflection only serves to increase doubt and fear!

ROSA. [*Enters R.H.*] Good afternoon, dear lady. You have not seen Florence yet?

LADY A. No, I arrived last night late, and they tell me she never quits her room 'till midday.

ROSA. Ah! Poor darling! She is inconsolable. Time, instead of soothing, seems only to intensify her grief. It is just a twelvemonth since we lost Arthur. This is the 23rd and the great ball she was going to have given to the Rifle Volunteers was to have been the 30th, and this is the end of all. As to my poor brother, his conduct completely mystifies me. He returned home an hour ago, after having been gone a month in search of some mysterious visitor, who came and went like a ghost on the very day of our great misfortune. Then there's Tabitha. She grows a deuced, crossed, old creature every day.

LADY A. If she makes you unhappy, Rosa, come to me.

ROSA. Oh! But she don't, bless you! I am her prime favorite but poor Sarah's the victim. I think she'll send that young woman to an early grave.

LADY A. Is not that Florence's step? [*Music pp.*]

ROSA. Yes, indeed it is. Oh, this day, this day! I almost dread to meet her! [*Enter Lady Florence L.D. in deep mourning. Lady Adela goes to her, while Rosa wheels arm chair to C.*]

LADY F. [*L.*] Ah! Dear Adela, you have arrived! How kind of you to leave the quiet, yet cheerful, comfort of your own home to visit so dull and dreary a place as Rosedale now. [*Seated C.*]

LADY A. Not dreary or dull to me, Florence, if I could see you more cheerful; but you *look* better, indeed you do. [*Rosa keeps behind chair*]

LADY F. [*Smiles faintly*] Do I? I hope I do, for my misery is not so selfish, but that I wish to be, and feel better for the sake of the dear few who love me. I will try, indeed I will, but I cannot forget that this—this—

LADY A. I know, dearest, this is the anniversary of that dreadful day.

LADY F. Yes! The long, dreary winter has passed; the beautiful summer has returned. The trees are green again, and the sweet flowers once more spring forth to life upon their delicate stems. But one rose, one little rose, whose blossoms lived through every season—my tree of life and love is gone! Yes, stems and flower have fallen to bloom no more!

LADY A. Come, come, dearest, you promised—

LADY F. I know! I know! Forgive me. There! I'm better even now. Have you seen Rosa? She is generally in my room early. Something keeps her at home this morning, I suppose—or is it—yes, I see—the foolish child fears to approach me on this day. She still persists in blaming herself. Poor girl, she does not know how deeply I love her or she would not.

ROSA. [*Has just come from behind chair*] Florence! Florence! [*Florence looks at her a moment and catches her to her heart*]

LADY F. There, there—and now—[*Rises and crosses to R.*] No other word on that subject today. These are my positive commands, and you know I will be a queen in Rosedale. Haven't you heard from Matthew?

ROSA. He returned today.

LADY F. And well?

ROSA. Oh, yes. A little fatigued, but—

LADY A. That is he crossing the lawn. Shall we go and tell him that you will see him?

LADY F. Yes, tell him to come to me here.

ROSA. [*To Lady Adela*] Poor fellow, he is almost as pale as she is. [*Exeunt Rosa and Lady Adela L.D.*]

LADY F. Dear, noble, high-minded Matthew Leigh! Every delicate act that true devotion could prompt he has lavished on me since that day, but no word of our engagement has ever crossed his lips; a true friend as well as devoted lover. He has respected the wretchedness he cannot alleviate. [*Matthew enters R.D.F.*] Oh, dear Matthew, how glad I am to see you again!

MATT. [*R. Kisses her hand*] And I, dear Florence, have had a weary, fruitless journey. I could have endured my disappointment better could I have found a shade more color in your face.

LADY F. But tell me—you have been—

MATT. Unsuccessful in my search! Alas! Yes, you know the whole truth about this man's visit and you can appreciate my state of mind.

LADY F. Matthew, if fate should throw your brother within reach of our sympathy for his unhappy lot and if our aid will make him fit for better things [*Colonel May enters R.H.D.F.*] we will do our duty. Do you hear me, Matthew? For it will then be *ours* and your—

COL. [*C.*] Will you pardon me for interrupting a conversation which I am sure must be agreeable to both parties? If I may judge by the familiar style of it. [*Elliot enters, unseen. R.D.*]

MATT. I beg, Colonel May, that you will not make an act of mine cause for a difference between your niece and yourself. I should indeed be sorry.

COL. Sir, you will excuse me if I say I cannot indulge in the luxury of your eloquence just now; and perhaps [*sic*] to come to the point at once I have long been aware of your pretensions with regard to Lady May, and I think it right and proper that you should understand at once that you cannot have countenance from me.

MATT. I shall imitate your brevity, Colonel, and simply assure you that *whatever* my pretensions may have been, I never had the slightest intention of submitting them either for your objection or approval!

LADY F. And as Colonel May appears inclined to make this a very disagreeable scene, suppose we change it, Mr. Leigh! Matthew, may I ask for your arm? [*Matthew gives his arm and they exeunt R.D.F.*]

ELL. [*Advances*] Very neat! Very neat, indeed!

COL. [*Crossing R.*] Oh, Mr. Grey, I'm afraid, sir, you were listening?

ELL. I am afraid I was. Yes, there's a pair of us. You see, Colonel, that I am a very intimate friend of both the lady and the gentleman, who have just left the room and my interest in their affection is so strong that I wished to gather your opinion also.

COL. Well, sir?

ELL. Well, I give my consent.

COL. Upon my word, sir, you are very liberal.

ELL. Why, yes; I think so—for I once had a penchant in that quarter myself. Now why can't you imitate my disinterestedness?

COL. I wish, sir, you would be good enough to attend to your own business.

ELL. I do! But, Lord, it amounts to so little that it hardly gives me decent employment. A small detachment—here under my command without a brother officer to speak to. The duty's so easy—

COL. Yes! So easy that you find time to gratify your elevated taste every now and then spending a few hours in the society of *play actors!*

ELL. What a funny thing it is, that when we are a little angry with that class of people we call them "play actors." As long as we are pleased with them they are "eminent artists" or "professional gentlemen," but the moment we wish to stigmatize them they are "play actors." Now I have seen a good many of them; they have their faults—oh, yes! But I have known men in other professions to be guilty of actions that "play actors" would be ashamed of!

COL. Sir, your manner would seem to imply some innuendo.

ELL. *Imply* some innuendo! Well, now, you do wound my self-conceit terribly. I thought my manner was quite significant enough to make you understand I was alluding to you. I flattered myself I was very pointed indeed!

COL. Sir, I'll take care to make you repent this insolence!

ELL. I dare say you will, by giving your consent to Matthew. I'll repent then and beg your pardon, too. If you don't, there's another niece of yours, quite as pretty as Florence. I met her at Brighton. I think she rather fancied me. Now if you don't behave like a worthy uncle in this matter, I'll marry that girl, become your near relation and then go on the stage. Wait till you see the bills—"Great novelty! Negro songs by Mr. Grey!"

COL. [*Much irritated*] You—

ELL. "A near relation of Colonel Cavendish May!"

COL. By Heaven, sir, you shall hear of this! [*Exits R.D.F.*]

ELL. "The gentleman will accompany himself on the banjo." There, I think I've made him comfortable for the day; Matthew and Florence gave him his dinner—and I just came in nicely for the dessert! [*Enter Corporal Daw. R.D.F.*] Well, Corporal, what news?

CORP. All right, sir; the party has been tracked.

ELL. Well?

CORP. Well, sir, I'm not good at long stories, so I got our sergeant, who's a schollard, to write a description of the place and the people. Here it is, sir. [*Gives him paper*]

ELL. Very good. I think you told me you had preserved the clothes you wore when you first came and asked to join the regiment?

CORP. Yes, sir.

ELL. If I required you to lend them to a friend of mine for a day or two, to do me a service—

CORP. Anything, Mr. Grey, to serve you; you've been the making of me.

ELL. Well, that will do.

ROSA. [*Enters at door L.D.*] Oh! You're busy—I'll go—

ELL. I beg you'll do nothing of the kind—

CORP. Any further commands at present, sir?

ELL. No, Corporal, you may go. [*Corporal salutes and exits R.D.E.*] A queer fellow that. When first he joined the regiment he was about as rough a customer as you would wish to look at. He has been a little of everything that is bad, I suspect, but now I believe we have made a good soldier of him, and a thorough soldier must be an honest man. Well, and how is poor Florence? I saw her a short time since, but I had no opportunity of speaking to her.

ROSA. [*R.*] Oh, she is as well as she can be on this day.

ELL. [*Sitting C.*] On this day?

ROSA. Yes, don't you remember?

ELL. Remember what?

ROSA. Good gracious! Do you forget that it is exactly one year today since we lost our little darling?

ELL. Oh, by-the-bye, so it is—yes!

ROSA. "Oh, by-the-bye—yes!" Really, Elliot, one would think you didn't care two straws about the matter.

ELL. Why?

ROSA. Why? [*Mimics*] How provoking you are! Why, because your tone and manners are so indifferent, that is why! And then, look at your conduct. While Colonel May and Matthew and everybody in the village was seeing the dreadful Black Pond was dragged and searched in every direction you never gave the least assistance.

ELL. What was the use of dragging a piece of water that we all knew was almost unfathomable?

ROSA. Well, you might have shown some interest in it, at any rate; but, oh, dear no! You must stay at the house all the time to comfort Florence.

ELL. Well, under such an affliction comfort is a necessary thing, isn't it?

ROSA. Yes, but not too much comfort. There's no occasion for kissing everybody that is miserable.

ELL. Kissing?

ROSA. Yes, you might have been sorry for Florence without kissing her!

ELL. Kissing her? Did I? Why, yes, I believe I did!

ROSA. I know you did. And then, your conduct since. You go to balls and parties and private theatricals. Poor people can't afford time for such things. I'm too busy at home! I'm dear Matthew's little cook now. Tabitha's going away for a week and Sarah's only fit for upstairs work. We poor people can't afford to be fine, Mr. Grey.

ELL. *Mr.* Grey! Oh, now you're angry! Come here, Rosa, and listen to me.

ROSA. Upon my word! "Come here, Rosa!" Your condescension is quite refreshing. No, sir! If you wish to be confidential, I think you may come to me.

ELL. Well, I've no objection.

ROSA. "No objection!" Haven't you, really! How very kind!

ELL. Rosa, have mercy; don't be so sarcastic.

ROSA. [*Contemptuously*] Sarcastic?

ELL. Yes! You're withering me into a cinder.

ROSA. You haven't enough *fire* in you for a cinder!

ELL. Oh! Now I'm ashes.

ROSA. Oh, go along!

ELL. Rosa, there's to be a ball on the 30th. I'm directing the preparations.

ROSA. Last year on the 30th there was to have been a ball. I should have been there—[*Cries*] poor Florence gave me a beautiful dress last year. Ah, I shall never wear it now. I shall never go to another ball.

ELL. Ball! You shall go to this one.

ROSA. I'll never go to another.

ELL. Yes, you will!

ROSA. I won't!

ELL. We shall see.

ROSA. What is it you wanted to say to me?

ELL. When?

ROSA. When? Why, just now when you had the assurance to tell me to come to you.

ELL. Oh, yes! I had something particular to request of you.

ROSA. Well, Elliot [*Going towards him*], you know very well [*Gradually nearing him*] that any request of yours will be cheerfully granted—but you shouldn't expect me to obey your orders like a child [*Sitting on stool at his feet*] because that is unreasonable, isn't it, Elliot?

ELL. Outrageous! And so, you see, I've come to you!

ROSA. Well, you needn't triumph over me, if I am a little fool.

ELL. You're a little darling! Now tell me what that pretty old-fashioned air is that you are continually singing about the house when I visit you in the village—

ROSA. Oh! I dare not sing it *here*. It was our darling boy's favorite song; he used to make me sing it to him two or three times every day.

ELL. I wish you'd teach it to me.

ROSA. For your private theatricals, I suppose?

ELL. Yes, I want to introduce it in a new part that I am going to play.

ROSA. What is it?

ELL. A sort of low comedy serious part.

Rosa. Well, tomorrow—

Ell. That won't do! Today! Now!

Rosa. But Florence—if she was to hear me she'd go distracted.

Ell. She's not in the house. Come! I've no time to lose.

Rosa. Well, it begins so [*Sings*]

"Lord Bateman he was a noble lord,
A noble lord he was of high degree;
He determined to go abroad
Strange countries for to see!"

Ell. [*Sings*] "Lord Bateman was a noble lord."

Rosa. [*Sings*] "A noble lord he was of high degree."

Ell. [*Sings*] "A noble lord he was of high degree."

Rosa. Yes, it goes up [*Sings*] "A noble lord he was of high degree," don't you see? [*Sings*] "of high degree."

Ell. Oh! I see! I didn't take my high degree.

Rosa. No! Try it again.

Ell. [*Sings*] "A noble lord he was of high degree."

Rosa. That's right! [*Sings*] "And he determined to go abroad, Strange countries for to see."

Ell. [*Sings*] "And he determined to go abroad, Strange countries for to see!"

Rosa. No! No! No!

Ell. What's the matter?

Rosa. You're all abroad.

Ell. Well, he went abroad.

Rosa. Don't be silly, now. [*Sings*] "Strange countries for to see." There's where you were wrong. [*Sings*] "to see."

Ell. "To see"—I see!

Rosa. Now try it all.

Ell. [*Sings*] "Lord Bateman was a noble lord
A noble lord he was of high degree.
And he determined to go abroad,
Strange countries for to see."

Rosa. That's it, exactly.

Ell. That's right, I believe. Ha! Ha! Ha!

Rosa. I'll write out the other words for you.

Ell. Umph! One o'clock! I must be off. Adieu for the present. Rosa! Rosa, dear, perhaps I may not—"perhaps never." [*Kisses her hand*]

Rosa. Why, Elliot—

ELL. [*Sings*] "And he determined to go abroad"—There, good-bye! Don't forget the words for me. Good-bye. [*Exit R.D.F.*]

ROSA. How very odd his manner was! What could he mean by "perhaps never"? What curious creatures men are!

ELL. [*Sings outside*] "I'll go strange countries for to see."

ROSA. Oh! That's all wrong. [*Runs to window, puts her head out and sings*] "Strange countries for to see!"

ELL. [*Sings outside*] "Strange countries for to see!"

ROSA. [*Sings*] "See!"

ELL. [*Sings outside*] "See! See!"

ROSA. [*Sings*] "See!"

TAB. [*Enters L.D.*] See! Yes, I see! What in the name of common sense are you doing, Miss Rosa?

ROSA. I was just speaking—

TAB. Nothing of the sort. You were singing. Where's your brother?

ROSA. He was here, but he went out with Lady May.

TAB. Umph! Ah! I dare say. I want to see him particularly. He must know of my intention of going away for a short time.

ROSA. He does know of it. I told him of it the moment he arrived.

TAB. But he must know why I go.

ROSA. That I couldn't tell him, for I don't know myself.

TAB. I'm going to look at a cottage twenty miles from this.

ROSA. Bless me, what a curious reason! There are plenty of cottages here, ain't there?

TAB. Miss Leigh, I wouldn't be absent if I were you. I'm going to look at a cottage *that is to let*.

ROSA. For a friend?

TAB. Nothing of the sort! For myself.

ROSA. Now, Tabitha, don't be wicked and cruel and talk about leaving us. I'm sure there's enough misery here.

TAB. Ah, you wouldn't care if I *did*.

ROSA. Oh, you dreadful old woman. I'm ashamed of you.

TAB. You think of nothing now but fine people, and their griefs and troubles—or—yes, one thing perhaps occupies you more. But what's a poor, old, affectionate, foolish nurse to a young dragoon officer?

ROSA. Now, Tabitha—

TAB. Never mind; I must see your brother before I go. He and I must have a serious conversation about you. If he's been blind, I haven't.

ROSA. What's the matter with you, Tabitha? You know and *see* his attachment for Lady May, and *that* don't trouble you at all.

TAB. He's a man. He can take care of himself. I've known him since boyhood and I love him too! But I nursed you, I—I—I—Oh! You naughty girl to love anything better than me.

ROSA. Tabitha, you'll put me in a passion presently. [*Cries*] I'm getting very cross; I should like something now.

TAB. [*L.*] Well, then, don't cry, and I'll do anything. Don't. There's a dear. Come, we'll go and find your brother together. Come now, don't cry. I can't bear that!

ROSA. Well, then, don't think unkindly of Elliot.

TAB. Ugh! He's a nasty—

ROSA. He isn't!

TAB. Careless—

ROSA. Rather—

TAB. Impudent—

ROSA. A little—

TAB. Handsome—

ROSA. Very!

TAB. Teasing wretch!

ROSA. But he *loves me* dearly!

TAB. Bless him! Bless him! Bless him! Bless him! [*Exeunt L.D. The scene gradually disappears revealing Scene 2*]

SCENE 2: *The gypsy dell by starlight. Gypsy music. A picturesque group. Docksey leaning on seat L. Romany leaning smoking against rock R. Mother Mix seated at back of fire C. A gypsy in front of tent, half lying back to audience, and another between second tent and fire. One leaning against wing L.2.E. One on second rock piece L.H. swinging leg. One back to audience facing another man, L.1.E.; one man seated on steps R.H.; one leaning against upper end of step.*

DOCK. [*L.*] Hey! Mother Mix, you know the stars. When's "big pal" to come back?

MOTHER M. [*C.*] When he comes, he comes. Let that content you. D'ye think his comings and goings are to be talked on by such as you?

ROM. [*R.*] That's right, mother; give it to him, he's always prying.

DOCK. Well, if I pry, I don't prig.

MOTHER M. No! You're one of the small curs. You let the big hands find the prey and you pick the bones.

DOCK. Ecod, mother, I wouldn't pick yours. There ain't nothing on 'em.

ROM. If you insult the mother, I'll crack your topknot.

Dock. Well, what's she always backing up everything the "big pal" does, for? He ain't no conjurer to be never wrong. I'll tell you I don't like him to be so near the place where soldiers are quartered, and I don't see what's the sense—[*Low peculiar whistle is heard L.H.*]

Rom. Hush!

Dock. By jingo, that's his pipe! [*Whistle again*]

Rom. All right. [*Imitates whistle*] Now Docksey, if you've anything to say to the "big pal" here he is. [*Music. Enter Miles McKenna L.U.E.*]

Miles. Well, my jolly birds, my Romanys, my night rabbits, how goes it in the burrow?

Rom. All right here. Watches awake, women and kinchen asleep.

Mother M. Who's with you?

Miles. Well done, old mother, you can tell firm footsteps on the green turf while the rest of the rabbits have their ears flat on their backs. Hist! Pals vanish! Gentry cove to palaver—quiet and easy! [*Exeunt gypsies R. and L.*] Now for my gentleman partner. Come across, sir. Come across. The bridge is safe, though slender, and it spans a wide gap. There, all right! Here you are!

Col. [*Enters cloaked L.U.E.*] Now, my friend, as few words as you will, and as much said as possible.

Miles. Just my way, Colonel.

Col. Why have you not applied to me for the money?

Miles. I didn't earn it.

Col. What! You had no hand in—

Miles. No! D'ye think I'm a fool? Abduction's cheap at 500 pounds, but murder—

Col. Hush!

Miles. Oh, don't you fret; my rabbits know me. I serve eavesdroppers a short, sharp meal.

Col. But you saw—

Miles. I saw him *sink*.

Col. And made no effort to save him?

Miles. Not a step; though if I had his mother would have come down handsomely; and that's why I think you still owe me 500 pounds as a debt of honor.

Col. Here's a check for the money. [*Gives it*]

Miles. Ah, ha! [*Takes it*] You're flush. They'll lend to the *heir direct*, eh?

Col. You can earn double that—

Miles. Let it be quickly, then, for I want to get out of England.

Col. Hush! Hark!

Rom. [*Enters L.U.E. down steps*] Stranger cove, with the password.

MILES. Send him 'round to the bridge. [*Exit Romany L.U.E.*] Now, Colonel, quick, now while they're coming 'round. Tomorrow at this hour.

COL. Tomorrow! [*Exit L.U.E.*]

MILES. What does he want now? Umph! Oh, I see—that talk we had about the Leighs, my *family* secrets! But what the devil are they to him? What shu' he care?

ROM. [*Enters L.U.E.*] Stranger cove!

MILES. Unarmed?

ROM. Searched him! Not so much as a hazel twig on him.

MILES. Right!

ROM. [*Calls*] Come! [*Enter Elliot, L.U.E., disguised as Coll, the Crack*]

MILES. Welcome!

COLL. Daws the ticket.

MILES. 'Tis "Coll, the Crack"! Glad to see you, my pal. Tip us your flipper. Here, my rabbits, my Romanys, up and hither! [*Gypsies all enter*] Quick, a hand and a can for Coll, the Crack! [*Gypsies get cans and bottles from tents R. and L.*] The knowingest lad, the downiest cove, and the best crib cracker in London. [*Gypsies all group around Coll*] Another grip of your mawley, my lad; here's to your good health, and welcome to the burrows! Good health and welcome! [*All drink*]

ELL. Thank ye, my boys, thank ye. Daw told me that I should find a jolly roaring lot! Thems the coves for Coll.

MILES. And what's the lay now, Coll, in this toggery?

ELL. Worn out sojer. Come home from the Crimea in very bad health.

ALL. Ha! Ha! Ha!

ELL. Got the consumption. [*Coughs*] Ugh! Ugh! Ugh!

MILES. There's a new pal, boys. I'll forgive Johnny Daw anything now, after sending us such a cove. I say, Coll, this beard grew out of that last affair, eh?

ELL. Why yes. You see in that affair at Mit Chain I not only cracked the crib, but I cracked the old gentleman's skull. So the perlice air uncommon active after me this time.

MILES. And Corporal Johnny Daw, like a faithful old pal, told you where you'd find friends and shelter and told us to expect you.

ELL. That 'ere is just the very way of it. Give us a drop more tipple if this is the way the rabbits lush, I vish I vas a hare.

ALL. Why, Coll, why?

ELL. 'Cos he's a size larger and can take in more on it.

ALL. Ha! Ha! Ha!

ROM. It's high and jolly with the boys tonight. Let's have a song.

ALL. Aye, aye, a song! A song!

MILES. Coll, give us the "Crackman's Chant." That's the flash jingle in London now.

ELL. Oh, hexcuse me.

MILES. Come now, no nonsense!

ELL. I'm so aged 'orse.

ALL. Oh, never mind—do it.

MILES. Come, Coll, chaunt! Here wet your whistle again!

ELL. Vell, 'ere goes. Now pals mind the chows. [*Sings. Song, "Luddy Fuddy"—The Cracksman's Chant*]

1.

"I seed three p'licemen in the Strand,
Luddy, fuddy, oh, poor Luddy, heigho,
I seed three p'licemen in the Strand,
And I know'd as they'd got a chase on hand.
Luddy, fuddy, oh, poor Luddy, heigho.
Luddy, fuddy, oh, poor Luddy, heigho.
Chorus

2.

"And I seed as they axed each passer-by,
Luddy, fuddy, oh, poor Luddy, heigho,
And I seed as they axed each passer-by,
And I knew as the cove what they wanted was I,
Luddy, fuddy, oh, poor Luddy, heigho.
Chorus

3.

"First they axed a Frenchman they chanced to meet,
Luddy, fuddy, oh, poor Luddy, heigho,
First they axed a Frenchman they chanced to meet,
'Il est là! vous le trouverez toute de suite.'
Luddy, fuddy, oh, poor Luddy, heigho.
Chorus

4.

"Then they axed a Dutchman, 'Ya mynheer,'
Luddy, fuddy, oh, poor Luddy, heigho,
'I see jist sesh man bass py here,
Vile I sits at mein door and trinks mine peer.'
Luddy, fuddy, oh, poor Luddy, heigho.
Chorus

"Now why did this throw them off the track,
Luddy, fuddy, oh, poor Luddy, heigho,
Now why did this throw them off the track?
'Cos Frenchman and Dutchman was both 'Coll, the Crack'!
Luddy, fuddy, oh, poor Luddy, heigho."

Chorus

ALL. Bravo! Good!

MILES. And now, my covies, let's go to roost. Coll's had a long tramp and must want a snooze. Back to earth my Romanys. [*Exeunt gypsies. Music*] Now, Coll take as best you can, a nest. I must across the bridge and watch the lane. All's fair with the Romany boys. Each must take his turn to watch. 'Tis mine tonight.

ELL. Oh, I shall snooze a down 'ere, I shall.

MILES. Good night then and a good sleep on your first night in the warren.

ROM. [*Enters R.U.E.*] I'm certain I heard—hello! comrade, not asleep?

ELL. Vhy no! You see ve old 'ands like to make ourselves comfortable under all circumstances.

ROM. All right. Only don't go it too loud or you'll wake the women. [*Exit Romany R.*]

ELL. [*Sings*]

"Lord Bateman was a noble lord,
A noble lord he was of high degree.
And father to a pretty boy
Whom all his friends thought might drowned be."

[*By this time he is seated on a stool R.2.E. Arthur gradually steals across the grass. Elliot sings*]

"But one there was for reasons good,
Who thought this boy alive and well,
And so he came to the wild, wild, wood,
To find and take him to his mother dear.
A false face did this friend put on
The little child full soon the truth did find,
And when he—"

[*Child has removed beard and kneeling on his R. reveals the features of Elliot Grey*]

ARTHUR. Elliot!

ELL. Hush, my darling! Oh, I was right! Thank God! Thank God!

ARTHUR. Oh, dear Elliot, have you come to take me home?

ELL. Hush! Yes, but you must be very quiet, very quiet, or we shall never get safe away. Now answer my questions. First, do you remember playing hide-and-seek with Rosa? [*Music. Romany enters R.U.E., sees them —glides rapidly across stage at back and off L.H.*]

ARTHUR. Yes! Oh, yes!

ELL. Did you go near the Black Pond?

ARTHUR. Not very near. I was hiding in the hawthorn hedge when someone crept close to me. I thought it was Rosa and laughed, when he threw a coat over my head so I could not cry out and then he ran off with me—while—

ELL. That will do.

ARTHUR. Oh, dear Elliot, I thank you so much for coming to me. I've cried for my mamma and Rosa; oh, such wicked men as these gypsies are. They have tried to teach me to lie and steal!

ELL. But you did not?

ARTHUR. I did not lie—but once I did steal.

ELL. What?

ARTHUR. But you won't be angry with me when you know—[*Miles and Romany enter L.U.E. Miles has a heavy bludgeon. Romany exits R.H.U.E.*]

ELL. Faith I was just in time with—well—well—we'll hear all that by-and-bye. Now, Arthur, you must mind me and do exactly what I tell you. Miles McKenna, who stole you, is a dangerous man. [*Miles has quietly come down L.*]

MILES. Very! [*Chord*]

ARTHUR. Ah! [*Gets R. of Elliot and hides face in Elliot's breast*]

MILES. Very dangerous under the present circumstances. Do you remember what you said to me the last time we met? "My friend, I'll trouble you for that child."

ELL. And do you remember what you got for trying to keep him?

MILES. I'm going to show you whether I do or not! Perhaps you recollect the purpose of my visit to you that night?

ELL. Perfectly well, and a very disagreeable one, too; still it was a visit and I thought I would return the call.

MILES. Upon my soul you're a game chicken and I could almost find it in my heart to let you go.

ELL. Thank you! I mean to go, and take this young gentleman with me!

MILES. Oh! You do?

ELL. Yes! I've got my right hand again.

MILES. And I've got twenty right hands! [*Whistles. Music. Enter gypsies R. and L.*] What say you to my rabbits?

ELL. I say, up Lancers!! [*Soldiers appear with torches, R. and L. on rocks and wherever there's a chance. Lights up. Corporal Daw gives Sword to Elliot*] What say you to my Lancers?

TABLEAU. QUICK CURTAIN

ACT V.

SCENE 1: *Room in Matthew Leigh's cottage. Same as Act II. All the furniture clear of grooves. See inkstand on desk. Rosa discovered.*

ROSA. It's of no use, I can't remain in the kitchen, stuck there at the back of the house. Oh, dear! I'm afraid poor Matthew will find sister Rosa's a very careless cook. But those curious words of Elliot's when he left me, absolutely haunt my mind! What did he mean by that look? And, "perhaps I may never—never—"; "perhaps I may never"—I'll just have another look and then go for the—[*Goes up to D.F.*] Why here comes Mr. Bunberry Kobb. Dear me! I must receive him, I suppose, so I can't begin my pie yet. Oh! My apron! I'll just take that off, and then,—Ah! I remember, old Kobb said he was coming to see Tabitha Stork and ask her if she would like to take charge of his house. He told me he was quite taken with her stately appearance. My gracious! I do think he wishes to marry her! Oh dear! [*Exit R.D.*]

KOBB. [*Enters D. in F.*] Miss Stork at home?

ROSA. [*Outside R.*] Oh, yes, Mr. Kobb. Please sit down—she'll be with you in a minute.

KOBB. Thank you. Yes, Colonel Sir Cavendish is a devilish high-minded man. Here he is, by this child's death, positively heir presumptive to the estates and money as well as possessor of the title, and all must come to him if he resolutely sets his face against the widow marrying—and yet he gives me hope—absolutely hopes the lady—But—well, I think my chances are fair. I have seen the errors of my ways in the matter of dress and I think my future get-up in that department will show I have not been to London for nothing. Yes! When I do take courage to speak, I'll have everything cut and dried; I'll offer her an establishment equal to her own; a husband whose personal *appearance* the advance of age has hardly touched. Horses! carriages—servants —ah, servants! Now I want very much to tell her that Miss Tabitha Stork will superintend that department. I've profoundly respected that woman ever since I felt the sting of her traps. Yes, I'll question—by jingo! there she is! [*Enter Tabitha R.1E.*] Good morning, Miss Tabitha. Miss Leigh has told you of my desire for a conversation?

TAB. Yes, sir.

KOBB. Pray be seated.

TAB. Nothing of the sort, sir! I know my place.

KOBB. [*Seated at table*] Ah! Miss Stork, I trust this will not always be your place.

TAB. [*Aside*] That's a hint, at any rate.

KOBB. As you are prepared for what I am going to say I shan't beat about the bush, but come to the point at once.

TAB. [*Aside*] Upon my word, I feel a little flustered. [*Aloud*] If you please, sir?

KOBB. Miss Stork—ahem—Tabitha!

TAB. Sir:

KOBB. Oh! come, you must allow me to call you Tabitha, in anticipation that it will soon be my right.

TAB. Upon my word, sir!

KOBB. Tabitha, I want you to change your home.

TAB. [*Aside*] The girl was right, he does want to marry me.

KOBB. And have the control of mine. Now, what do you say?

TAB. Of course I did not understand Miss Leigh?

KOBB. What did she say?

TAB. She said that you were pleased to admire my general appearance.

KOBB. All right—I do.

TAB. And that you wished to elevate me by placing in my hands the keys to Kobb Hall.

KOBB. Quite right, I do. Now your answer?

TAB. Well, Mr. Kobb, my answer will be a decided one. I thank you very sincerely for the compliment, though the communication was somewhat sudden.

KOBB. Oh! no, we won't do anything suddenly; marriage is my ultimate intention, to be sure, but—

TAB. Sir!

KOBB. But, my good creature, there are many things to be thought of first.

TAB. I don't quite—

KOBB. Why, you'd better come to Kobb Hall at once and see how you like the place.

TAB. What?

KOBB. It is necessary we should find out how we get on together.

TAB. Eh!

KOBB. Because neither of us would like to buy a pig in a poke.

TAB. Why, you—

KOBB. So, you'd better live with me a month or so before the marriage takes place. Do you see?

TAB. Yes, I *do* see! I see plain enough you are a villain!

KOBB. Hello!

TAB. A wicked, old hypocritical—

KOBB. [*Jumps up*] Why, what the devil's the matter with you?

TAB. But you've got the wrong sort of person to deal with.

KOBB. [*Aside*] She's cracked!

TAB. Now I understand the story about that before—Dolly Darkins—

KOBB. What d'ye mean, woman?

TAB. Woman! Nothing of the sort! But no matter—quit the house!

KOBB. With much pleasure! [*Going*] but—

TAB. And quickly or I may forget my sex.

KOBB. You needn't trouble yourself. [*Aside*] I'll send a policeman to look after her.

TAB. You're an impudent, rascally libertine! But I'll go to the child—she that misunderstood your motives. Give me a house!

KOBB. Yes, I would—

TAB. Ah!

KOBB. In a lunatic asylum!

TAB. Ugh! You hardened sinner! [*Exit D.R.1.*]

KOBB. I've made a pleasant day's work of it. [*Going. Is met by Lady Adela and Colonel May R.H.D.*]

COL. Hello! You're in a hurry.

KOBB. Well, I *was* but now there's some protection for life and limb; I'm not so pressed.

LADY A. [*Crosses to C.*] Life and limb? Why what's the matter, Mr. Kobb?

KOBB. Matter? Why, that dreadful old person who caught me in her traps is now more inclined to murder me than not.

LADY A. What has happened?

KOBB. No matter—Hello! an idea strikes me; by jingo! I believe the dragon thought at first I was going to marry her!

LADY A. Oh, nonsense!

COL. Upon my word I shouldn't be at all astonished; these Leighs are a pushing family, and the quality may extend to the domestics.

LADY A. [*C.*] Why, how do you mean?

COL. I have reason to know that the doctor's pretensions to my niece are unequivocal, and his sister, not to be behind-hand in presumption, looks to no less person than Elliot Grey, Esquire, a lieutenant in her Majesty's Lancers!

Lady A. Ah!

Col. You may well be horrified, my dear Lady Adela.

Kobb. Horrified? I should think so! But Elliot would never demean himself by such a thing.

Lady A. Pray be quiet, Mr. Kobb!

Kobb. But, confound it, my lady, I am a connection of the family and I feel it a degradation.

Lady A. Rest satisfied; this union *never* shall, *never* can take place!

Col. Ah, my dear friend, you don't know what has been going on in your absence.

Lady A. Oh! this is too dreadful! But I deserve it for leaving them near one another. I must at once see to this! Sir Cavendish, pray give me your arm to the carriage—this—this has somewhat overcome me!

Col. My dear Lady Adela, you are faint—let me call—

Lady A. No! No! No! Action! Action! I must go at once and find Elliot. Great Heavens! I dare not think of this. I must at once make sure! Come, sir, pray come. [*Exit with Colonel R.D.F.*]

Kobb. I'll go with you. I'll see to this, too! What! A member of the oldest family in the country! How dare you? But there's no fear of Elliot—he has lots of pride, and oh, by the lord! but we'll settle these Leighs and confound the old woman and all her works.

Rosa. [*Enters R.H.D.*] Yes, he's gone! Well upon my word I never saw or heard of such a queer end of such a pleasant beginning. Tabitha's in an awful temper. I wonder what he said? She says he's a villain and I'm never going to speak to him again. Well, now I can't get my flour—and—ah! there's the gate open again. [*Runs and opens door R. flat*] Here comes Florence, I declare; and so early. What can it mean? [*Florence enters R.D.F.*] Come in, dear, I'm all alone and I am so glad to see you. Now you must consent to go to the ball.

Lady F. The ball! Impossible!

Rosa. Well, at least you'll put on the dress and sit for the picture?

Lady F. Well, well—I'll see about it.

Rosa. Ah! there's somebody. [*Runs and opens door. Meets Colonel as he enters abruptly*] Oh! [*She shows disappointment*]

Col. Sorry I'm not a young lieutenant of dragoons instead of an ex-officer of the guards, my dear young lady, but so it is—unfortunately. I saw you, Florence, at a distance and followed you here because I wished particularly to speak to you—if Miss Leigh will kindly give us permission?

Rosa. Oh! certainly, Colonel. [*Aside*] Matthew's pie must wait a little while longer. [*Aloud*] I have business in the kitchen and shall be occupied for the next ten minutes; so pray make yourself at home here. [*Aside*] I'll go into the garden and watch for Elliot. [*Exit R.D.*]

LADY F. [*L.*] We are alone, sir! What is the subject of—

COL. [*R.*] I should suppose the place in which we meet might have suggested it, so let us approach it without further, or false, delicacy.

LADY F. Oh, don't fear on that point. I am aware that delicacy is quite thrown away on you!

COL. [*Aside*] Sarcastic little devil! [*Aloud*] Well, then—as business will soon call me to London, I think it right, before I go, to reiterate my fixed determination never to consent to your marriage with Mr. Leigh.

LADY F. Well, sir?

COL. I have nothing to add, Florence, except that I really regret that my *duty* compels me to this decision! [*Matthew enters R.D.F.*]

LADY F. Your regret, sir, is very consoling—and doubtless sincere, but Mr. Leigh [*Matthew comes forward on hearing his name*] can afford to dispense with your sympathy. In return for your candor, pray accept mine! My word is pledged to Matthew Leigh—I shall not belie it!

COL. [*Aside*] Victory! Victory! [*Aloud*] Oh, I never presumed otherwise and as the property—excuse my abrupt business way—will then be mine, I shall make you and your husband such an allowance—

MATT. [*Comes forward*] Indeed, sir, you will not!

LADY F. Matthew!

MATT. One moment, dear Florence. I'm not much of a tactician, sir, but I think I see the drift of your maneuver; however Lady May will not be my wife. She refuses me.

LADY F. Matthew!

MATT. She refuses to see me pointed at as the man who selfishly sacrificed a fine property to a sentiment he could not conquer. She refuses to place the noble old home of her husband's ancestors at the disposal of a gamester. She refuses to relinquish the bounteous name of doing good to the suffering poor around here—that a few fakes and spendthrifts may be the better for it—and last of all, she refuses to see her husband the recipient of your allowance!

LADY F. Matthew!

MATT. Florence! Dear Florence! I am still your friend—your lover—your adorer. I will ever be near you to guide, console, advise, and can consecrate a life to you! But my life shall wither, and my spirit break before you become the victim of that man!

COL. Outmaneuvered for the present!

ELL. [*Enters R.D.F.*] Good afternoon, Florence. Gentlemen, your most

obedient servant. Why, what's the matter? Very lóng faces for such an afternoon. Oh, I see—the renewal of a former discussion.

COL. [*R.*] Yes, sir, and with the same result!

ELL. Oh, I hope not.

COL. Your hopes will not stand in the way of my determination, believe
me.

ELL. [*Crosses to Lady Florence*] Florence, I have something very particular to say to your uncle. Don't think me rude if I ask you and Matthew
to walk quietly to Rosedale, and wait for me, if you arrive there first. I ask
this as a favor.

LADY F. Nay, Elliot, I fear a quarrel.

ELL. What, between the Colonel and I? Bless your soul, impossible. I
know the Colonel—his motives and disposition at this moment better than
anyone except himself. We shall understand each other in five minutes.

LADY F. Whatever be the result of your understanding with him, my resolve is taken. As a relative I disown him! As a friend, an acquaintance even,
I renounce him! And I will never of my own choice exchange one word
with him again! Matthew, I shall await Elliot's arrival at Rosedale. [*Exit
R.D.F.*]

ELL. And Matthew, permit me to thank you for giving me the use of your
parlor—to your own disturbance, perhaps?

MATT. Not at all. [*Crossing hastily and abruptly to R.H.D.*] I have business in the surgery.

ELL. It is very essential to me and to Florence—do you mark me?—to
Florence, that you should at once dress for our ball at the barracks tonight—
and be ready to go with me to Rosedale. I cannot explain now. Enough that
I tell you it is most important that you should do as I desire.

MATT. All right! I'll do it! [*Exit Matthew R.D.*]

ELL. Now, Colonel May!

COL. Excuse me—it's rather bad taste to press one's title—still I should
prefer to feel that you are quite aware to whom you are speaking. *Sir* Cavendish May, if you please.

ELL. I shall remember and whenever necessary observe the correction.
Now, for business—I want you to give your consent to your niece's marriage
with Matthew Leigh.

COL. And, what claim have you, sir, to interfere in my family affairs?

ELL. I don't interfere, observe that I simply request.

COL. And I simply refuse.

ELL. If that poor child were alive, you would consent.

COL. Never, sir!

ELL. Your plans will fail.

COL. My plans?

ELL. Both of them! Shall I tell you what they are? If they marry without your consent—we know your advantage. If they don't, you know, that though elderly, you are well preserved, and you think you'll break her heart, and possess Rosedale after she's gone! But, lord bless you! I've known Florence ever since she was a child. She has an enormous constitution and—candor compels me to say—that you are getting shaky.

COL. Sir, you are—

ELL. Well, ask Matthew, he's a medical man.

COL. Sir! I will endure no more of this impertinence. [*Rises and gets near door R.F.*]

ELL. One moment's look at this paper—it is important. [*Gives paper*]

COL. My written consent to the marriage. [*About to tear paper*]

ELL. Stay, 'till I have explained.

COL. I will not listen. [*Going*]

ELL. Miles McKenna is arrested! [*Colonel stops*] Don't go, Colonel! [*Colonel comes back*] Miles McKenna has made a confession! Sit down, Colonel! [*Colonel sits R.*]

COL. Well, sir, how does this concern me?

ELL. You shall hear. According to his confession, Miles McKenna—*who will persist in believing you caused his arrest,* says he promised to take away the child, if you would give him 500 pounds. The proof of your consent was initials cut in the old willow, near the Black Pond. At first you were virtuously indignant, but at last the *willow was cut,* and the child was to have been abducted, had he not otherwise been disposed of.

COL. Balderhash! What *proofs* that *I* cut the willow?

ELL. Only these! Your valet being asked, says you were never known to carry a knife since he served you! But you bought one in the village the very day the child was lost! Will that do? No? Well, you have visited Miles McKenna since his arrival in this neighborhood. Will that do? No? There's the check you gave him, with your signature—will that do?

COL. Damnation!

ELL. Ah! Ha! That will do! Colonel May, sign that paper!

COL. And if—

ELL. There's no *ifs!* Sign that paper and I'll give you this. I can, for I bought it. Refuse and you shall be in jail in half an hour.

COL. Will you listen to no terms? Stay! It is signed—there!

ELL. And there! [*Gives check*] And now, as through circumstances you'll be hard up—you had better try to earn your bread in an honest way. But I would not advise you to go on the stage. You've lowered one profession, don't disgrace another. [*Exit Colonel R.D.F.*] I think I may consider that portion of our home affair as settled in a satisfactory manner, although I hardly thought it would happen here. I hope Rosa has attended to all instructions about the ball. She is no doubt dressing by this time and [*Rosa enters R.D. with flour board, etc.; sees Elliot, screams, drops rolling pin and tries to rush into his arms, but is prevented by flour board*]

Rosa. Elliot! There, now just look at what you've done. Now, sir, pray where have you been these two days?

Ell. Employed in particular service.

Rosa. Particular service, indeed! Sending me your watch and frightening me to death.

Ell. Well, never mind that. Tell me, have you persuaded Florence to dress for the ball?

Rosa. Oh! No! I did not dare to do that, but I persuaded her to sit for her photograph in the dress she would have worn last year, and she is to try it on tonight.

Ell. That will do! Now, Rosa, be on your guard. I'm going to astonish you—Arthur May—

Rosa. Elliot!

Ell. I never believed him drowned. I had my suspicions of a certain Miles McKenna. I employed a faithful corporal in my regiment, who had formerly been a comrade of McKenna's. He ferreted out all the other's movements, and my suspicions were confirmed. I studied a new part, went out among the gypsies—

Rosa. And you found—

Ell. Exactly!

Arthur. [*Outside, R.*] Rosa! Rosa!

Rosa. [*Overjoyed*] Oh! [*Throws herself into Elliot's arms with a scream, whitens him with flour. He gets away from her. She runs off R.D.1. calling*] Florence! Florence! [*He follows her. Closed in*]

Scene 2: *A sort of folding door on a gigantic scale, forming a means of opening or shutting the conservatory.*

Sarah. [*Enters R.*] Well, I think as how I *do* look smartish. So I be to keep the ladies' dressing room at the grand ball. I a main heap sooner take of the gentlemen's hates for them. Maybe some young officer would take a fancy to me for I know I'm parsonable. I'm better looking any day than Dolly Darkins, the housemaid at Kobb Hall. She that they said Squire prom-

hate you, but I know you have a true heart; you loved her, ha! ha! ha! You loved her, and your happiness is gone! [*Exits L.1.E.*]

LADY F. Come, Elliot, look upon her. She is still your sister.

TAB. Nothing of the sort! She's my daughter! [*General surprise, all but Matthew*] I told you I had my revelations to make, as well as other people. Mrs. Leigh died abroad. I, the widow of a poor tradesman, came to live with Parson Leigh soon afterwards; on learning I had a little daughter, he proposed to adopt her. Well, poor people are as liable to temptation as rich ones, I suppose. To see my Rosa a lady, I consented.

MATT. This is true! I have known it for some time, dear Rosa; it has not changed my love for you one jot.

ROSA. Still my dear brother!

ELL. He shall be, and pretty soon too! If we are not speedily married, we shall change into somebody else!

ROSA. Oh, Elliot!

ELL. Besides, though I have respect for you personally, I can't stand Stork. No! no! Rosa Leigh, you have been by suffrage, and Rosa Leigh you *shall be by right*!

TAB. But I—

ELL. My dear Mrs. Stork, you shall have the largest cupboard in Great Britain, and I will buy up all next year's pickles to fill it.

TAB. And now—

ELL. And now, dear Florence, for my accommodation—the ball is going to take place here!

LADY F. Elliot—

ELL. Here, I tell you, at Rosedale. The guests have all arrived—the arrangements have been going on for a week past, and you are dressed.

LADY F. And would you have me—

ELL. Yes, I would, and I will! How do you think I got those papers? They were stolen from that fellow who calls himself Miles McKenna, by a little boy. Would you like to see the thief?

LADY F. What do you mean?

ELL. Good people, retire while I produce the thief. You'll be contaminated by the proximity of such a character. [*Exeunt Matthew, Tabitha, and Rosa R.1.E.*] Florence, you bore your surprise well—can you be as courageous?

LADY F. Elliot! Do I—are you—

ELL. Dear Florence, imagine the greatest joy that could befall you— [*Enter Rosa with Arthur*] Think of a delight that would thrill from your own heart to that of every friend you have.

LADY F. Elliot!

ELL. You understand me—I have not been too abrupt—

LADY F. [*Sinking on her knees*] Elliot! Elliot!

ELL. From the dear hands of her who lost the treasure, take it back again! [*Rosa puts Arthur in her arms—she bursts into a passion of joyful tears, at same time two livery servants enter R. and L. At a sign from Elliot they lay hold of large handles on scene, and flats open displaying* SCENE 3: *The Conservatory, brilliantly illuminated, filled with ladies, rifle officers, civilians, servants, etc. Music. Kobb enters L.1.E. dancing. Elliot advances to meet him*]

ELL. Ah! Bunberry, here? you *are* got up regardless of expense.

KOBB. That's a fact! I have an object in view; we are all so happy in the recovery of the dear child! Now we shall enjoy the dance with more spirit. [*Trying to pull on glove*]

ELL. You are looking wonderful well, but you are having a hard struggle with your glove. .

KOBB. Indeed I have—all owing to a careless mistake of a stupid boy. I sent him for a pair of "9's," and that he might not forget the number, I put the figure "9" on a bit of paper, and the foolish fellow handed it to the shopkeeper upside down—so they sent me "6's" in mistake!

ELL. Surely you know the new dances, eh?

KOBB. To tell you the truth, I am a little doubtful about them but to prevent mistakes I have a book here with directions, which I can keep in my hand. So I've only got to look at my book to keep all right, and put me straight again!

ELL. Well, then—partners! partners! but Mr. Kobb, take care of your book! [*Music. Dance commences, and Kobb turns and slides to L. corner, looking at his book to see if he is correct; puts book in his coattail pocket and dances over to R.H. corner. Whirls around and glides to C.; seems puzzled; scratches his pate and pulls out book—appears reassured, and replaces book in pocket, resumes dance; strikes an attitude in L. corner. Arthur quietly enters from R. and abstracts book and retires behind the dancers. Kobb searches for book and is dumbfounded to find it gone. Starts towards Arthur who is laughing at him, and tries to catch him. Arthur tantalizing him by showing book, and runs off R.1.E.; Kobb follows. They run across several times while dance is going on; at last Arthur brings on footstool and places it C. Kobb enters and falls over it. General laugh; dance is broken up, and all surround Kobb as the act curtain descends.*]

TABLEAU

QUICK CURTAIN

ACROSS THE CONTINENT;
Or, SCENES FROM NEW YORK LIFE AND THE PACIFIC RAILROAD

By James J. McCloskey

CAST OF CHARACTERS

JOHN ADDERLY, *who keeps a saloon at Five Points*

GEORGE CONSTANCE, *who patronizes the saloon*

THOS. GOODWIN, SR., *merchant prince*

THOS. GOODWIN, JR., *son of the merchant by adoption*

LOUISE, *Goodwin's adopted daughter*

AGNES CONSTANCE, *a broken-hearted wife*

DENNIS O'DWYER, *a good-natured Irishman*

MADALIA O'DWYER, *his wife, not so good-natured*

LORENZO McGONIGLE, *an Irish-Dutch watchman*

JAMES WALSH, *guest of Adderly*

MASTER JACK, *no lines*

JOE FERRIS, *called "The Ferret"*

JOHNNIE O'DWYER, *a chip off the old block*

GIOVANNI, *a son of Italy*

PABLO, *Giovanni's brother*

HERR GLIMP, *called "Dutchy the Dutchman"*

"BILLY," *keeper of the Underworld Parlor*

THE DUDE, *and nothing else*

DOLORES, *a street urchin*

CAESAR AUGUSTUS, *called "Coon" because he is one*

"VERY TART," *a Chinaman*

AUNTY SUSANNAH GOODWIN

"CHIEF BLACK CLOUD," *heap big Indian*
    and to which are added

MEN, WOMEN, INDIANS, SOLDIERS

SYNOPSIS OF SCENES

ACT I. *A street in full stage, with a house on either side. Interior of these houses with first and second floor may be seen by audience. At the back in the house, L., a window looks out on street. A door at back leads to the rear room. In the house on the R. there is a kit of shoemaker's tools, upstairs. There is also other plain furniture. Downstairs in this house, are the rooms of the Constances. There is a bundle of straw in one corner, and a box with lighted candle in another. In the house on the right, only the second story is visible to the audience, and a pair of stairs, outside, lead to a door up on landing. Inside of this house—upstairs—there are tables, chairs and glasses with liquor, etc., etc.*

ACT II *is twenty years later, first act being practically a prologue. There is a street, in about one and a half.*

SCENE 2 *is the interior of a barroom, with doors right and left, tables and chair and the usual bar furnishings.*

ACT III *is a parlor in Goodwin's home. There are doors right and left leading to outside and other parts of the house. There is a curtained arch in the center. A mantel and fireplace up against the right wall, with a chair near the mantel. Across the corner of the upper left there is a sofa. Over on the right, down stage, is a table and two chairs, and on the left near lower corner, a stand. Other suitable furniture may be added.*

ACT IV *represents the exterior of the U.P. Railway station, with all the trunks, boxes, trucks and such other things that are found at this period. The back drop is a wood, or rocky pass, and there are trees, rocks, etc., etc., to give atmosphere of the surroundings. Near the station, but down stage, on the right, there is a box with a cover large enough to hold a man lying down. Railroad rails are in evidence, running across stage and telegraph wires run from left to right, down stage.*

ACT I.

SCENE: *At rise, John Adderly, discovered upstairs in house on R., with two other men, Adderly sitting opposite the door. In the house upstairs on the left is O'Dwyer, and downstairs in this house George Constance is discovered asleep on the floor. Agnes is sitting on box in center of room. Children are near her.*

GEO. [*Half-rising*]   Agnes, Agnes, where are you?

AGNES.   Here, George, here. How do you feel today?

GEO.   Oh, hellish. My throat is parched and burning, and my blood courses through my veins like molten lead. See—see—look there—[*Points to corner*]

AGNES.   I can see nothing, George.

GEO.   Can you not see them writhe and twist, and dart out their tongues like streaks of flame? Oh, God!

AGNES.   No, no, George—it is only the imagination of your heated brain. Try and calm yourself.

GEO.   Have you any money in the house?

AGNES.   Not a penny.

GEO.   What has become of the money I got for shovelling the snow on Chatham Street?

AGNES.   Gone—all gone. Spent by yourself at Adderly's for liquor.

GEO.   Is there nothing in the house?

AGNES.   Nothing. And the children and I are starving.

GEO.   Go and get a pint of Adderly's best—that is the stuff to invigorate you. You won't want anything to eat then.

AGNES.   O George, how can you speak so.

GEO. [*Desperately*]   Get a pint of Adderly's best and tell him to chalk it up behind the door. [*Falls back on floor*]

AGNES.   Oh, must I sit here and see my children die for want of bread? No, I will make one more effort to get them food, though it be a fruitless one. [*Rises*] I will go, if I have the strength. [*Takes off shawl and puts it on children. Exit to stairs and starts up*]

ADD.   Well, boys, as this is my birthday we are celebrating, as well as the event of my leaving this place, I will give you a toast. Here is to my little son sleeping yonder. John Adderly, Jr. [*Drinks*] His father has known nothing but prosperity for the last twenty years, and now I leave this place a rich man—worth at least $20,000.

WALSH. Your success only verifies the old adage.

ADD. What is that?

WALSH. That the devil always takes care of his own. [*All laugh*]

ADD. But do you know, one of your street missionaries told me the other day that he wouldn't accept the sum twice told, with all the curses clinging to it. But I wouldn't give the old fellow a chance.

WALSH. No, I should say not. [*Agnes raps*] What's that.

ADD. Some leather-headed policeman, I dare say, to ask us to keep quiet. Who's there? [*Loudly*]

AGNES. 'Tis I.

WALSH. Oh, it's some poor devil looking for their share of the liquor, of course. [*Throws open the door. Agnes steps just inside the door*]

ADD. Surely I should know that face.

AGNES. If you have a conscience, you should—John Adderly.

ADD. You're George's wife, ain't you?

AGNES. Today I am. Tomorrow the grave may claim me for its own.

ADD. Well, we want none of your preaching here. What do you want?

AGNES. Food for my starving little ones and myself. [*Stretches out arms in supplicating manner*]

ADD. And for your drunken husband, too, I suppose?

AGNES. [*Staggers back*] Oh, no—[*Fiercely*] Who made him so? YOU, John Adderly, and when I begged you on bended knees to sell him no more liquor, you laughed at me and drove me from your door. You have taken the money week after week that should have gone to clothe his children, and when there was nothing else, you accepted even the poor covering from our bed to pay for liquor. And now when I ask for food to keep our little ones from starving, you taunt me with your drunken laughter.

ADD. Begone, woman! I haven't time to listen to you.

AGNES. I go, but mark you, John Adderly, the day will come when the accuser and the accused stand together before that dreadful bar. What, then, will be your answer, when—like another CAIN, you are asked, "What hast thou done with thy brother?"

ADD. Begone, I say—before I brain you. [*Grabs a bottle*]

WALSH. [*Interposes, and Agnes leans against the door which is left open. She stands just inside and against it*] Here, Susie or Jennie, or whatever your name might be, take this and drink it—it will do you good. [*Pours out drink. Agnes shakes her head*] Oh, very well, then—take it home to the old man. It's the last drop of liquor you'll ever get in this house, for Adderly leaves us tomorrow forever. Come—give us a toast.

AGNES. I will—from a broken heart, perhaps a dying one. May the wealth you have acquired by such unhallowed means melt from your grasp, as I now pour out this poison. [*Pours liquor on floor*] May the shrieks of your victims ring in your ears till your dying day. May that boy—[*Pointing to where baby is supposed to lie*] whom you call your son, live to turn you from his door. And may YOU—in your dying moments, CURSE him as I now CURSE you! [*Adderly strikes her—swears at her. Walsh stops him from striking her the second time. Agnes starts out of door and gets downstairs with difficulty*]

AGNES. [*As she comes down*] May God forgive him for that blood! Oh, my children! [*Falls at foot of stairs. Denny O'Dwyer entered room above while she was talking to Adderly, and works at bench*]

DENNY. [*When she falls*] What's that? [*Has strong Irish accent*]

MAD. You want to know too much.

DENNY. I do, I do, I do. They are carousing over at Adderly's tonight. Ah, Madalia, it's a good thing for many a poor soul that Adderly is going to leave the place—for it's many a one he's put under the sod. What a blessed thing it was that Lazarus Gilhooley got me to jine Father Abbott's Society.

MAD. What's that?

DENNY. Don't ye know what that is? That's the Father Abbott's Timperance Aid and Relief Society—and I've known nothin' but luck since I jined it. Look at that man downstairs. There's a man fer ye, who—ho, ho, ho—had an eddication like Socrates, the philosopher.

MAD. Who's Socrates?

DENNY. Don't ye know who Socrates was, ye ignoramus? He was a famous politician who used to play polo and lawn tennis along with Van Pell and the rest of the gang. Why, the last loaf of bread I took down to her saved his poor wife and babies from downright starvation. Have you any more bread in the house, my darling?

MAD. Yes, but I've only got enough for the children's breakfast, and I don't know where we will get any more.

DENNY. [*Takes bread from table*] There was never a door shut up but what there was another one open.

MAD. Would ye be after takin' the bread out of your own children's mouth?

DENNY. Go to sleep, my cuckoo. Your dreams will be all the swater fer partin' wid' half a loaf.

MAD. I wouldn't think you could sleep at all for robbin' yer own flesh and blood.

DENNY. That'll do now. I'll give ye a slap in the jaw.

MAD. [*Jumps up and Denny sits down on the bench*] Ye'd better not, or I'll put such a head on you that yer mother wouldn't know ye.

DENNY. [*Laughing*] Look at the old woman—Ho, ho, ho—ho—look at her. [*Jumps up with the bread in his hand*] Sit down. [*She sits*] Ye's gettin' altogether too acrimonious. [*Starts out*] You will lose me before long, and when you lose me you will lose a soft snap. [*Exit*]

MAD. Faith, and he takes better care fer them brats downstairs than he does fer his own. [*Takes drink out of bottle in her pocket*]

DENNY. [*Enters room by back door*] O-oo, but it is cold out! Ah, there's the poor father layin' stiff-drunk on the floor, and the poor wife—Heaven knows where she is! [*Picks up candlestick bottle*] Oh, my—Little Tootsy Wootsies! They are twins—there is a pair of thim. They look so much apart, ye can't tell thim alike. Here me little darlin's—here is some nice bread I brought down to ye. [*Throws it down*] I've got five mouths of me own to feed, but I'd stay up and work all night to keep your mouths agoin', me little darlin's.

GEO. [*Starting up*] Who's there?

DENNY. Why, me dear man, ye nearly gave me palpitation of the heart.

GEO. Give me brandy—anything to quench this awful thirst.

DENNY. If ye are dry, go outside and get a schooner of snow. There is some bread. I brought it fer yer wife and children's sake.

GEO. Oh—curse your bread!

DENNY. Oh, me dear man—may the Lord forgive ye fer sayin' that!

GEO. Give me brandy—brandy or I will die. [*Catches hold of Denny. Denny throws him off and he falls back into corner*]

DENNY. Die, thin. Ye'll get no brandy out of me.

GEO. [*Starts up again*] See—See!

DENNY. Where?

GEO. In the bottle. There's snakes in it. [*Falls back. Denny sets bottle down hastily and exit. Goes upstairs*]

DENNY. That man down there has got the snakes.

GOOD. [*Comes from L.U.E. Is full, and singing "Rolling home in the Morning, Boys." Runs against stairway*] Ah—beg your pardon. [*Backs up against door of Room 2*] I beg your pardon, sir. I wonder where I am. [*Looks around*] Why, it's the Points. Come, come, old fellow, you ought to be ashamed of yourself. [*Keeps well to opposite side of stage from where Agnes lies*] If my friend Major North could see me now, what would he say, I wonder? But this settles it. This is the last spree for me. To be sure, this is only a genteel drunk—a champagne drunk, but it's a drunk nevertheless. Well, they say that evil often results in good. And what good will come out of this? Hello, what's that? Some drunken policeman snoring at his post. Will they ever have a well-regulated police force, I wonder? Like all other great cities. By George, if they did, I wouldn't be here. The mayor says that drunkenness has become so prevalent of late that it must be stopped. Hmm—I'm afraid he'll never stop it by fining me. Let me see—how are the finances? [*Fishes out ten cents*] Ten cents—well, never mind—there's plenty more where that came from. Ah—that sound again—sounded like a moan, and a woman's voice, too.

AGNES.   Oh, sir—[*Coming to*] If you would be a man—and help me.

GOOD.   Here is one that answers to that name. [*Raises her up*] Who are you, my good woman? And why are you lying here on the ground such a fearful night as this?

AGNES.   I am a wretch—cold—chilled and dying.

GOOD. [*Takes off overcoat—puts it around her*]   Cold and chilled? There, there—now you're all right. The champagne may have got into my head, but it shall never drive humanity out of my heart. But come, my dear woman, you must not lie here. Have you a home?

AGNES.   I had one once, but that time is past. Oh, my children! I feel that the hand of death is on me. [*Sinks back on ground*]

GOOD.   Why good gracious! The poor woman will die here on the ground if she isn't removed to a warm place. [*Yells*] Watch—Watch—Watch—Watch—[*Exit R.1.E., still yelling*]

DENNY. [*Jumps up and tries to get on his coat—Madalia helps him*] What's that? This is the greatest place fer picnics I ever saw. [*Can't get coat on; smashes at Madalia; sits down again. Watchman enters R.1., having Goodwin by the collar*]

GOOD.   Let go—let go, I tell you. [*Jerks loose*] You've got the wrong pig by the ear. I was merely calling for aid. I wish to get the poor woman, who is actually dying here on the ground, to a comfortable place.

McG. [*Broken German*]   Let me take a look at her. [*Looks*] That's a strange face around here. I think she has been drinking a little too much whiskey.

GOOD.   No, no—I could stake my life to her honesty. There is something about her that is superior to the rest of the denizens in the neighborhood. Come, lend me a hand and we will get her to a comfortable place. We will take her in here. [*Points to Room 2*]

McG. I'll help you. [*They take her into Room 2. Agnes sits on box in middle of room*] Oh, say, mister, look at the two little kids in the corner. [*Laughs—sees George*] Hello—here's the old man drunk on the floor. I'll just lock him up. [*Proceeds to do so*]

GEO. You have come to drag me to the scaffold, have you? [*They struggle*] Well, you will find in me the strength and fury of a demon. [*Breaks away. Walsh leaves Room 3 and comes downstairs. George exits near door in Room 2, and McGonigle exits side door onto stage. Catches Walsh and hustles him off R.1.E. Denny opens window of Room 1 and fires old shoes at them. As he exits R.1.E. Walsh runs across stage R.U.E. to L.U.E., McGonigle after him. McGonigle does not catch him and comes back L.U.E. toward R.1.E. Denny pelts him again with old shoes. As he gets close to R.1.E., dances up and down on one foot, looking at Denny, who closes window and laughs, but opens it again quickly*]

DENNY. Go on, ye Jumpin' Jack, ye! [*Motioning up and down to indicate the Dutchman's hopping*]

McG. [*Walking toward him*] Here, here, here, here.

DENNY. Wah-ay, wah-ah, wah-ah—

McG. Say, I got my eye on you.

DENNY. Well, thin, take it off again.

McG. I'm lookin' right at you.

DENNY. Ye must be cross-eyed, ye ould Dutchman, ye. Lookin' over there —[*Points to rear*]

McG. Say, look here, you Irish flannel-mouth mick.

DENNY. [*Turning around*] Madalia, is there any flannel in my mouth? [*Madalia shakes her head*] Say, you Pete Wienerworst—

McG. What's that, you Irish potato?

DENNY. Oh, potato, potato—[*Gets another shoe*]

McG. If I come up there, I'll break your jaw.

DENNY. Well, if I come down there I'll put a lump on yer face the size of a freight car. [*McGonigle works to the corner of the house, partially out of range*]

McG. Come down here.

DENNY. Come up here. [*Fires shoe at him—then catches broom and fires that. Walsh enters L.U. Crosses to R.1.E. McGonigle picks up broom, drops his club, strikes at Walsh, who dodges and runs. McGonigle falls—gets up and chases Walsh off R.1.E. After Denny throws the broom, he gets excited and tries to throw the bench—then catches Madalia by the neck and seat and tries to throw her. She hits him bang in the eye*]

MAD. I'll teach you manners, and not to take liberties with me!

DENNY. Ow, ow—Madalia—see if ye can find me eye—and where. [*Mc-Gonigle enters R.1. Denny takes his sign down and throws it at him. McGonigle picks it up and marches off R.1., and Denny closes window*] Did ye see the six of thim pile on me at once, Madalia? But I'm sorry ye overheard the conversation, for ye're a lady.

MAD. I am.

DENNY. Ye are. And I trate ye like a lady.

MAD. You do.

DENNY. I do—

MAD. NOT.

DENNY. And I am a gintleman. Look at me Napoleon moustache.

MAD. A gintleman indeed! I had four brothers and ye couldn't hould a candle to any of them.

DENNY. You did. And thim same byes could drink more whiskey in one day than a ward politician could drink in a month. You're gettin' entirely too superfluous, and ye're not stylish enough fer me, anyway.

MAD. Well, I won't be after takin' a back seat fer your sister Johanna, and she gets blind drunk, too.

DENNY. Shut up. Don't you say a word about my sister. She's a lady and she's married to a decent respectable man, too. A better man than your husband ever dared to be. [*Madalia laughs. He sits on bench—jumps up*] Oh-oo —Madalia, did you put that awl in the basement of me pants? [*Shakes her head and laughs*] It's very funny, ain't it? Is there any wood in the house?

MAD. [*Excitedly*] There is only wood enough in the house to make a fire for breakfast in the morning. [*Denny takes bundle of kindling from table*] You'll be wantin' me to chop some more in the morning.

DENNY. You'll not. Who chops the wood, I'd like to know? You nivver chopped a stick of wood since I had you. I'm goin' to take this down and build a fire for them sweet little babies.

MAD. You take everything and give it away. Faith, you'll be takin' me next.

DENNY. Who'd take you, I wonder?

MAD. You took me once. [*Whimpering*]

DENNY. Faith, I did. I took ye fer better or worse.

MAD. For better or for worse. [*Squalls*]

DENNY. [*Mocks her*] And before I had you very long, I found you were a great deal worse than I took you for. And what's more, ye can't go in the same society that I can. My language is too diminutive for your copious denunciation. [*Exit*]

ADD. [*Excuses himself and comes downstairs, saying*] Confound the woman! I didn't mean to hurt her, but she had no right giving me her chin. I don't see anything of her about here. I guess she has gone home to her own house—at least I hope so. [*Looks into Room 2*] Confound the women, anyway! They are more trouble than they are worth. [*Walks toward R.1.E. Goodwin enters R.1.E.—runs against him*]

GOOD. I can't find a physician anywhere. Oh, beg your pardon, sir—can you tell me where I can find a doctor about here?

ADD. In bed, where you ought to be.

GOOD. Or in jail, where YOU ought to be.

ADD. What's that? [*As if to strike*]

GOOD. I said this snow might turn into hail. [*Denny enters Room 2—rear door. Goodwin enters just after. Adderly exit R.1.E., and afterward walks across from R.U.E. to L.U.E. Goodwin speaks to Denny, who has his back to him, and whose coat is split up the back*] What's that up your back?

DENNY. I've got me back-bone up me back—what do ye suppose?

GOOD. No, I mean this. [*Points to wood*]

DENNY. That's some wood I brought down to make a fire. [*Suddenly*] Who the devil are you?

GOOD. I'm here on a mission of charity.

DENNY. Well, this is a queer time of night for a commissioner to be snoopin' around—

GOOD. You misunderstood me, my friend.

DENNY. [*Grabs him*] That'll do, now. Shut up, or I'll make ye. I'm not your friend.

GOOD. You are mistaken, sir. Chance brought me to this place.

DENNY. Well, if I'd been here I'd a throwed you and chance both out.

GOOD. And a lucky chance it was, too, for I found the poor woman perishing in the street. She spoke of her children, and I think this is where she resides.

DENNY. I don't know where she resides, but this is the house she lives in.

GOOD. You know her, then?

DENNY. Faith, I do—and a good woman she is, too. She's too good for these parts. [*Picks up candle*]

GOOD. O-ooh-oo—[*Candle comes in contact with his nose*]

DENNY. What's the matter with you—have you got the hydrophobia? I'll light the fire. [*He does so*]

GOOD. But see—she revives. [*Kneels down and supports her*]

AGNES. Where am I?

GOOD. At home with friends.

AGNES. Have I then passed the portals of death, and sharing with the departed their perfect rest?

GOOD. No, no—my good woman—I trust it may be many years yet ere you do that.

AGNES. You are a stranger—I don't know you.

DENNY. [*Grabs him and hustles him to the door*] Get out—get out— What the devil are you doing in here, when nobody knows you? [*Shakes him*] She don't know you—she knows me. If she knew you like she knows me, you'd be all right, don't you see. See, now, how well she knows me— [*Stands before her*] You know me, ma'am—now don't you—now—see—

AGNES. [*Looks up*] I don't know you—who are you? [*Goodwin laughs*]

DENNY. Why don't you laugh? You needn't never know me, ma'am, but I'll tell you who I am. Me name is Denny O'Dwyer. I live on the floor beyant. Patent-leather boot and shoemaker. Half-soling and heeling done at short notice, and invisible patches put on by Madalia O'Dwyer.

AGNES. Oh, I do not deserve such kind words of comfort from you, while he whom I might have expected them from lies there. But for your kindness, myself and my children would have been dead ere this.

DENNY. Oh, don't talk so before the commissioner. Don't you believe her, Mr. Commissioner?

AGNES. 'Tis only too true, and while we have eaten the bread of charity, he who should have provided for us has come home night after night, helplessly intoxicated. Look around you—look at the place we live in—Look at it—Look at it. [*Buries her face in her hands—they stare around the room and then at each other*]

DENNY. Well, what are ye lookin' at me for? I'm no curiosity. Why don't you look around that way? [*Sits on box in corner—back to audience. Puts on his hat, which has a large hole in the top, and shows his bald head through it*]

GOOD. Here, my good woman, take this ring—I have no money with me —and try and get some good brandy.

AGNES. No, no—it has been our bane—not mine, but my husband's. What has reduced me to the abject wretch you see before you? What has changed my husband from the upright, honorable man he once was, to the drunken sot you see him? What has brought our children to the very verge of starvation? Why—Drink—Drink!

GOOD. [*Who has knelt beside her*] This has been a bitter lesson for me, and I here swear that not another drop of liquor shall ever pass these lips.

DENNY. That's right. [*Shakes hands*] Come out wid me and we'll join the Knights of Labor.

AGNES. That man Adderly is the cause of all my misery, curse him!

DENNY. Ah, me good woman, ye have no time for cursing now. Ye'd better be prayin'. [*Puts on Goodwin's hat*] I'll go down and get Levy Cassiday the hostler. [*Exits onto stage. Picks up policeman's club and trots off R.1.E. The watchman spies him from L.U.E. and gives chase. Exit R.1.E.*]

AGNES. Father in Heaven, accept my suffering here as atonement for him who needs Thy mercy. Be Thou a Father to his little ones, and should temptation assail them, Oh, deliver them from it. Oh, my children, let me kiss you once more before I die. [*Kisses them. To Goodwin*] Stranger, to your care I commit them. Do not let them bemoan my fate. Take them away from this place. Do not let them breathe its fetid atmosphere—for to them it is the morning of life.

GOOD. And for you—

AGNES. The evening of death. [*Sinks back*]

FIRE—FIRE—FIRE—Woman in nightdress runs from R.U.E. Bright light back of houses. Firemen C. Denny rushes from R.1. and motions for Madalia to throw him something. Not knowing what else to do, she throws a pillow at him.

ACT II.

SCENE 1: *Twenty years after. Street scene between 1st and 2nd entrance. At rise: Enter Johnnie O'Dwyer L.1.E., with advertising boards, hung one in front and one behind him. This can be utilized for a genuine ad. John Adderly enters after him.*

ADD. Come, Jack, you had better accept my proposition. Then you can dress like a gentleman and no longer be obliged to carry those signboards of degradation.

JOHN. My name isn't Jack—my name is Johnnie. J-o-h-n-n-i-e.

ADD. Well, then, Johnnie, what do you say?

JOHN. Look here, John Adderly, I don't want nothin' to do with you. Everybody that has had anything to do with you has gone to the bad. There was poor Bill McLaughlin—what did you do with him? And then Joe Ferris, one of the best-hearted boys that ever lived—Didn't you send him up the Hudson for three years? Why, I'd rather wear these signboards of degradation, as you call them, than be the scoundrel we all know you to be. [*Adderly starts as if to strike*] Ah—just try that and I'll keep the flies off from you. [*Adderly turns his back*] All I want is my little old six square meals a day, nine schooners of beer, a bottle of pickles and a plate of ice cream. And say, young fellow, if you ever stop me on the street again, I'll break your jaw. [*Exit R.1.E.*]

ADD. So he doesn't think it worth while to accept my Chatham Bar? If he had, I could have got young Goodwin in there, and got him to sign his father's name to more checks. I fear this coal speculation of mine will fail, and unless I can induce old Goodwin's daughter to marry me, I shall have to leave this part of the country, and that soon, too. [*Exit R.1.E. Tom Goodwin, Jr. and Joe Ferris enter L.1.E.*]

TOM. I won't take No for an answer. I gave up your checks with instructions to have your baggage sent up to the house at—

JOE. What will your father say to your bringing me, an entire stranger, into his house?

TOM. That my friends are his, and can make his house their home.

JOE. Ah, home! What a sweet sound the word has, and how lucky the man that has one. I never knew what a home was, unless a gambling house could be called one.

TOM. But I say, old fellow, how is this for a trip to Saratoga? [*Taps breast pocket*] The folks said the trip would do me good, and it has its advantages. I have returned with loss of appetite, and nerves all unstrung—

JOE. And a pocket brimful of money. [*They walk arm in arm*] Do not forget that I was your physician in the latter case.

TOM. Yes, indeed. Your advice to forsake the king and stick to the queen came just in time.

JOE. Her Majesty never deserts me, but the king often refuses to show his ugly face when I am most desirous of seeing him. But, come, Tom, as I am to become an inmate of your home, give me a sort of a panoramic view, as it were.

TOM. Well, home, they say, is where the heart is.

JOE. Quite right, but I would hear of the inmates of that home whom I am likely to meet.

TOM. Well, there is the Old Top.

JOE. Stop! Now whom do you designate as the Old Top?

TOM. Why, my father, of course.

JOE. You should speak more respectfully of your father.

TOM. Very well, then. My father takes off his hat.

JOE. That will do. No more "Old Top."

TOM. No more. A mother's care and love I never knew.

JOE. That shot struck me, too. And who else?

TOM. Let me see, now—there are the girls.

JOE. [*Rubs hands*] Ah, that's it. Tell me about the girls.

Tom. Well, there's Louise, my own sister—she's a dear good girl, always covering up my little failings.

Joe. In fact, she is so near and yet so far. [*Laughs*]

Tom. Then there is Clara.

Joe. [*Feints*] Oh.

Tom. What's the matter?

Joe. You shouldn't mention two such girls in a breath. It's more than I can stand.

Tom. Clara is my adopted father's own daughter.

Joe. She adopted you and your father?

Tom. No, no. She's my adopted father's own daughter.

Joe. So near and yet—[*Confused*] Shakespeare!

Tom. Oh, get out.

Joe. But tell me, old fellow, are there any visitors at your house whom I am likely to encounter?

Tom. Yes, there is one man, and to tell the truth he is not a favorite of mine.

Joe. What are his characteristics?

Tom. Well, he is a dark sort of a person.

Joe. Not colored, I hope?

Tom. No, I mean his actions.

Joe. What are his peculiarities?

Tom. Well, he is very reserved, rarely smiles, and has nothing to say—and—in fact I could give you no better description.

Joe. That's enough. I take a sudden antipathy to the man from your description. But did you ever hear my nickname?

Tom. No.

Joe. I had a great knack of finding things that were lost, when I was a little boy, and if any article of value was lost in the neighborhood, little Joe Ferris was called in to find it, and from my success in finding such things, I got the name of Ferret. That name has clung to me ever since. Now the ferret is a shrewd, cunning little animal, and if this man meditates any evil, rest assured I will find him out.

Tom. But we may wrong him.

Joe. True. But in every happy home that seems to remind us of Eden, where all is joy and peace, we should guard it from intruders and be more than careful of our friends, for the man will come who will sow discord, and perhaps ruin its peace and happiness forever. I am at war with all such men. I cannot say it is something unseen or unheard—it may be my destiny—but I will keep an eye on this man.

TOM. Come, let's go after a glass of sparkling champagne, and a puff of Reina Victoria. We will devise other sports. If we cannot find them here, we will seek them in green fields and pastures new. [*Start to Exit R.1.E. They run into Johnnie O'Dwyer*] Oh, wouldn't that fellow be a picnic for me! [*Squares off*]

JOE. Excuse me a few moments, Tom, will you?

TOM. Certainly. But mind you don't fail me. I shall expect to see you at the house soon.

JOE. All right. [*Exit Tom. To Johnnie*] Hello, sonny!

JOHN. I don't know you, and my name ain't Sonny, neither.

JOE. Oh well, I guess I'll go on, then—You don't know me?

JOHN. Your face is kind of familiar, but your feet have grown entirely out of my recollection.

JOE. Ha, ha—well—well—[*Takes off his hat*] You can't remember me, then?

JOHN. Well, if it ain't Joe Ferris! [*They shake*]

JOE. Johnnie, how are you?

JOHN. I'm red hot and still a-hottin'. [*Strikes pose*]

JOE. How are all the boys?

JOHN. The boys is all right—all except Aby.

JOE. What's the matter with Aby?

JOHN. [*Jerks his thumb over his shoulder, and makes a choking sound*]

JOE. What? Hung? What did they hang him for?

JOHN. Oh, the same old complaint—nothing.

JOE. Oh, go on—what did he do?

JOHN. Well, you see, Aby was coming down this way with a little bit of a knife in his hand.

JOE. How big was the knife that Aby had?

JOHN. It was a little bit of a knife—only about so long. [*Hands close together—then spreads them out*] That's all.

JOE. I see.

JOHN. Well, Aby was coming down this way with a little knife in his hand, and there was a young fellow coming in the opposite direction with a big boodle of money.

JOE. How big? A boodle? A New York boodle?

JOHN. No—bigger than that. Almost as big as a Chicago boodle.

JOE. Oh.

JOHN. And the young fellow ran right into the knife, and the knife ran right into the young fellow, and it got stuck right in his heart, and he got the heart disease and he went to his grave and died.

JOE. And they hung Aby for it?

JOHN. Yes, sir, they hung him.

JOE. Well, that's a shame. He was such a good boy, too. He would give anything away.

JOHN. Why, he would give himself away.

JOE. He would that.

JOHN. He was so generous that if he had two apples and your mouth was watering for one, he would eat one and keep the other for himself.

JOE. He would, indeed.

JOHN. Aby was a good friend of mine, too. I will never forget him. [*Takes Joe's handkerchief out of his pocket and weeps*] He owed me a dollar and a half.

JOE. You should seek consolation in the old adage, Johnnie, which says "forget and forgive." Therefore you should forget the dollar and a half.

JOHN. How am I to forget the dollar and a half, when he wasn't forgiving the dollar and a half? [*Joe pulls handkerchief away and pulls Johnnie's cap over his eyes in place of it. Johnnie gets through weeping, and tries to put the cap back in Joe's pocket, when he notices that Joe has changed them*] You got ahead of me that time, Joe.

JOE. That is because you were committing a capital crime. [*Pulls cap down*]

JOHN. Oh, my! [*Bends over*]

JOE. Come—brace up.

JOHN. I can't—I've busted my suspenders. [*Straightens up*]

JOE. Aby was generosity personified.

JOHN. Aby was generosity personified.

JOE. In fact I never saw generosity so well personified as in Abraham.

JOHN. In fact I never saw generosity so well ex—ah—ah—oh Joe I can't say that word.

JOE. Why not?

JOHN. It tickles my tongue.

JOE. He was a young man worthy of emulation.

JOHN. He was a young man worthy of emigration.

JOE. I could stand here and expatiate at large upon his many good qualities, and if I could find words to express myself, I could make the welkin ring with its praise.

JOHN. Keep away from me. [*Gets over to L.I.E.*] You've got them bad. Don't come near me.

JOE. Why?

JOHN. I ain't been vaccinated.

SCENE 2: *Bar with bottles and glasses, sandwiches and apples, seltzer bottles and a couple of Indian clubs made to look like bottles, all on bar. Curtain painted to resemble back of bar. Window in curtain. Chairs, table-doors. When curtain rises, Dolores and other young women seated in chairs. In chair in front of bar is dummy representing young woman. Billy is behind the bar. Young woman comes in and sings. Dutch song-and-dance man does a turn and waltzes with dummy from the chair, and retires with it under his arm. He also comes out with a coat on in which the sleeves are six or eight feet long and have large hands sewed on the ends. Inside the sleeves and fastened to the hands, are sticks by which he can hold the hands up and make them look very natural. He sings "Only to See Her Face Again," and at each pause lets the arms out a little way until finally they are stretched to their full limit. Very funny. After this a nigger song and dance, and the play goes on. Giovanni enters door R., and advances to center of room.*

GIOV. [*To Dolores*]   Come here, and give me the money. [*She advances and gives him some silver*] Is this all you have got? [*He speaks very broken Italian*]

DOL.   It is, indeed. It is all I have. [*Young women all retire into R.U. corner*]

GIOV.   I think you steal from ˜me. [*Catches her by the hand—jerks her around—then goes to table and counts money*]

DOL. [*Kneeling down*]   There is nothing I wish to steal from you, except myself. [*Clasps hands*] And if I left him, where would I lay my weary head? [*Goes over to where the rest of the women are*]

BILLY. [*Comes out from behind bar—slaps Giovanni on back*]   So, Signor —you like this country?

GIOV.   Yes, me like the country. Me maka da plenty money.

BILLY.   But don't you think these girls steal from you sometimes?

GIOV.   Oh, everybody steal in dees country.

BILLY.   What's that, you Italian organ-grinder and ring-tailed monkey-dancer? Take back those words or I'll make you eat them.

GIOV. [*Jumps up*]   Never! I no take back.

BILLY.   Well, take that, then! [*Strikes him*]

GIOV. [*Stabs him. The Dude enters L.2.E.—catches Billy as he falls and carries him out. Dolores exit D.R.*] I stab him to ze heart. I fiddle—everybody dance. [*Sits down opposite R.1.E. Music—waltz. Johnnie enters door R. and the Dude L.2.E. They both take partners and waltz. Nigger picks up chair and waltzes. Music stops*]

JOHN. [*Has on new suit. Slaps Giovanni on back*] Where is the bartender? [*Giovanni jumps up, but sits down again. The Dude sits down at table when Giovanni jumps up. Johnnie backs across room and runs into Dude. Dude holds table between himself and Johnnie*] [*To Dude*] Where is the bartender?

DUDE. The barkeeper has retired. [*Johnnie acts as if he were spoiling for a fight*]

JOHN. Oh, he's retired, has he? Well, I'll be bartender myself. [*Goes behind counter and takes off coat, showing undershirt without sleeves, and large muscles*] Come on up and take a drink. [*The Dude and Nigger get there promptly*] [*To Dude*] Well, what'll you have? [*Girls at bar also*]

DUDE. I'll take a little Lignumvitae Rye.

JOHN. Ain't got it. Anything else?

DUDE. Well, give me a little rye, then.

JOHN. Rye whiskey? Yes, sir. [*To Nigger*] What will you have?

NIG. Give me six cigars, a bottle of pop, and a package of cigarettes.

JOHN. I'll give you a smash in the eye. [*Dude drinks*] Pretty good stuff, that.

DUDE. Yes—it will do.

JOHN. Ten cents, please.

DUDE. [*Looks in pockets*] Ah-h—what did you say?

JOHN. I said ten cents, and I want it now.

DUDE. Well, give me a little more. I prefer to pay for mine all at once.

JOHN. [*Gives him another drink*] That's great stuff—twenty years old.

DUDE. [*Examining drink carefully*] Indeed, it's very small for its age.

JOHN. Want some more?

DUDE. Well, you might make it grow a little. [*Fills it up*]

JOHN. [*As he goes to drink*] Ah, look out there.

DUDE. What's the matter?

JOHN. There's a fly in it.

DUDE. Well, fill it up and let the fly float off. [*Johnnie does so. Dude drinks*]

JOHN. Twenty cents, please.

DUDE. [*Feeling in his pockets*] Ah, yes. By the way—do you know Goosey?

JOHN. No, I don't know Goosey, and I want twenty cents for those drinks right quick.

DUDE. Then you don't know Goosey?

JOHN. [*Threateningly*] Are you going to pay for those drinks?

DUDE. Well, Goosey is a very singular fellow. He walks off—like this—[*Exit L.1.E. Coon (i.e. "Nigger") laughs. Johnnie chases him with seltzer bottle. Coon comes back as soon as Johnnie gets behind bar. Enter Dutchman with water pail*]

DUTCH. [*To Coon*] Shoo-oo. [*Walks up to bar—hands pail*] Give me a pint of beer.

JOHN. You're in the wrong house. This won't hold a pint.

DUTCH. You got anytings to eat?

JOHN. Yes, there's some sandwiches and apples.

DUTCH. [*Takes sandwich and bites piece out*]

JOHN. Twenty-five cents.

DUTCH. What?

JOHN. Twenty-five cents for that sandwich.

DUTCH. [*Takes piece out of mouth and lays it and apple back*] I don't want it. Ain't you got no business lunch?

JOHN. No—and do you suppose I'm going to take that sandwich back after you have been chewing on it?

DUTCH. [*Picks up apple*] Say, how much are the apples?

JOHN. Same price.

DUTCH. Will you give me the sandwich for the apple?

JOHN. Why, yes—I don't care which you take.

DUTCH. All right. [*Hands him the apple and takes sandwich. He walks over to Giovanni*] Hello, Johnnie. [*Slaps him on the back*] Johnnie, get your hair cut, hair cut, hair cut—[*Takes hold of Giovanni's hair, which is long. Girls go R.U. and sit down*]

JOHN. You'll get your hair cut if you don't give me twenty-five cents for that sandwich.

DUTCH. I guess not. Vot's der matter mit you? Didn't I give you the epple for der sandwich? [*Walks up to bar*]

JOHN. You didn't pay me for the apple. [*Dutchie goes to explain, but gets a smash in the eye. He staggers over to Giovanni—pushes him out of chair and sits down. Giovanni reaches for knife, but thinks better of it*]

DUTCH. Oh, say, mister, find my eye, vill you? [*Joe comes out from bar and squirts seltzer at Coon, who retreats L.1.E. Dude stalks in, but gets contents of seltzer, and retreats L.1.E. Joe enters D.R. Dude enters L.1.E. and goes to right end of bar. Coon enters L.2.E. Giovanni's brother Pablo enters*]

GIOV. [*To him*] You see the bartender?

PABLO. Yes, I saw him. He is dead. Why did you kill him?

GIOV. Ah—he strika me—he have no right to strika me. Dolores, go out. I fear she will betray me. [*Exit D.R. Pablo exits L.2.E.*]

JOHN. Oh, Joe, you just ought to see me clean out the place. [*Swings arm around and hits Dude in the eye*] Well, you hadn't ought of been there.

DUDE. OW—OOO—OW! [*Coon gets him a chair center, opposite second entrance*]

JOHN. Oh, I can feel my muscle swelling.

DUDE. And I can feel my eye swelling.

JOHN. Well, Joe, you're just in time to take a drink.

JOE. No, thanks, I never drink.

JOHN. Then have something to eat.

JOE. What have you got to eat?

JOHN. Three kinds of pie—rice, custard and mustard.

DUTCH. Rice, custard and mustard?

JOHN. Yes, rice, custard and mustard.

JOE. Well, ha, ha, ha! I don't think I care for anything to eat. Come up, boys, and have a drink. [*Dude and Coon get there suddenly*]

JOHN. Look here, you fellows—[*Points seltzer bottle at them*] Get away from here—[*They hesitate*] Git—[*Seltzer*]

DUDE. [*Dude and Coon center of stage. Dude to Johnnie*] Ah, will you do me a favor?

COON. Yaas—do us bofe a favor, will you?

JOHN. Yes, I'll do you both a favor.

DUDE. Just come outside here, will you?

COON. Yaas—just come on de outside. [*Johnnie comes at them with a rush and they exit L.1.E.*]

DUTCH. Will you do me a favor? [*Opposite R.1.E.*]

JOHN. Yes, I'll do you a favor, too.

DUTCH. Ah, there—stay there.

JOHN. Come on up, Dutchy, and have something to eat.

DUTCH. [*Still nursing eye*] I want nottings to do mit you. [*Enter Dolores door R., running and screaming—Giovanni after her—center L.1.E. Giovanni's brother Pablo, Coon and Dude L.2.E.*]

JOE. [*Catches Dolores by the hand and steps in front of Giovanni*] Stop— what do you want with this child?

GIOV. Give her to me. She belongs to me—

JOE. No, you shall not have her. By what right do you beat and misuse these children?

GIOV. I bring her from home. Italy, Signor. She is my child.

DOL. Oh, no, sir, he is not my father. Do not let me go back to him.

JOE. No, you shall not. [*To Giovanni*] She says you are not her father, and I believe her. If you dare to lay a finger on her, you shall answer for it dearly. [*Giovanni throws down club and springs at Joe with knife. Joe knocks him down. The brother attempts to help, but Johnnie knocks him down and he retreats L.2.E. Giovanni exits D.R. screaming vengeance. Joe knocks Dude and Coon around just for exercise. Joe assumes to talk with Dolores, picks up club and looks at it; then leads Dolores to a chair opposite R.1.E., sits down and talks to her. The Dude has retreated—also Dutchy—after the fracas through L.1.E. Dude comes back and bows head on bar—Dutchy enters with dynamite bomb—explodes it back of Dude. It is filled with red fire. Consternation*]

JOE. [*To Dolores*]   That man is not your father?

DOL.   Indeed, he is not. He brought me from Italy.

JOE.   But your father—surely he would not let that man bring you away from Italy?

DOL.   He was killed fighting with Garibaldi.

JOE.   And your mother?

DOL. [*Hands to eyes*]   Dead.

JOE.   Poor child. [*Wipes away her tears*]   Your mother dead, too.

DOL.   She grew sick and died when she heard of my father's death. She placed her hand upon my head and said, "God guard my little one. God bless my little Dolores."

JOE.   But how came you in that wretch's power?

DOL.   Oh, there were a great many children brought over when we were. We played the harp and fiddle on the ferry boats and on the streets, anywhere to get money, and if we don't get two dollars every day, he kicks us and beats us and sends us to bed.

JOE.   What? Kicks you and beats you?

JOHN. [*Rushes from behind bar*]   Kicks and beats her—Oh, wait till I catch him—[*Starts for door R. Knocks down Dutchy and Dude, who get in his way. Exit D.R. Coon, Dutchy and Dude all go to bar and help themselves*]

DOL.   There was a little boy and girl who used to live with us and play on the streets. When they were coming home one night, they crossed the bridge and they were hurrying so, because it was after dark, that they both fell into the river and were drowned, and the next morning they were found locked in each other's arms. Oh, Barney was awful sorry. [*Dutchman brings chair to front center and goes to sleep. He has picked up the Dude's hat and has it on when he goes to sleep. The Dude picks up the Coon's hat—looks it over— then gets Indian club off bar—goes to Dutchman and strikes him in the stomach with it*]

DUDE.   That is not my chapeau. [*Changes with Dutchman*]

DUTCH. [*Now has Coon's hat—throws it on floor*] That is NOT my chapeau. [*Kicks at it and falls on his back. Coon fires Dutchman's hat also. Dude rushes up to strike Dutchy while he is on the floor. Coon does the Pocahontas act—gets on his knees*]

COON. Have mercy, sire, have mercy.

DUTCH. Does he have mercy? [*Gets on his knees*] I am shaved—I am saved. [*Dutchman gets in chair again. Dude lights cigar and smokes, sitting at R. end of bar. Coon is still drinking*]

JOE. He was sorry on account of their loss, of course.

DOL. Oh, no—because they had lost his best harp—

JOHN. [*Enter D.R.*] You just ought to have seen me lift him.

JOE. Did you catch him?

JOHN. I should say I did. I'd like to break my foot on him. I'd send him so high that his clothes would be out of fashion before he gets back.

DOL. Oh, you will not let him have me again, will you?

JOE. No, my child, I will see that you are provided for, and he will never misuse you again.

DOL. And my brother and sister! Oh, Barney will beat them worse than ever, now that I am gone.

JOE. But they are not your brothers and sisters.

DOL. I know it, but I love them just the same.

JOE. Well, I will provide for them, too. That wretch of an Italian shall not exercise his cruelty on them if I can help it.

JOHN. What are you going to do, Joe—steal a poorhouse?

JOE. Why, certainly not!

JOHN. Well, if you do, just put me down for a front seat. [*Discovers Coon, who is just putting bottle under coat. Johnnie commences to whistle—so does the Coon, who skips toward L.1.E. Johnnie skips alongside of him, imitating his gait and pointing back at bar. Continue this to entrance. Back to counter, leaving bottle there, Coon skips to L.1.E. Johnnie gets seltzer bottle—takes cigar out of Dude's mouth—Dude expostulates against it. Dude rushes out L.1.E. and back again, shouting*]

DUDE. The world is mine! [*Gets a facer from seltzer bottle, and retires. Johnnie turns attention to Dutchman, who enjoys the fun, but goes to sleep suddenly*]

JOHN. Oh—Oh—o—Three shots for five cents. [*Takes three shots with bottle. Dutchman and Johnnie fight. Dutchy exits. Report of a gun L.2.E. Coon rushes in L.2.E.*]

COON. Oh, you've done it! You'll catch it.

JOHN. [*Behind bar*] Done what?

COON. That young fellow went right outside and committed suicide. Blowed his brains out with a cigarette.

JOHN. Well, it ain't my fault.

COON. Yes, it is—all your fault. You'll catch it. [*Puts card on Johnnie's back marked LEFT. Johnnie repeats that it is not his fault, but Joe sides in with Coon and he is dubious. Play death march. Dutchman and Dude march in with sheet between them arranged to look as if they had a stiff on shoulders*]

COON. There is only one thing that will save that man's life.

JOHN. What's that?

COON. A bottle of brandy.

JOHN. Well, I'll give him that, if it'll do him any good. [*They take the bottle, and throw shutter off—Exit L.1.E. Johnnie comes out, but he is too paralyzed to do anything. When he turns up, shows card on his back "LEFT." Takes off card*] I'll get even with them fellows. [*Picks up pepper-box*]

JOE. What's that?

JOHN. Cayenne pepper.

JOE. What are you going to do?

JOHN. Make them a dynamite cocktail. [*Puts some in bottle*] Come on, boys, and have a drink. [*Coon and Dude enter and drink; turn wrong side out. Dutchman laughs at them—then drinks his—goes through same motions, his hair rising straight up on head. Dude and Coon carry him off, after he falls L.1.E. John Adderly enters D.R. and goes to take a drink. Johnnie grabs bottle*] We don't sell liquor to boys. [*Joe catches him—he struggles*]

JOE. Oh, you need not struggle—you are in a vise. Didn't I tell you that we should meet again, villain? [*Adderly breaks away and makes motion to draw weapon*] Why don't you draw your weapon? You are a coward as well as a villain, I see.

ADD. What has caused this change in you, Joe? Have we not always been friends?

JOE. Aye, friends. Who placed the money in my room for which I was tried and convicted? What could I do? My companions were of your stamp, whose words or oath would not avail me. Death was preferable to dragging out a miserable existence in prison. I escaped—went to California and there I met a wretch who was dying of some frightful disease. He was your accomplice, and it was he that told me who put that money in my room. It was YOU, John Adderly. And now what am I? An outcast—an escaped convict—a gambler without sympathy from the human race.

JOHN. Who says you got no sympathy? You, Jack Adderly? [*Joe quiets him*] Well, I don't take water from no such duck as him. [*Drinks out of dynamite bottle*] Oh, Joe, what do you think I did? I took some dynamite myself—

ADD. I did not do it. It was all a mistake.

JOE. Who caused the search to be made there?

ADD. Not I. Come, Joe, let us be friends again.

JOE. And you will give information, and have me sent back, I suppose?

ADD. I would never do that.

JOE. You better not. If I thought you meditated such a thing, I'd place the rope around your bull-neck with my own hands, as a terrible warning to all traitors.

ADD. Enough. Our paths lie in different directions.

JOE. [*Interrupts*] I trust that our paths may lie in different directions, but if in our walk through life we should ever meet, fear will never cause me to turn aside from avenging a wrong.

ADD. Nor me from avenging an insult.

JOHN. Oh, go West, young fellow, and shoot snipe.

ADD. I'll see you again, young man. [*Exit D.R.*]

JOHN. [*Follows him to door*] Oh, come and see me now. [*Giovanni's brother Pablo enters L.1.E. and picks up snipe lying in center of stage. Johnnie turns and sees him and shoots. He drops snipe and exits L.1.E. Dutchman then starts after snipe. Has on a small plug hat. Picks up snipe and starts off. Joe whistles—then hollers at him. Drops snipe and exits L.1.E. Johnnie shoots just before he gets out. He jumps—hair stands up straight—hat falls off. Johnnie puts on hat—picks up snipe—sits in chair opposite R.1.E.*] I'll do all the snipe-shooting round here myself.

JOE. [*With Dolores by the hand*] Poor child, there is something in her life that strangely resembles my own, for I am like a tennis ball—here, there and everywhere at times, and should misfortune overtake me I shall have at least the heartfelt prayers of one more homeless little wanderer. [*Exit Joe and Dolores L.2.E.*]

JOHN. Joe is a good fellow, and Joe thinks pretty well of me, too. Why, if I was starving and Joe had one sandwich I believe he would give me the mustard. Joe has got a heart in him as soft as a woman—some women. Oh, women, women, with your four-button kid gloves, while we poor men have to pin our suspenders to our pants! [*Goes behind bar. Women gather round bar. Lights down on stage, except light on L. end of counter. Adderly and Giovanni enter door R. and talk just inside. Dolores enters L.2.E. and listens. Gets close to them*]

ADD. He struck you down, you say?

GIOV. Yes—he knocka me down—so.

ADD. Well, I'd have his life for it. He is a bad character and I know it. You kill him and I'll swear you out of it.

GIOV. Ah—I keel heem—but how?

ADD. Ask them all up to drink—then turn down the light and stab him in the dark.

DOL. I have heard enough. I will put him on his guard. [*Exit L.2.E.*]

GIOV. See—my knife is sharp. I will do it.

ADD. That is right. Now here is money to treat with. Kill him and you will get your revenge and rid me of a dangerous foe. Call them up to drink and I will return just in time to see my friend the Ferret give his last kick. [*Exit D.R. Giovanni goes to L. end of bar. Dutchman, Dude and Coon enter R.L.1 and L.2., and get in front of bar. Giovanni's brother Pablo enters L.1.E. and stands next to Giovanni, who shows him his knife. It is quite dark. Enter Joe and Dolores L.2.E.*]

JOE. Why, you must be mistaken, there is no one here who means to harm me.

DOL. I am sure he will kill you, and all on my account. Oh, let me go back to him.

JOE. Why, I couldn't think of such a thing. Come, wait for me outside a moment. [*Takes her to D.R. Then walks up to L. end of bar. Giovanni turns out lights*]

JOHN. Look out, Joe. [*Giovanni strikes, but hits his own brother, who falls. Johnnie lights the gas*]

DOL. [*Enters D.R.*] Why, Barney, you have killed your own brother!

GIOV. No, no—I no keel my brother. I know my own brother.

JOE. Cowardly assassin—[*Grabs him*] You have killed your own brother in mistake for me, and you must answer to the law for your crime. [*Enter Adderly, door R. and looks at the dead man*] Ah, I see you were but the tool, and there stands the instigator. [*Adderly draws revolver, but the women who are nearest him grab him, and Dolores catches his hand and bites it until he drops the pistol*]

TABLEAU

ACT III.

SCENE: *Parlor in Thomas Goodwin's house.*

CAE. [*Enters R.C. with gas lights in hand*] Hang out your banners on the outer wall, and let the cry be "Onward!" But why should I play the Roman fool and die here upon me own sword? NO. Lay on, Macduff, and damn'd be he who first cries, "Hold—Enough!" [*Up and down—across stage—stab—fall*]

AUNT S. Why, Caesar, what in the world are you making such a noise about?

CAE. That ain't noise—that's ambition. "Lay on Macduff and damn'd be he who first cries, 'Hold—Enough.' " That's crushing genius through the mighty cranium.

AUNT S. Caesar, don't you know that Mr. Tom is expected? Go and see that his room is in order.

CAE. Ha—

AUNT S. Leave the room, sir.

CAE. I go, but of my own accord. [*Enter Louise L.1.E.*] Ha, ha, ha!

LOU. Go. [*Points*]

CAE. Great Heaven—I am crushed!

LOU. Now, Auntie, be good and don't insist upon my going to the entertainment with Mr. Ellerton.

AUNT S. But you must.

LOU. I hate him, and I won't go.

AUNT S. Mr. Ellerton is a very nice man, and I don't want to hear any more nonsense about him.

LOU. But I can't go with him.

AUNT S. You will.

LOU. I won't.

AUNT S. If you don't stop being saucy to me, I'll tell your father.

LOU. Well, I don't care, you are awful cross, and I despise Mr. Ellerton. Tom is the only fellow I care a snap for—he is just splendid. Say, Auntie, don't you think Tom is good-looking?

AUNT S. Young girls like you should think of something else besides good-looking young men. It is for ladies like me, and not young girls like you, to think of such things.

LOU. Well, I am bigger than you are and you are forty-nine.

AUNT S. You naughty girl—forty-nine! Why, the idea! It's no such thing. [*Enter Tom L.1.E.*]

LOU. Oh, Tom, I'm so glad you have come.

AUNT S. Thomas, kiss your aunt.

TOM. All right, old girl.

AUNT S. Thomas, what do you mean?

LOU. She has been scolding all morning, Tom, and I'll tell you all I know. She meets a red-headed policeman down at the gate every day and talks to him for hours.

AUNT S. Thomas, don't you believe a word she says.

TOM. I don't, I never saw a policeman talking to a woman in my life. [*Tom and Louise walk to rear of stage together*]

AUNT S. The idea! As if I would talk to a policeman, let alone a red-headed one! [*Enter Caesar L.I.E.*]

CAE. [*To Aunt Susannah*] There is a gentleman down in the garden wants to see you.

AUNT S. A gentleman to see me? [*Confidentially*] Now, Caesar, who is it?

CAE. It's the red-headed policeman. [*Aunt Susannah chases him out L.I.E. Louise and Tom laugh*]

LOU. [*Coming forward*] Now, tell me, Tom, did you enjoy your trip and did you find more attractive faces and friends there than at home? For I suppose you found time to amuse yourself, although you went for health.

TOM. No, my dear, here I find metal more attractive. [*Aside*] My father's money!

LOU. You mean ladies, of course?

TOM. Oh, yes. But by the way, does Mr. Ellerton call as frequently as ever?

LOU. Yes, he does, Tom, and I wish that he would stay away.

TOM. Why, I thought you were fond of him, and the thing as good as settled?

LOU. Oh, I could never marry that odious Ellerton, Tom. The man whom I marry must be one whom I can honor, love and respect. Mr. Ellerton is not such a man. [*Takes seat at table*]

TOM. But such a man I know—a noble, generous fellow, and though we have been acquainted but a few weeks, our hearts are joined together with links of steel. I have invited him here and am expecting him this evening.

LOU. I shall be glad to meet any friend of yours, but in affairs of the heart I prefer to be my own mistress.

TOM. Rest assured that father loves his children too well to ever force you to marry anyone you do not love.

LOU. Surely the father that has been so kind would not want his daughter to risk her happiness with such a man? [*Enter Caesar*]

CAE. The young gentleman is in the reception room and promulgates his wishes on this year card.

TOM. Why, it's Ferris. Show him up at once.

CAE. Safe conduct to his happiness! Ala ca Zam. [*Exit L.I.E.*]

Tom. Why, what's the matter with the fellow?

Lou. He has joined an amateur dramatic society. Why, the other day we heard the most terrible noise upstairs, actually thought the house was tumbling down, but upon investigation it proved to be poor Caesar—[*Rises and walks to rear*] rehearsing *Richard the Third*. He was running around the room, jumping over chairs and madly shouting "A horse—a horse—my Kingdom for a horse!" [*Comes forward laughing*]

Tom. And still the world turns round. A black Richard. We shall be having a black Juliet next.

Cae. [*Enter L.1.E.*] Room for me, Lord Duke Don Caesar De Pizaro Patsy Bol—bol—bol—Bolivar! [*Enter Joe L.1.E., and makes a quick move at Caesar*]

Tom. Leave the room, fool.

Cae. He who calls me a fool insults the lady I board with. [*Exit L.1.E. Louise R.C. Tom L.C.*]

Joe. [*To Tom*] What's the matter with the fifteenth amendment, Tom?

Tom. Oh, he's only a black amateur.

Joe. I should never take him for a white professional.

Tom. Mr. Ferris, allow me to introduce you to my sister Louise. [*Joe advances and they stand together*]

Joe. Miss Goodwin, it is indeed a pleasure to make your acquaintance.

Lou. The pleasure, Mr. Ferris, is mutual. I assure you I was chiding Tom for his selfishness in leaving me to be escorted by a man whom I abhor.

Joe. [*To Tom*] It is evident that you have neglected your sister. [*Winks*]

Lou. Why, he left us entirely alone last winter.

Joe. Did you leave your sister alone?

Tom. [*Desperately*] Well, what is a fellow to do?

Joe. You should emulate me. Never leave any fellow's sister alone.

Tom. Oh, pshaw!

Lou. Tell me, Mr. Ferris, what were the attractions at Saratoga? Were there any ladies who received Tom's special attention?

Joe. Yes, there was one in particular whom he was very devoted to.

Tom. [*Pulls his coat-tail*] Oh, come off, Joe.

Joe. Go 'way, you naughty, naughty man. She had lemon-colored hair and a pull-back, so.

Tom. Joe, for Heaven sake, draw it mild.

Joe. [*Taking hold of coat-tail*] You will draw it off if you keep on pulling it.

Lou. And what was her name?

Joe. Her name was—

Tom. [*Whispers to him*]

Joe. Did you hear what he said? He said her name was Augalusha.

Tom. Augalusha Snobbs.

Joe. She was the queen of the surf.

Lou. [*Walking past Joe to Tom*] And so you were playing court to the queen, Tom?

Tom. Why, certainly. [*To Joe*] I trust we may not meet as strangers when I am united to royalty.

Joe. I hope not. [*Aside*] Ah, Heaven grant that those words may not come back tenfold to repay for my raillery!

Cae. [*Enters L.1.E.*] Sir, your generous father requests your presence in the ante-chamber.

Tom. What's that?

Cae. Your father wants to see you.

Tom. Tell him that I will join him at once. [*Joe, Tom and Louise gather opposite R.L.E. and stand talking*]

Cae. Such proclamations shall be made. [*Makes a run at them*] Ha— beware. She has deceived her father and may be—

Tom. Leave the room.

Cae. [*Singing*] "There Is a New Coon in Town, There Is a New Coon in Town." [*Exit L.1.E.*]

Tom. Pardon me for leaving you, but I must pay my respects to my father. I'll leave you to the tender mercies of Louise. You will stay with us, I hope, while in town, as per agreement, you know. [*Exit R.2.*]

Joe. [*Follows him to the door*] Thanks—perhaps I will. [*Gets chair at back of stage*]

Lou. Your family, then, do not reside in New York, Mr. Ferris?

Joe. [*Brings chair to her side*] Pardon me if I intrude my domestic history upon you. My father and mother both died when I was a little boy, and I have been compelled to fight my way all alone in the world.

Lou. I can sympathize with you, for I, too, and my twin brother, were left alone. And had it not been for Mr. Goodwin, who took our mother from the snow-covered street where she had fallen exhausted, brought her home and warmed us back to life, I fear our history would have been a sad one. But ever since that night when he adopted us he has been the kindest of fathers. I trust that you will remain with us and meet my father, who will, I am sure, be delighted to make your acquaintance. Our circle of friends is very small, and with the exception of Mr. Ellerton we have very few frequent callers. [*Enter Caesar L.1.E.*]

CAE. Mr.—Mr.—Damned if I haven't forgotten the gentleman's name. [*Exit L.1.*]

JOE. [*Aside*] Ellerton—why, that is the very name that Johnnie said Adderly had assumed. The wolf in the fold of the lamb. Can it be possible? But, caution, Joe—caution. [*To Louise*] Do you know Mr. Ellerton's occupation?

LOU. To tell the truth I do not, and were it not for the business relations he has with my father, his presence here would be a cloud upon our sunshine. I think I can dispel the cloud and then the sun will shine brighter than ever. Oh, villain—villain!

CAE. [*Enters*] Mr. Ellerton is without and craves admission to your ladyship.

LOU. Show him in.

JOE. What—Ellerton here? He must not see me. What shall I do? [*To Louise*] I wish to speak to your brother a moment. [*Goes to R.2.E.*] I think I can find him.

LOU. Wait until Caesar returns and he shall show you the way.

JOE. I wish to see him at once, and I think it is quite unnecessary, as I can undoubtedly find him. [*Opens door*]

LOU. You will find him on the second floor to the left.

JOE. Thanks. I trust I shall have the pleasure of seeing you again.

LOU. Will you not stay for the evening?

JOE. I will. [*Aside*] Would to Heaven it were for life! [*Exit R.2.*]

LOU. Why, what a nice young man he is! Tom is very fortunate in having such a man for his friend. [*Enter Caesar L.1. and behind him Ellerton*]

CAE. Behold the most conglomerate of his race. [*To Ellerton*] "Mark where she stands. Around her awful form I draw the holy circle of our church. Step but one foot within that circle, and on thy head—yea, even though it wore a crown, I'd launch the curse of—"

LOU. [*Sharply*] Caesar! [*Exit Caesar whistling L.1.*] He is becoming unbearable. I am afraid we shall have to discharge him.

ELL. Not on my account, I trust. I like his nonsense rather than otherwise. Your father is at home, is he not? In fact he is always at home to me.

LOU. He is, and he bade me say that he would receive you in the library when you called. And there you might transact any business you may have with him.

ELL. [*Draws chair closer to Louise*] Business, Miss Goodwin, is a very cold word to be used between friends and does not sound well when coming from your lips. [*Essays to take her hand*]

Lou. [*Rising*] Pardon me, Mr. Ellerton, but my friends I have already selected. [*She sweeps from the room and exits through arch*]

ELL. [*Getting up and gazing after her, and putting chair at rear of stage*] I'll lower her tone, the haughty beauty, and that before the day is over. [*Sits at table. Aunt Susannah enters L.1.*] There's that crazy old maid. I'll pretend to be asleep.

AUNT S. [*Just inside entrance*] Oh—it's a man! [*Goes forward*] Why, it's that dear delightful Mr. Ellerton! He's asleep. How sweet he looks. I've a good mind to kiss him. I believe I will. [*Kisses him—he jumps up. Looks from behind fan, coquettishly*] Peek-a-boo!

ELL. Crazy!

AUNT S. Did I frighten you?

ELL. Bless my soul, no! It takes more than that to frighten me. Do it again if you want to. [*Aunt Susannah with a little scream starts to do it again —he holds her off*] But not now.

AUNT S. I hope you will forgive my little indiscretion. [*Turning herself around and back again like a schoolgirl*] Girls will be girls, you know!

ELL. Yes, a nice old girl. [*Aside*] I suppose I'll have to make love to the old aunt in order to get the niece. [*To Aunt Susannah*] I have business with your brother which brings me here quite often. [*Steps toward her. C. front*]

AUNT S. Don't you tickle me, sir—don't you tickle me! [*Wriggles*]

ELL. I understand your warm and gushing nature. [*Arm around her*] It has been chilled by contact with the cold and cruel world. If I but dared to reveal to you—

AUNT S. Oh, do.

ELL. Oh, no.

AUNT S. Oh, Mr. Ellerton, isn't this too real to be sweet!

ELL. It IS too real to be sweet.

AUNT S. Oh, will you return my love?

ELL. Certainly I will. I've no use for it.

AUNT S. Will you love me when I'm old? [*Draws it out*]

ELL. That's about the only chance I have. Allow me to kiss—[*She puts up her face*] your fair hand. [*Gets away from her a little*]

AUNT S. I must go now. [*Edges up to him and holds her dress in the hand nearest him, as if to detain herself*] Now, don't you hold me back, for if my brother knew I was alone with you, he would scold me for being so giddy.

ELL. [*Puts his arm around her again*] Your giddy brother shan't scold you, for I'll protect you from his wrath.

AUNT S. Oh, wouldn't we make a pretty tintype!

ELL. A great big chromo given away with a pound of tea. [*Lets go of her*]

AUNT S. Now, Mr. Ellerton, how old do you suppose I am? Guess.

ELL. Well, there is a question about ancient history. I guess you are about eighteen.

AUNT S. Oh, somebody told you. [*Goes for him—he holds her off. Caesar enters arch*]

CAE. Oh, Lordy! [*Jumps behind sofa*]

AUNT S. Why, I thought I heard someone speak. [*Goes to L.1.E.*] Goodbye. [*Throws kiss*] Oh, you dear man, I shall never forget you! [*Exit L.1.*]

ELL. Well, I'll never forget *you*, that's sure.

LOU. [*Enters arch*] Why, Mr. Ellerton, you here yet?

ELL. I still trespass upon your valuable time.

LOU. [*Calls*] Caesar—[*He jumps from behind sofa*] Caesar is here. Caesar, show this man to my father's study.

ELL. This gentleman can find the way to your father's study. [*Bows—goes L.2.*]

CAE. Goest thou to speak to my lord Hamlet?

ELL. Go thou to the devil. [*Exit L.2.*]

CAE. Lead on—I'll follow thee. [*Exit L.2.*]

LOU. [*Sits at table*] I know it was wrong to speak to him as I did, but there was something so sinister in his looks and actions that I could not help it. I have made an enemy of him for life—of that I am sure. [*Enter Caesar L.2., with letter on tray*]

CAE. A letter from my lord Duke.

LOU. [*Takes letter*] Caesar, you are a fool.

CAE. My proud girl, you shall yet be humbled. Go, get thee to a nunnery. Be thou as chaste as ice, as pure as snow—go—go—go. [*Runs into door jamb and Exit L.1.*]

LOU. A letter from my brother. [*Reads*]—and that man here too, closeted with my father at this time. I feel that something terrible is going to happen. I fear his devilish look—his cunning smile. [*Enter Joe D.R.*] Oh, Mr. Ferris, I think that Heaven has sent you here for me to confide in. I need your assistance.

JOE. I always act on the first impulse. I find it is the best way.

LOU. I will trust you. Mr. Ellerton is now closeted with my father. That man has long been a suitor for my hand, but without the least encouragement from me. And now I get this letter—read it. [*Hands him letter*] Oh, I feel there is something deep laid underneath all this. Oh, I know that it is some game.

JOE. [*Glances at letter*] You may be sure there is, and you may also be sure that I am just the man to spoil his little game. [*Hands back letter*] I am not a lawyer, no one knows that better than I, and if this man has any business with your father, the latter will come out second best, you may be sure. Is there a door or a window through which I could hear their conversation? It would enable me to act with more certainty, for, believe me, we have a desperate man to deal with—a perfect tyrant and one who will not leave his prey while a drop of blood remains.

LOU. I will tell you what we can do. I will scream and alarm the inmates of the next room. You conceal yourself behind the sofa. They will rush in here. You can then step into the next room. I will give them some explanation for my fright and you can overhear every word that is said.

JOE. [*Goes toward sofa*] What a wonderful faculty for invention has a woman, and what a dear delightful creature she is! Well, who knows, something good may come of it, after all.

LOU. Are you ready?

JOE. All ready. [*Joe hides behind sofa—Louise screams. Ellerton and Mr. Goodwin enters L.2.E. Tom enters D.R. Caesar and Aunt Susannah L.1.*]

OMNES. Why, what in the world is the matter?

LOU. Oh, dear me—look under the table! [*Joe sneaks into L.2.E.*] I was so frightened.

AUNT S. What was it?

LOU. It looked for all the world like a great black cat.

AUNT S. A great black cat. [*Picks up skirts and runs out R.1.*]

MR. G., ELL. *and* TOM. A great black cat! [*All look at Caesar*]

CAE. A great black cat? Well, what are you all looking at me for? I thought he had a touch of E Pluribus Union! [*Exit L.1. Louise and Tom are at table*]

ELL. [*To Louise*] I trust that you will be better presently.

LOU. I have every reason to believe I shall be better presently.

ELL. Your father was afraid that some calamity had befallen you.

LOU. [*Going up stage—looking at father, who is on sofa*] And I was afraid some calamity had befallen my poor father. Come Tom, I am all right now. And of one thing you may be sure.

ELL. And that is—?

LOU. [*Bowing herself out with Tom*] That the black cat will never frighten me again. [*Exit through arch*]

ELL. What a fuss she makes about nothing—and what does she mean by a black cat, I wonder? Well, Mr. Goodwin, let us resume our conversation which was just interrupted.

Good. [*Rising*] Yes, let us come to the point at once. We are ruined.

Ell. Excuse me sir—YOU are. I offered to take a share of the risk, but you declined.

Good. But you said the stocks were firm and the supply was inexhaustible.

Ell. There you are—wrong again. Their circular said so.

Good. But you gave it your support.

Ell. True—and at that time I thought so. But come, sir—your son.

Good. Ah, yes. Five years ago I left him in undisturbed possession of a house that had stood the shocks of thirty years. Young in years but old in mercantile experience. During the panic of '73, while other houses were tottering and falling about us, ours alone stood—like the giant oak, it defied the storm. And now, what do I hear? Rivals say its time has come at last. That proud old fabric is levelled with the dust. [*Turns, with hands up*] Oh, Heaven, do not now desert me! In the evening of my life sustain me as thou hast in other days! [*Sinks on sofa*]

Ell. Would it not be better to act for yourself than to leave everything to Heaven? [*Snaps fingers*]

Good. I confess, 'tis to you I owe all my misery. Your oily tongue first counselled me to risk my all, and when I warned my son to beware of you, he only laughed.

Ell. But you didn't warn him in time, or he wouldn't stand the chance he now does of ending his days in the State's prison.

Good. [*Catching him by the collar*] Unsay those words, villain, or, old as I am, I'll strike you dead at my feet!

Ell. Your indignation is very natural, sir, but I have proof of what I say.

Good. You have proof?

Ell. Yes, sir, right here. [*Takes note out of bill book—puts book back carelessly, so it can be easily gotten at*] Look at this signature and tell me if it is yours?

Good. It is my writing.

Ell. Look again and be sure.

Good. No—this is not my writing. It is a forgery.

Ell. So you see that the great house of Goodwin has a worse enemy than I am.

Good. Oh, wretch! And my son, too! [*Turns to exit, rear arch*] This matter shall be laid bare.

Ell. Stop! [*Holds up check*] Here is the proof against your son. Render ME powerless?

Good. I do not understand you.

Ell. Make it to my interest to destroy this note and conceal this evidence.

GOOD. I am still in ignorance.

ELL. In other words, give me the right to call Louise my wife.

GOOD. [*Coming back slowly*] What—Louise your wife? You, marry Louise? Never! She loathes—she detests you.

ELL. I may not be able to inspire love, but I have the power to command respect. We shall see. [*Goes to rear arch*]

GOOD. Oh—stay—!

ELL. Come—I will do better. I will advance money to meet your creditors—destroy all proof against your son. We'll infuse new blood in the firm of Goodwin and Company, and it shall live again as Goodwin, Ellerton and Company.

GOOD. Oh, anything to save my children from misery—myself from despair!

ELL. I thought you'd change your mind. Come, sir—sign this paper. [*Takes out book and lays it on table*] And you flourish again like a green bay tree.

GOOD. [*Reads paper*] Ah, your schemes were well laid and you have me in your power. But as long as you hold that forged check in terror over my head I will not sign.

ELL. [*Tears note up*] Behold my magnanimity. [*Aside*] I didn't tell him, though, I had a second one. [*To Goodwin*] So you see the devil is not always as black as he is painted. [*Goodwin starts to sign. Enter Joe L.U.E.*]

JOE. Stop! [*Tears up paper*] And now, sir, you behold *my* magnanimity.

ELL. The Ferret here?

JOE. Yes, the Ferret—right here.

GOOD. Who are you, sir?

JOE. I am the man who scared away the black cat, and there he is! [*Points at Ellerton and laughs. Ellerton annoyed*]

GOOD. But I never saw you before.

JOE. Let it suffice for the moment that I am here as your best friend, and Heaven helping me, I'll prove myself one by thwarting yonder devil. Let us call him by his right name for once. DEVIL, did I not tell you that you should feel the weight of my arm—while you rioted at your ease on the ill-gotten gains wrung by the father from the poor starving wretches of Five Points? My mother went to you for assistance after your accursed place had swallowed up my father's all, and when she asked for help, your father struck her. I then, boy as I was, registered a vow to be even with you for that blow, and Heaven has sent me to right the wrong, and drag the guilty one to justice.

ELL. Do not believe him—he is an escaped convict.

JOE. But come, John, tell me what has become of John Adderly?

JOHN. Oh he's ruined—turned respectable. He's up to some game.

JOE. Evidently, as he never would have done so from choice. But tell me—what do you know of him?

JOHN. Well, you see I was walking down Wall Street the other day.

JOE. What were you doing on Wall Street?

JOHN. I was over there to get a check cashed, to buy five cents' worth of chewing gum.

JOE. Oh, yes, I saw your bank on Wall Street.

JOHN. Well, you see, as I was walking down the Street, I saw Adderly coming in the opposite direction, talkin' to a rooster.

JOE. Come now, stop right there. Do you think that I am from the country and you can stuff that down me? I would like to know in what language a man could carry on a conversation with a rooster?

JOHN. He could cackle to him, couldn't he?

JOE. I bow to your superior knowledge of cackleology.

JOHN. Oh, don't. [*Gets weak*]

JOE. [*Holding him up*] Can it be possible that my cackalogical phraseology has upset your equilibrium?

JOHN. Joe, don't give them to me in clusters—give them to me one at a time.

JOE. How do you feel now, Camille?

JOHN. Look in the pupil of my eye and you will see a little black spot, and underneath my thumbnail a thin blue line. I cannot marry you.

JOE. Why?

JOHN. I am an octoroon.

JOE. That's foul.

JOHN. Well, then, that's two I've got on you.

JOE. That's so, the other rooster and this one makes two. [*Puts up two fingers*] All right, we've got two roosters. Now, go ahead.

JOHN. No, the last one wasn't a rooster, so we let her lay. [*Puts one of Joe's fingers down*] Well, Adderly and this rooster were talking, when up comes the Shrimp and introduces Adderly as Ellert.

JOE. He's sailing under false colors, then. That looks bad. But come to the underground parlor, Johnnie, I want to have a long talk with you.

JOHN. This coat ain't good enough to go to the parlor, Joe—it's queer.

JOE. It is a dizzy coat.

JOHN. But, Joe, it's not the coat that makes the man.

JOE. [*Sincerely*] You're right. It's not the coat that makes the man.

JOHN. It's the pants. [*Exit both R.1.E.*]

GOOD. No, impossible!

JOE. Through his hellish machinations and perjury, too, he confines me to the loathsome cells of the State's prison, but I have a paper signed by his confederate, and attested to by the judge of the court before which I was tried, proving that I was innocent and he the guilty one. And he must take my place in that same prison. That is your doom, John Adderly.

ELL. No—no—Joe—stop. Don't say that.

GOOD. What, the son of John Adderly that kept a place in the Five Points?

JOE. The same. And you see the father well represented in the son.

GOOD. Merciful Providence, how wonderful are thy ways! Twenty years ago, and the night of the great fire, I knew of a similar act done by his father. I heard a cry of distress, and following the sound I found a woman in distress. Aye, dying in the streets. I afterwards learned she had gone to him, asking for a mere pittance. Bread enough to keep herself and two children from starving, after her husband had been ruined by rum, and she thrown from his door and left to die in the street. Those two children are now mine, by adoption, and living under this roof.

JOE. [*To Ellerton*] Oh, villain, pray that it may not fall and crush you!

ELL. Joe Ferris, you have been the bane of my life. YOURS shall now answer for it. [*Draws revolver. Joe takes it from him, and holds picture, hesitating to fire*]

JOE. You deserve death for being such an infamous coward. But I'll not cheat the hangman of such a precious package as you are. [*Gives revolver to Goodwin*] He would become a murderer as well as a forger.

GOOD. WHAT? A forger?

JOE. Yes, forger! I know something of this coal transaction. He calls himself the coal agent, but I call him the coal fraud. Why, the coal only exists on the char that he carries in his pocket. Why, he's the whole coal company; transacts all the business. In his pocket, are all the stealings, rolled up in a little bit of a lump. Give it a toss and away it goes. [*Indicates tossing a ball away*]

ELL. But I never forged my father's name.

GOOD. But the proof of that has been destroyed.

ELL. So you think, but I have another check. [*Shows book that he sticks, carelessly, in his vest pocket. Joe jerks it out*]

GOOD. Villain, you have deceived me in that also! [*Enter Policeman, Louise and Aunt Susannah*]

ELL. What, a policeman here? Arrest that man! [*Points to Goodwin*]

JOE. [*As he tears up check taken from Ellerton's pocket, Tom Goodwin enters L. and stands behind Goodwin, Sr.*] What for?

ELL. For forgery.

JOE. That proof has been destroyed. Arrest THAT man! [*Points to Ellerton*]

ELL. ME? What for?

JOE. For murder. You instigated the Italian to strike the cowardly blow that your arm failed to strike. ARREST that man!

ELL. [*Crossing to Goodwin, Sr.*] But you yourself saw him *destroy* the proof against your son!

JOE. A father will not convict a son.

ELL. But my *oath* will.

JOE. But you are a criminal, and your oath will not be taken seriously. [*Women come down and congratulate Joe, as Policeman goes down and puts handcuffs on Ellerton, who stands amazed. Goodwin embraces his son, as curtain falls*]

ACT IV.

SCENE: *A Station house at a Union Pacific Railroad station. See front of script for description of set. At rise, Joe, a Chinaman and three ladies are discovered, and as curtain ascends, they give three cheers.*

JOE. [*Calls*] Come, boys, get those trunks off. [*Johnnie and several supers enter, and take trunks off left, followed by the ladies, Johnnie, and the Chinaman. But as Joe calls Johnnie, and ladies stop*] Johnnie, you escort the ladies over to the ranch, and you'd better stop on your way back, and tell the Chief to send me a few of his braves. Black Cloud and his band are reported at Station 42, and it is possible they may come here. I don't want them to catch us without a guard, as it might invite attack.

JOHN. All right, Joe. Catch on, girls! [*Offers arms, which two girls take and they exit, followed by other girl and Chinaman, off R.1.E. As Tom Goodwin enters up R. and comes down and slaps Joe on back*]

TOM. Are you the station agent?

JOE. I believe I am. [*Turns*] Why, Tom Goodwin!

TOM. Joe Ferris, I'm delighted. [*Shakes hands*]

JOE. Where'd you come from?

TOM. Why, from the train, of course!

JOE. And I not there to meet you!

TOM. What in the world brought you out here?

JOE. Oh, Tom, don't ask me. How could I stay in New York after what happened in your house?

TOM. How can I ever repay you for what you did? In a moment of madness I forged my father's name, and you saved me from disgrace and ruin.

JOE. It was a terrible sacrifice, for in doing so I forfeited the good opinion of your family, by revealing the name and conditions of my associates.

TOM. But I investigated, and found you innocent of any crime.

JOE. But I was a gambler, and my associates were men of the lowest stamp. But, remember, I was left alone when a mere boy. I found myself in the streets one night, with clothing scarcely sufficient to protect me from the cold, while vice rolled by me, wrapped in furs. I resolved I would lead such a life no longer, and I became a gambler. My wits were as sharp as theirs. They didn't thrust me aside, but even then, the money wrung from my dupes seems to melt in my hands. So, after passing through an eventful life I have at last settled down as station master at 47th U. P. Railway. By the way, Tom, what ever became of Adderly? You know, he was sentenced for five years for that affair with the Italian. I suppose he is still serving the State?

TOM. About six months ago an uprising took place in the prison, and after killing one guard and nearly killing another he escaped by jumping into the river. Nothing was heard of him for a long time, but just before I left New York I read in the papers that he had been seen around his old haunts.

JOE. He is free, then. That man bears me no good will.

TOM. Yes. They never succeeded in capturing him. But tell me, do you feel contented out here?

JOE. How could I be contented? I sometimes long to be back in New York and I sigh for my old associates—but always the GOOD ones, Tom, remember that. But, Tom, come into the station. [*Starts*]

TOM. But I must go and bring Louise and the rest of the folks.

JOE. What? Louise *here?*

TOM. [*Points to them, as Louise and Aunt Susannah enter R.U., followed by Chinaman*] No, THERE! Louise, allow me to present you to a very dear friend.

LOU. Why, Mr. Ferris! I'm more than pleased to meet you here. [*Shake hands*]

AUNT S. Why, Mr. Ferris! [*Tries to kiss him, but he dodges her*] How do you do?

LOU. AUNTY! Oh, I'm so glad to find you here ahead of us, Mr. Ferris, for this is to be our new home. And Aunt Susie was afraid we'd have no neighbors, and no one to entertain us. But tell me, how is it that we find you here?

JOE. I have learned that an honest day's work is the best nurse for a good night's sleep. [*Chinaman has been trying to pull ribbons off Aunt Susannah's hat, she turns, frightened*]

AUNT S. What in the world is *that?*

JOE. Well, we haven't named it yet.

AUNT S. Well, it looks exactly like a Chinese firecracker.

CHI. Me no firecracker, me skyrocket. [*Sits on box, and gets his finger pinched in lid*] Oh, oh, oh. [*Joe points to show him he's sitting on the lid*]

JOE. See. [*Chinaman gets up. Joe shows him the end-pieces on the box. Chinaman sits again and grins*]

LOU. May I have a word with you, Mr. Ferris?

JOE. Certainly. [*Tom and Aunt Susannah retire to boxes at back of stage*]

LOU. Why did you leave New York so suddenly, without a word of farewell?

JOE. I loved one far above me. Do you remember, when I sat in the witness box giving evidence against that man, and every word I spoke was carrying me further and further away from her, until I had revealed myself a gambler and the accomplice of this unprincipled man? Then I realized the position in which I stood, and not until then did I realize how hopeless was my love. Even as I sat there I held in my own hand that priceless boon —my pardon signed by the governor, who had heard my prayer, and with tears in his eyes, he bade me "Go and sin no more." That was why I left New York.

LOU. But she whom you had loved—Had she loved you in return and bade you to stay—?

JOE. Then I would have died at her feet.

LOU. You were wrong not to disclose your love, for had she been a true woman, she never would have refused such a noble heart as yours.

JOE. Had you been that woman, would you *then* have spoken thus?

LOU. I would, indeed.

JOE. Then, 'tis you I love. But until this moment I never even dared to hope to win the love of one so pure and good as you. [*Louise turns toward him*]

LOU. Oh, what can I say? That I never loved until I saw you—never knew happiness until you came to our house! [*He kisses her*]

CHI. Oh, shamee—shamee—[*Hides face. Aunt Susannah comes forward with Tom*]

TOM. What does this mean?

JOE. It means that your sister has consented to become my wife—and that I am the happiest man on the U.P. Road.

AUNT S. [*To Louise*] Then 'tis you he loves. [*Kisses her. Tom and Joe go up and sit at back*] But don't you know that that is very naughty?

LOU. Yes, I know it's naughty, but it's nice. [*She goes up-stage and joins Tom and Joe. Joe springs to meet her*]

AUNT S. I wish I had some nice—

CHI. [*Runs up to her*] You like some ricee—[*Aunt Susannah turns back on him and walks to box opposite R.2.E. Sits down and takes drink out of bottle*]

CHI. Ah ha—Melican woman like jig water. Me likee, too. [*Takes bottle out of her hand and drinks. Offers it back several times, but fools her and drinks himself, talking Chinese all the time, and keeps this up till the bottle is empty*] Me makee mashee. [*Sits beside her*] Ah, there my sizee—me stealee you. [*Tries to put his arm around her. She jumps quickly—he falls, then chases her*]

JOE. Here—what is the matter, Tart?

CHI. [*Joe comes forward with Tom*] Melican woman fightee.

JOE. Come here, Tart. [*To others*] Watch me telephone to China. [*Takes Tart's cue*] Hello, Tart!

CHI. Hello!

JOE. You're crazy.

CHI. Me, too. [*Joe turns away laughing*] Now me talkee. [*Takes end of cue*] Hello—hello—hello—[*Jerks his cue—disgusted—jumps on box*]

JOHN. [*Enters R.2.E.*] Supper is ready, Mr. Joe.

CHI. Hello, Johnnie. Me makee mashee.

JOHN. Who is it? The old girl? [*All exit R.3.E., except Joe and Louise and Chinaman, who is on box. Enter Caesar with baggage*]

CAE. Say, look here—[*They are just disappearing in the station*] Where is the colored population goin' to roost? [*Joe and Louise stop at door of station. Chinaman hollers and skips R.1.E.*]

JOE. [*To Caesar*] Why, I thought I would leave you out here to amuse my Indian friends.

CAE. Injuns around here? [*Looks scared*]

JOE. Lots of them. You ain't afraid of Indians, are you?

CAE. What—me afraid of Injuns? Well, I guess not. Why, my maw used to keep an Injun boarding-house.

JOE. Where?

CAE. In Indianapolis.

Joe. [*Quickly*] What's that?

Cae. [*Jumps*] Oh, Lord!

Joe. You ain't afraid?

Cae. No, I'se just a little bit skeered, that's all. [*Exit Louise R.2.E.*]

Joe. [*Comes forward and takes Caesar by the arm*] You must be very circumspect. There is an Indian around here ten feet high, and mark you, Caesar, he eats a nigger every morning for breakfast.

Cae. He eats a nigger every morning *before* breakfast?

Joe. Yes, sir.

Cae. That settles it. This nigger don't get up till after dinner.

Joe. [*Crosses to R.2.E.*] Look out for that hat. [*In deep tone*] The bell has rung for it and the Indians are death on a white hat.

Cae. Oh, Lord!

Joe. What's that behind you? [*Exit R.2.E.*]

Cae. Oh—[*Jumps. Chinaman enters R.1.E., runs into Caesar and exit L.2. After this Caesar is about scared to death. It gets dark*] I wonder what's the matter with that hat. The boys in St. Louis used to holler "Who skinned the cat, Nigger wid the white hat." Oh, how dark it's getting! I wish when I come out here I'd stayed home. If any of them Indians eat this nigger, I'll be doggoned if I don't lay heavy on their stomachs. Oh, but I'm sleepy. I'll go and get something to eat, and then with the blue sky above me and the green grass beneath me, I don't think an earthquake would scare me. [*Indian war-whoop*] Oh, Lord, what's that? [*Exit R.U. Enter Indian L.U., goes to station—looks around—beckons. Adderly enters L.3. followed by Chief and Indians. Indians squat around at back of stage. Adderly opposite R.2.E., Chief opposite L.2.E.*]

Chief. White Brother so—

Add. Don't call me White Brother—call me Indian like yourselves. I would not have the keeper of the station here know that a white man had led you on the war-path.

Chief. Did he not say that he would lead the Indian where he could avenge the wrongs of his race? Have we not done so? Has he not seen the Pale-faces scalped—their homes burned, and their women and children carried away captive to the wigwams of Black Cloud's braves? And now, more of the white race turn their faces to the west. Where can the Red Man go? What spot can he call his own? None—but his Mother Earth, to sleep his last sleep. Behold, there is another reason why we must fight. The Iron Horse comes thundering across our plains. Our warriors look aghast, and in vain does Black Cloud tell them that these were the hunting grounds of their fathers, and belong to them. They are filled with fear. And what has the white man given us for all this? Ugh—his fire-water. It steals away the brains of my people and excites them to deeds of violence. The Red Man's hours are numbered.

ADD. You are right, and nought is left but revenge.

CHIEF. Yes—spare neither age nor sex. Kill all.

ADD. But what is to become of the white family that we tracked here?

CHIEF. Their fate will be sealed by the rising sun.

ADD. Yes—kill all. But the women—what of them?

CHIEF. They shall be carried away captives to become the squaws of Black Cloud and his braves.

ADD. That is good. There is much plunder here. Provisions, ammunition, money. All this shall belong to you.

CHIEF. White Chief speak good. Indian take all—and kill.

ADD. All but the women, for the Chief himself wishes one for his squaw.

CHIEF. The White Chief shall have one for his squaw. Indian kill all the rest.

ADD. Yes, kill all that I shall name. The station-keeper is my deadly enemy. Kill him.

CHIEF. Black Cloud kill him.

ADD. He may take away your hunting grounds and not pay you for them, but pay your great Father in Washington and leave you to freeze and starve. Now, the keeper of the station is as cunning as a fox. We must return when all have gone to rest. Fire the station—stampede the horses, and when the sun rises, not one of their cursed tribe shall be left alive.

CHIEF. When does the Iron Horse come back?

ADD. At this time tomorrow, and they must find naught here but smouldering .ashes.

CHIEF. White man is black. But they are our enemies and must perish. I will teach them that the Indian, too, knows how to punish and avenge. [*Adderly goes to door of station. Chief steps back a step or two, then quickly forward with a yell to his followers, who all spring forward, but Adderly stops them*]

ADD. Back! Lights are still moving around the station. Back—and defer our purpose for a while.

CHIEF. The White Chief speaks good. Back until I give the signal. Then spring upon them like wolves. [*All back to L.U. and L.3. and exit, Adderly being the last. The first Indian who entered runs back to Adderly and raises his knife—wants to enter the station. Adderly catches his arm and forces him off L.U., following him and looking back, shaking his fist at the station*]

JOHN. [*Enters R.2., with revolver in hand*] Oh, why didn't he wait a minute! Just a minute and I would have plugged him. I wonder where I've seen that face before. In some jail, I guess, for a more hang-dog looking countenance I never saw before. [*Peers around carefully*] That settles it. The first Mr. Injun I see around here will get perforated. [*Chinaman makes noise at L.2. Johnnie watches with gun ready*]

CHI. [*Lying down*] Don't shootee.

JOHN. Come here, Tart. [*Enter Chinaman, L.2.*] You seen anything of Black Cloud around here?

CHI. Me no likee Black Cloud.

JOHN. No, you bet you don't. Black Cloud is a very tart Indian.

CHI. Me tart. Mashee woman.

JOHN. Yes, you are a very tart washerwoman. Say, what did you put starch in my sox for?

CHI. Me no putee starchee sockee. Me putee sockee starchee.

JOHN. [*Mimics him—shows him revolver*] Do you know what that is? That is a young man's Christian Companian. And it's five volumes all bound in one, and it's all loaded with slugs plumb to the muzzle.

CHI. Muzzle—sluzzle.

JOHN. Yes, muzzle-sluzzle. And if I ever draw a bead on Black Cloud I'll give him a new set of shirt studs.

CHI. Shirtee studee?

JOHN. Yes—you want one?

CHI. Me no wantee. [*Caesar enters R.1.*]

CAE. It's no use. I can't sleep for those dol-garned mosquitoes.

CHI. Oh, Black Cloud—Black Cloud—

CAE. [*Falls on his knees very frightened; holds up hat*] Oh don't shoot me—don't shoot me—shoot the hat.

JOHN. That ain't an Injun—it's only a nigger.

CAE. Yes, I'se only a nigger.

JOHN. Well, it's a good thing, for if you'd been an Indian I'd of blowed the whole top of your head off.

CAE. Well, thank the Lord, I'se only a nigger!

JOHN. Where did you come from?

CAE. The railroad, of course.

JOHN. Don't get funny now.

CAE. I come along wid the white family what's inside.

JOHN. How many of them are there?

CAE. About a hundred and fifty.

JOHN. Count them.

CAE. Well, dar's de old man and de young man, de two young ladies, and de old woman. Two dogs, a Thomas cat, Big and Little Casino. . . .

CHI. Fullee hand.

JOHN. That's only a hundred and forty-nine.

CAE. An' one respectable gentleman. That's a hundred and fifty.

JOHN. We don't count niggers out here.

CAE. You don't?

JOHN. No, we don't.

CAE. Well, I guess you counted 'em last election just the same.

JOHN. Did you ever play smarty?

CAE. No, but I've played Richard the Third.

CHI. Oh shootee—shootee!

JOHN. I'll shootee. You shut up. [*To Caesar*] Say, you want to be mighty careful round here. This place is surrounded by Indians. [*All close together, C.*]

CAE. Oh, Lord!

JOHN. The very trees is full of them.

CAE. Den, fo' de Lord's sake don't shake dat tree.

JOHN. How are you heeled?

CAE. How is any nigger heeled? Got a razor.

JOHN. [*To Chinaman*] You—are you heeled?

CHI. Allee samee Melican man.

JOHN. I'll tell you what we'll do—we'll go hunting for Indians. [*They creep around stage*]

CAE. I pray de Lord we don't find any. [*Music all through this. They get startled at loud strains. Business and ad lib. Do this once or twice. Chinaman and Caesar almost fall. At last all three form in line at rear of stage, trot to front with music and sing song. Exit R.1.*]

ADD. [*Enters L.U.E.*] I had almost forgotten the accursed wire. I must destroy it, for Ferris will telegraph for help. Come here. [*Calls to Indian, who enters L.1.E.*] Well, you must cut that or the chief of the station here will telegraph to his brother, far away, and get help. Do you understand?

IND. Yep, me know. Indian climb like squirrel. See. [*Runs off R.1.E.*]

ADD. Now, Joe Ferris, your hours are almost numbered—you who have thwarted me so often. Through you the plans I have laid for years have been almost dashed to pieces. And now to come here and find everything as if I had planned it. The daughter who so despised me, the father who hated me, and the son who escaped with me! All here, and at last in my power! Oh, I could shout with very joy until the rocks re-echo with laughter! Rejoice, you red-skinned devils! For this I have sold myself to you, and become one of your tribe. My measure of crime is almost complete, for, with the wealth which I now possess and the gold, I am told, is hidden here, I will return to civilization. Then who will recognize me, the elegant gentleman of the East, as the renegade of the West? [*Click, click, click, three blows outside, and the sound of the wire falling*] All hope has fled you now. That little wire held your hopes, but *it* is severed now and eternity yawns at their very feet. [*Looking in station door. Indian now enters R.1.E.*]

IND.   Indian do what white man tell him—climb pole—cut wire—so.

ADD.   You have done well. But see, lights are still around the station. Come, let's get back for awhile. [*They exit L.U.E. at same time. Johnnie and Chinaman enter R.1.E. and Joe enters with lantern, at R.U.E.*]

JOE.   You must be mistaken, there are no Indians around here. Forty-two reported them in *that* vicinity yesterday.

JOHN.   Can't I believe my own earsight?

JOE.   Well, what did you hear?

JOHN.   I don't know, ask the Chinaman. He's just as big a liar as I am.

JOE.   Well, Tart, what did you see? Come, speak up!

CHI.   Me see Indian white man—Black Cloud.

JOE.   Are you sure it was Black Cloud?

CHI.   Me saby, Black Cloud.

JOE.   Then there is, indeed, danger. Johnnie, go and destroy all the liquor in the storehouse. [*Johnnie exits R.*] China, you go and attend to the horses. [*Chinaman exits R.U.E.*] I'm afraid Black Cloud means trouble. [*Picks up wire*] Why, the wire has been cut! This, then, is positive proof that white men are directing the Indians' movements. No Indian would have been cunning enough to cut that wire, and I may expect them down on me at any minute. What shall I do?—I have it! I'll tap the wire here and telegraph to Station 46, and have the train sent back, and perhaps it will get here in time to save us. [*Shaking fist threateningly L.1.E.*] Ah, you red devils, you thought to get ahead of the Ferret, did you? Well, I'll show you the Ferret is a match for sixty red-skinned devils. Now, then, for the apparatus. [*Exits R.1.E., as Chinaman enters R.U.E.*]

CHI.   Melican man like fightee. Chinaman like sleepee in box. [*Gets in box R.2. Caesar enters R.U.*]

CAE.   I just went and put on my new Rip Van Winkle wig and whitewashed my face, and if any of them Indians scalp dis child—Oh—they'll get fooled. Oh, I fixed myself! [*Pulls back coat—shows two big horse-pistols*] Dat am a gun—and dat am a son of a gun. The last time I shot dat one was last Fourth of New Year's, and I was laid up for just seven weeks. If I turn dis one loose on an Injun, and he don't drop, I'll turn Old Faithful loose, and if he don't drap, then I'm goin' around behind him and see what's holdin' him up, that's all. I'd just like to try this here one on an Injun—just to see how quick he'd move. [*Chinaman raises top of box and lets it drop. Caesar drops on his knees, shaking. Finally looks around, and gets up—sees that there is no one there—is completely changed and scared*] Injun see nigger—Injun run. Injun not run—nigger run. Oh Lawd—here comes one now with a seven pounder on his back. [*Exit R.U. Enter Joe with instrument R.1.E. Puts it on barrel—connects wire and works instrument*]

JOE. Station 46—[*Speaks while working instrument. He is supposed to be telegraphing. Stops and examines gun—looks around—telegraphs again*] Come, old man, wake up—wake up! [*Stops and waits again*] Oh, why don't he answer me? [*Very anxious*] Patience, Joe, patience. Don't talk of patience to a man of my temperament! Leave patience to the saints. [*At last machine answers—he listens eagerly*] What do I want? I'll tell you what I want. [*Telegraphs*] Has the U.P. train yet passed your station? Answer me quickly. [*Turns off key of instrument and waits*] God grant that they have not passed there, for before they could reach the next station, which is a great way off, I fear the crisis would have passed and the murdering savages have done their work. [*Instrument on barrel begins to work—tick, tick, etc. He speaks, translating the message as it comes over the wire*] "The train is just entering the station." Thank God for that! [*He goes to instrument and telegraphs*] "Get help and send back the train at lightning speed. I am surrounded by Indians. I have two helpless women to protect, and only about four fighting men. Lose not a moment if you would save human life." [*Stops telegraphing*] There, my pretty little piano, that's the sweetest tune you ever played. And if I am ever a father, you are the only instrument my little ones shall practice on. Now, if they will wait until I get rid of my instrument, I'll promise to handle them a little rougher than their great Father in Washington. [*Rolls barrel off R.1.*] If we are lucky, I guess we will get out of this with a whole skin. [*Indians appear at L.3. and L.U. Joe enters R.1. Tom R.2. Johnnie R.3.*] Give them a warm reception. [*All advance and chase Indians off, fighting. Tom and Black Cloud enter R.2., struggling for gun. Black Cloud gets gun and Tom retreats to L.U.E., firing a revolver. Black Cloud levels gun and snaps it as Tom exits L.U.E., followed by Chief Black Cloud. At the same time Caesar enters R.U.E. Falls in C. of stage—kneeling and praying. Indian enters R.1. and rushes to Caesar, scalping him, pulling off the Rip Van Winkle wig which Caesar has over his regular wig. Indian exit L.1. as Caesar jumps up and fires revolver after him. Indian returns and gives a war-whoop, which frightens Caesar, and he runs off R.3.E. Indian follows chasing him, and Caesar re-*

enters R.1., followed by Indian, who chases Caesar off L.1. Aunt Susannah comes out of station in nightgown and exits hurriedly L.1.E. Chinaman opens box and shoots at her as she runs off. She returns and runs out R.3.E. Chinaman fires another shot and goes out after her. Caesar enters L.2. followed by Indian who catches him, as Johnnie enters L.3., and grabs Indian. All exit. Adderly enters R.3.E., dragging Louise by arm. Black Cloud enters R.U.E. Joe enters R.2., and releases Louise. Johnnie enters L. and shoots at Black Cloud, who chases Johnnie off L.2. Joe and Adderly indulge in a fist fight. Adderly finally falls. Johnnie returns—hands Joe a revolver. Tom and Chief enter R.2.E. Chief and Adderly stand at bay. Train comes on here and stops, and soldiers from train fire at Chief and Adderly, both of whom fall. Louise rushes into Joe's arms, forming the picture as down comes

THE CURTAIN

DAVY CROCKETT;
Or, BE SURE YOU'RE RIGHT, THEN GO AHEAD

By Frank Murdock

PROPERTY PLOT

ACT I.

Plenty of dry leaves to cover the stage—four guns to load—powder-stuffed squirrel—water pail, sidesaddle.

ACT II.

Four buffalo robes—Cot C.—bar to break—bundle of twigs for Davy—snow to blow in door—six pieces of wood—Scott's poem of Lochinvar—an axe.

ACT III.

Same as Act II.

ACT IV.

Large pictures on easel—pen and ink and document for lawyer—table L.2.E.

ACT V.

Lighted candle in window—rifle on wall—small book for Parson—legal papers for Crampton.

SCENE PLOT

ACT I.

A clearing in the forest with cottage R.2.E.—Well, rope and bucket L.2.E.—Rustic bridge from R. to L.U.E.—Steps L.C.—Window in cottage—Dried leaves cover the stage—Bench in front of cottage facing audience.

ACT II.

Interior of Crockett's hut—Fireplace L.2.E.—Door opening down stage R. 2.E.—Sockets for the bar to fasten it.

ACT III.

Same as Act II.

ACT IV.

Handsome C.D. Room.

ACT V.

Interior of Crockett's house—Door L.2.E.—Table C.—Window of C. flat.

CAST OF CHARACTERS

DAVY

OSCAR CRAMPTON

NEIL

MAJOR ROYSTON

BIG DAN

BRIGGS

YONKERS

BOB

QUICKWITCH

WATSON

PARSON

ELEANOR

DAME

LITTLE SAL

ACT I.

SCENE: *A clearing in the forest, with Dame Crockett's cottage, set R. Well L.*

CHORUS. [*Before rise of curtain*]
> When high o'er the mountain
> Field, valley and crag,
> The sun gilds the fountain
> We watch for the stag—
> Crack! Crack! 'mid the covers
> Our free rifles ring,
> Far flies the wild, wild plover
> The eagle takes wing.
> A thousand bold echoes
> Roll round at our hand,
> And the startled air owns us
> The Kings of the Land.

Discovered: Dame, at window.

HUNTERS. [*Without*] Hello!

DAME. Didn't I hear voices, singing and hollering? There again—my old ears ain't what they once was, but I reckon I can tell Big Dan's voice a good quarter of a mile or so yet.

HUNTERS. [*Without*] Hollo! Hollo!

DAME. Yes—there they come—as wild a set as any in the settlement, and as hungry, too, I'll be bound—for they never come this way without empty stomachs. [*Exit into house. Enter Hunters, Big Dan, Briggs and Yonkers*]

BIG DAN. Hollo, Crockett! Hollo—nobody's to home.

BRIGGS. What did I tell you?

BIG DAN. Hollo. Marm Crockett. Commissary, hollo—o—o—

YONK. Dan your lungs is in your stomach. You never yell that way except when vittles is wanting. [*Dame appears*]

BIG DAN. Ah—there she is. I know'd if she was anywhere in the settlement I'd fetch her.

DAME. Why, where's my Davy?—ain't he with you?—I allow'd he was.

YONK. Ain't seen him these two days.

DAME. He started for the ridge this morning 'fore daybreak! Well, boys —what luck?

YONK. Bad enough—here's three on us been out on a tramp arter a bear since sun-up and nary a squint of the varmint—and now look at us—tired out and as hungry as catamounts—so how about provender, mother?

DAME. Oh, plenty, boys and something worth eating this time.

OMNES. What, mother?

DAME. Well, don't ax—just wait till I get it ready. [*Exit*]

BIG DAN. There goes the biggest-hearted woman in these parts.

YONK. You are right there. [*Enter Little Bob*]

BOB. Hollo, Big Dan.

BIG DAN. Hollo, yerself, Bob.

BOB. Hey—Sal—here's Big Dan. [*Enter Little Sal and Tot*]

BIG DAN. Come here, Sal.

BOB. Go to your sweetheart, you Sal.

SAL. He ain't neither my sweetheart. Davy's my sweetheart.

BOB. Davy's your uncle—how can your uncle be your sweetheart?

BIG DAN. Oh, Davy's the man—we are square on that point. Say, Sal, what's for supper?

BOB. I know, she don't.

OMNES. What, Bob?

BOB. Broiled bear steaks.

BIG DAN. Briled bar steaks—do you hear that, boys? Bob, where did that bar come from?

BOB. Davy killed him last night.

OMNES. Last night! I'm an Injun if I don't think it's the same critter we have been arter. Say, Bobby, what did the varmint weigh?

BOB. It warn't a varmint, it were a bar.

OMNES. Ha—ha—

BIG DAN. Bob, kin you hit a squirrel yet?

BOB. I bet you I can, right in the eye, too.

YONK. Oh, Brag is a good dog, sonny.

BOB. Well, who said you weren't?

OMNES. Ha, ha!

BIG DAN. Oh, he—he can do it. I've seen him afore.

BOB. Hey—yonder's one now.

OMNES. Where?

BOB. Up there in the big chestnut tree, yonder. Give me a rest if you want to see me fetch him.

BIG DAN. Steady, Bob.

BOB. You steady your own self.

YONK. He can't do it.

BIG DAN. He can. I tell ye he can. [*Bob shoots and runs off*]

YONK. Hit, by thunder! [*Re-enter Bob*] Well, what's the matter? You fetched him, didn't you?

BOB. Yes, but it ain't in the eye. But I can do it, I can.

BIG DAN. Never mind. Maybe I moved a bit.

YONK. Yes, you moved—but it's a pretty enough shot as it stands. Ha, ha! These Crocketts do beat all creation.

DAVY. [*Without*] Hollo.

BOB. That's him. That's our Davy.

YONK. Yes, that's his voice—as clear as a bell and as sharp as the crack of a rifle—not another one like it in the settlement, and yonder he comes with a two-year-old buck over his shoulder—good for you, my boy! [*Music —quick and lively—Auld Lang Syne. Enter Davy*]

DAVY. There you are, Mother. Forty-two, how's that? Why, hollo, boys, how are you?

YONK. In luck again, eh?

DAVY. Yes, the red fools, they will come my way. Well, it's what they are made for, I spec—but for all that I never drew my knife across the throat of one of 'em without a shudder. Don't seem like a square fight, no-how. Well, boys, how are you, anyhow?

DAME. Hungry as you be, I spec', and supper just about ready.

OMNES. Ha! Ha! [*Exit*]

DAVY. [*To Bob*] Where are you going?

BOB. To get some supper.

DAVY. No siree. You and me waits.

BOB. I want some of that bar.

DAVY. You talk to me about bar in that way, I'll sew you up in the skins.

DAME. [*Appearing*] Come, Davy, there's a nice rib and slapjacks piping hot.

DAVY. Now, you go in with the boys—you know, I never eat except when I'm hungry—[*Sees Bob. Business*] What's the matter with you? What are you hiding behind the well for? Come right here to your uncle—what have you got behind you? What's that—a grey squirrel? Who killed it—you, did you? Well, what's the matter with you?—Oh, you don't mean to tell me you have missed the eye, eh? Let me look—now what kind of a shot do you call that? A good inch from the eye—and after all my teaching too! Is it all to be throw'd away on you like that? Here—I'm ashamed of you—I am indeed —I don't think you are a Crockett arter all. I reckon you must have been changed in the cradle.

BOB. Well, they ought to have watched it, then—I say, Davy, what did they do with the other one?

DAVY. The other what?

BOB. The other baby, the one that was took out?

DAVY. Young man—yer mind's wandering—go in and get some supper. [*Exit Bob*] Ha, Ha! Just like that boy. [*Enter Dame, with pail. Goes to well*] Hold on, Mother, that's my work. I say, Mother, I've got some news for you. Squire Vaughan's daughter's coming home.

DAME. What! Little Nell?

DAVY. Well, Little Nell, as she used to be called. But I reckon it's Miss Eleanor Vaughn now. Mother, do you remember she was took across to forren parts to be eddicated by her father? You remember, don't you?

DAME. Yes, and he died then—poor old man.

DAVY. Yes, died and left her an orphan to the care of a guardian. I think that's what you call it. Well, he's fetching her home now, and that's why they are fixing up the old house so nice of late.

DAME. Son, I wonder if she will remember the time when you and her were sweethearts, eh, boy?

DAVY. Why, Mother, how you talk? Oh, dear—no—I reckon she's gone and forgot us by this time.

DAME. Well, I allow you're right. [*Goes to door, takes pail from him*] Ah, thank you, son, you're allus good to your old mother. [*Exit*]

DAVY. [*Solus. Business*] What am I for if I shouldn't be good to you? Bless that dear old face—she's getting on in years, and by and by she'll need a son's hand to keep the wolf from the door.

NEIL. [*Without*] Hollo.

DAVY. Strange voices.

MAJ. R. [*Without*] Hollo.

NEIL. Can you hear us?

DAVY. Yes, I reckon we can. Hollo, what's the matter? What do you want?

NEIL. Assistance. We have met with a serious mishap. [*Hunters appear*]

DAVY. Hold on, boys, I'll see what's wrong.

BRIGGS. Who can it be?

YONK. Strangers here, sure.

DAME. [*Entering*] Tinkers or peddlers. Such folks is allus getting into some sort of fix or other—there they come—why, ther's a gal with 'em—a real lady! [*Enter Major Royston leaning on Davy*]

MAJ. R. Is it much further to this place of yours?

DAVY. Oh, no—right here. [*Eleanor and Neil enter. Crossing bridge*]
Take care—look out. [*Neil falls. Davy catches Eleanor*] That's slippery where
you are.

NEIL. Yes, I perceived so as I fell.

EL. I'm very much obliged to you, but don't you think it would be just
as well to put me down?

DAVY. Oh—yes.

EL. Thank you. [*Goes to Major Royston*]

MAJ. R. Take care.

DAVY. What's the matter? Sprain, I allow.

MAJ. R. To be sure—you see that just leaning my weight on that ankle
sends a shoot of pain all through me. See that?

DAVY. Yes. But if I were you, I'd lean my weight on the other leg.

MAJ. R. Sir!

EL. Oh, be patient, guardy.

MAJ. R. Patient? Haven't I a right to stand on which leg I please—on
my right leg or my left leg?—I'll stand on my head, if I like—then, sir,
what do you say to that?

DAVY. Oh, that's good, if you like it.

MAJ. R. I don't know, sir, but you are right. My name is Royston, sir.
Hector Royston, ex-major in the Continental army, at your service or anybody's.

DAVY. Well, my name is Crockett.

EL. What?

DAVY. Crockett, Miss—

EL. Not Davy Crockett—not my old friend, Davy Crockett?

DAVY. Well, Davy's the name, but as for the old friend—

EL. Ah—you have forgotten me, while I knew your face before your
name recalled it. Don't you know me? Who am I, now?

DAVY. Why, Mother, look—it's Nellie Vaughn!

EL. Yes, the same saucy Nell as of old, and this is your good mother?
Have you forgotten me, too?

DAME. A thousand welcomes *home*.

EL. Home—yes, it was home while my poor father lived, but now—

DAME. Oh, miss—I didn't mean—pray, forgive.

EL. For what?—For recalling him to me?—I rather thank you, for his
memory is the one green spot in my lonely life—no, not lonely, for here is
his worthy representative. [*Goes to her guardian*]

MAJ. R. Take care—

DAME. I beg pardon, sir, but did you say your foot was sprained?

MAJ. R. No, marm, I did not. I said it was turned—there's a difference between a sprain and a simple turn—it was all the fault of that accursed saddle.

EL. Oh, Guardy—

MAJ. R. Eh—wh—I beg your pardon, madam, for the expression, but it was all the fault of the lady's saddle—the girth broke—the saddle turned—she turned with it—I turned to save her, my foot turned under me and, confound it, we all turned topsy-turvy together.

EL. Oh, Guardy!

DAME. He'd better step indoors. A basin of cold water and a bandage will set that all right.

MAJ. R. I thank you, madam, and I will take your advice.

EL. Assist him, Neil. [*Neil comes to him. Major Royston limps toward door. The children stand in front of him*]

MAJ. R. Get out! [*Children laugh. Major Royston falls and gets up*] Why don't you come, some of you, and pick me up? [*All laugh*]

EL. Oh, how beautiful it all seems! I declare, the place has changed just as little as its inmates—and what little folks—are these all Crocketts?

DAVY. Yes, all!

BOB. All 'cept me.

DAVY. What?

BOB. I was changed in the cradle.

DAVY. Oh, clear out.

BOB. Well, Davy says I was.

EL. Not yours, Mr. Crockett?

DAVY. Good Lord, no!

EL. Of course not. Well, come, little folks, I am the visitor and you must show me the way. [*Exit with children*]

BIG DAN. Davy Coo-Coo—Ha! Ha!

YONK. Davy Coo-Coo—Ha! Ha!

BRIGGS. Davy Coo-Coo—Ha! Ha! [*They all scamper off. Chorus—music. Repeated outside*]

DAVY. Mighty, but she's pretty! I feel just as I did when a little boy no bigger than Bob. Dear me, I forgot them horses! They'll want a feed—and while I'm about it I'll fetch up that damaged sidesaddle. I reckon I can tinker it up a bit, and maybe I'll get another of them looks in pay—pay—great Lord, that gal could buy me out, body and soul, for next to nothing, and I ain't for sale generally. I ain't, neither. [*Exit. Re-enter Eleanor followed by Neil*]

NEIL. So you have known these people before, Eleanor?

EL. Yes, and I am proud to know them still. I love their honest simplicity, rugged though it be. It refreshes me like a draught of pure spring-water, or a breath from this fresh mountain air. Why do you smile?

NEIL. You will hardly expect me to share your enthusiasm.

EL. Certainly not. Our tastes are very dissimilar.

NEIL. I am very sorry if our engagement has become irksome to you. It was no fault of mine, when abroad I was well enough—but now—

EL. [*Rises, sits on bench in front of cottage*] I see you are determined to be ill-natured. I wish you would go and look after my saddle—you know it must be mended before I can remount.

NEIL.—Oh, yes—[*Goes up*] I declare I am quite turned about. Which way did we come?—I think this way.

EL. I think the other.

NEIL. Yes, I daresay you are right.

EL. Well, why don't you go?

NEIL. You won't be afraid?

EL. Afraid of what?

NEIL. Of being alone.

EL. Why, I was born in these forests. I am the daughter of a backwoods-man.

NEIL. Very well, I'll hurry back.

EL. You needn't.

NEIL. Eh?

EL. Oh, do go and look after my saddle.

NEIL. Yes, I will. [*Exit*]

EL. This marriage with Neil Crampton is a mistake—a fatal error—I do not love him—I cannot love him—and if I am to understand this letter I am not so much to blame. A strange, ambiguous letter.—It is from Mr. Dunforth, poor papa's solicitor—it puzzles and disturbs me.—Let me read it again for the hundredth time: "My dear Miss Vaughn: You start to-morrow for your old home in the west. As your father's old friend and your legal advisor I feel in duty bound to offer you a word of caution. I have reason to believe that measures are afoot to coerce you into what I believe to be a matrimonial speculation." [*Enter Davy*] "If you doubt me I will only suggest that you keep one eye on your guardian's movements, another on those of Mr. Oscar Crampton—." Oscar Crampton, a man I never liked from the beginning, and yet Guardy trusts him—I can comprehend nothing—absolutely nothing. [*Enter Davy with saddle. Eleanor mistaking him for Neil*] Now, what in the world has he brought that saddle here for?—I thought I told you not to hurry back—now, don't say I didn't—I told you so very distinctly—not that

your society is so distasteful to me as you imagine—but because—because—
Oh, do put it down! [*Davy drops saddle*] Umph—he obeys me like a dog—
well, what you brought it for at all I don't know, I don't want it—[*Davy is
taking it off*] Well, you need not trouble yourself to take it back—[*Pause*]—
My smelling salts. Now, don't say you haven't got them. I'm sure I gave them
to you this morning—Well, why don't you—? [*She turns and sees Davy*]
Oh! Oh!

DAVY. I'm afeared you got the wrong pig by the ear.

EL. Oh, sir, I didn't mean—I—I—did you bring my saddle?

DAVY. Yes, but I'd just as leave take it back if you don't want it.

EL. Oh, no, I like to have my saddle with me. No, I mean I thank you
very much.

DAVY. You're welcome, miss—I heard the old gentleman say the saddle
was a little bit damaged, so I thought I'd just fetch it up and tinker it up a
bit—that's all.

EL. How good!—I thank you—I—oh, dear, I don't know what to say.
What's the matter with it?

DAVY. The belly-band's busted.

EL. And do you think it ought to be mended?

DAVY. Well, if you are going to ride on it again I think it might as well.

EL. Do you mend saddles?

DAVY. Well, I don't do it for a steady living, but I do sometimes, just to
keep my hand in—

EL. I wonder if I could—

DAVY. I don't think it would be just a lady's work.

EL. Oh, I like to do odd things, and I think I could do this.

DAVY. Well, go ahead—let's see how you'd do it.

EL. Oh, there's no difficulty about that—the girth is broken.

DAVY. Eh—yes, busted off there.

EL. Well, then, I would get a piece of leather, a real strong piece of leather
—and a needle and some thread—some real strong thread—then I would
make some holes in the leather—then—then—I would sew it right on there
and then I am sure it would buckle just as well as ever. There—why he's
laughing at something—is it so *very* funny?

DAVY. No, it ain't funny at all. [*Laughs*]

EL. Isn't that right?

DAVY. Yes, that's first-rate. [*Laughs*]

EL. Is there another way?

DAVY. Yes, I'm afeared there is, miss.

EL. A better way?

DAVY. I don't know that it's a better way—but it's a shorter way.

EL. How would you do it?

DAVY. I'd just let it out a couple of inches on the other end.

EL. Why, to be sure—how stupid I am!

DAVY. Yes.

EL. Sir!

DAVY. No, miss, only a trifle green.

EL. Thank you, sir.

DAVY. Oh, it's quite natural, miss. You haven't been used to this kind of work, and that makes a great difference—[*The Dame appears at window*]

DAME. Miss, the old gentleman is coming out. Won't you come and help him?

EL. Certainly. I shall be back soon. [*Exit with Dame*]

DAVY. I didn't think you could get so much fun out of saddle-mending. [*Enter Oscar Crampton*]

OSCAR. Hollo.

DAVY. Hollo.

OSCAR. Well, sir, can't you come to me?

DAVY. No, I'm busy. You ain't, so you can come to me.

OSCAR. You are very independent. I only wished to—

MAJ. R. [*Within*] Take care.

OSCAR. Ah! I know all I want. I will trouble you no further. [*Retires back*]

DAVY. Well, there's a man I reckon don't say his prayers every night. [*Crosses L. to Neil. Enter Major Royston, Dame and Eleanor*]

MAJ. R. I declare, madam, your bandages have worked quite a miracle. The pain is quite gone.

EL. We cannot sufficiently thank you, madam.

DAME. Don't try, miss—better let me make you up a couple of beds— going to be a bad night—snow on the mountains, sure.

EL. Thank you, madam. Much as we thank you, we are compelled to decline—

MAJ. R. The fact is, marm, we are expected by a friend—

OSCAR. [*Advancing*] By a friend who has anticipated your arrival and has hastened to meet you.

MAJ. R. He, here? [*Eleanor shudders*]

OSCAR. Well, old friend, a thousand welcomes—Miss Eleanor, your blooming looks are the best vouchers for your health. I am rejoiced to see it, but where is Neil, my nephew? I long to embrace the dear boy. Well, old friend, everything goes to a wish.

Maj.R. A word with you, my dear friend.

Oscar. That's right. Call me your friend—your dear friend—[*They go up*]

Davy. That's all counterfeit—the men are playing 'possum—but the gal is in earnest. I can see it in her eyes.

El. [*Aside*] My guardian seems distressed at this meeting, but why— why—?

Oscar. Everything is to a wish—the house is arranged as much to her taste as if she were in reality its mistress.

Maj.R. As if she were its mistress?—do you dare—? [*Offers to strike him*]

Oscar. [*Seizing his hand*] Be calm, my dear Royston—you were always so passionate—take my arm, I insist—I command—ha—ha—you see how impossible it is to resist me! [*They exit. Bob enters stealthily—watching*]

Davy. Bob—come here—[*He gives him the saddle. Bob goes off with it*] There's a screw loose somewhere.

El. Yes, there is some mystery here—my guardian's agitation, nay—posi-tive terror—this warning letter. I begin to doubt. Oh, for some friend! [*Crosses L.*]

Davy. [*Coming forward*] I beg pardon, miss, but I think you called my name.

El. Can this be intuition? It is, and I will follow it—Mr. Crockett, Davy—

Davy. Yes, that's it, call me Davy—that's my name.

El. Yes, that's the name I once called you by—then we were children and playmates.

Davy. Yes, little fellows—I remember.

El. If the occasion offered, *could* you defend the woman as you once pro-tected the girl?

Davy. *Could* I?—just try me!

El. I take you at your word, Davy Crockett.—Do you see this letter?— It concerns the happiness of my whole future life, and yet I cannot compre-hend it—here, you read it—and advise me. No, do not hesitate. Your strong man's nature will make all clear. Read it, for I trust you, Davy Crockett.

Davy. Well, miss, I'd like to do what you ask, but I'm afraid it's im-possible.

El. Oh, you refuse to befriend your old playmate?

Davy. No, miss, it ain't that—I've looked into them eyes and I've seen thar what I never see in the eyes of a living woman before, and I'd lay my life down this minute—I would—as I'm a man—but take back your letter and find a better friend than Dave Crockett, for I'm a backwoodsman—and I cannot read—

EL. He cannot read—[*Re-enter Neil*]

NEIL. I cannot find your saddle in that direction. I must take the other path.

EL. Ha! Ha! I fear your chance has gone; someone has been before you—

NEIL. Eh, who?

EL. Who?—Why—Davy Crockett. [*Re-enter Major Royston and Crampton, Dame and children*]

MAJ. R. Madam, good-bye—we are to be neighbors and we will see more of each other. Good-bye, Mr. Crockett. Good-bye, Davy.

OSCAR. [*To Neil, who is about to offer arm to major*] No, no, my arm alone shall support our dear friend. Your arm where it is due—lean on me, my dear friend. [*Exit Major Royston and Crampton. Neil gives arm to Eleanor—they go up. Bob follows with side-saddle on shoulder*]

EL. Not a word—not a look—[*Exit. Music soft—"Annie Laurie." Davy is rushing after them*]

DAME. Good Lord, what's the matter with the boy?—Davy, there's a queer look in your eye—what's the matter, nothing wrong, is there?

DAVY. No, Mother.

DAME. Where are you going?

DAVY. I don't know, Mother.

DAME. When are you coming back?

DAVY. I couldn't exactly say.

DAME. Davy! [*Business*]

DAVY. What, Mother?

DAME. Do you remember the time when you were a little boy no bigger than Bob? You used to go out in the woods and set your traps for rabbits. Sometimes it was pitch dark—What allus kept you from being scared and brought you back to your mother's side? What was it, boy?

DAVY. The light in the window, Mother. [*Warning for curtain*]

DAME. Davy, that light is there for you still. It will always be there for you—remember that it will always be there for you—

DAVY. I know it, Mother. [*Business*]

DAME. Now, son, where are you going?

DAVY. I don't know, Mother.

DAME. And when are you coming back?

DAVY. Mother, what's allus been mine and Father's motto? Ain't it been "Be sure you're right, then go ahead"?

DAME. But are you sure—dead sartin sure you're right this time?

DAVY. By the Eternal, Mother, I think I am—[*Ring down very quick curtain*]

DAME. Then go ahead! [*Swell music on curtain*]

ACT II.

SCENE: *Interior of Davy Crockett's hut. Enter Davy.*

DAVY. Lord, how it do snow! I'm a good mile ahead of them, and they have got to pass this way. I'll allow, they'll be pretty glad of a shelter. Now, there's comfort—just a handful of twigs and everything outside wet through with the snow. Davy Crockett, you're a careless varmint—just enough to start a blaze and little more. [*Enter Neil*]

NEIL. Help—help!

DAVY. Well, I declare! It's that man!—Where's the girl?

NEIL. Out there, fainting—freezing—

DAVY. Freezing? 'Tarnal death! [*Exit. Neil crawls to corner of stage*]

DAVY. [*Re-enters bearing in Eleanor in his arms*] Not dead—but—dear me, how cold she is! Miss, try and rouse yourself. What am I to do for more wood? Oh, here—it is the bar of the door, but no matter. [*Breaks it*] Thar's something big enough to barbecue an ox. Another minute I'd have been too late. Too late—the word sends a cold shiver all through me.

EL. Oh—Oh—!

DAVY. Did you speak, miss?

EL. Oh, my feet—

DAVY. Thunder and lightning, what am I going to do now? Well, it's got to be done, so here goes—[*About to take off shoes*]

EL. What are you doing?

DAVY. Nothing, miss, nothing.

EL. Oh, my head—

DAVY. Yes, miss, and them feet, too. Do try and rouse yourself, for them shoes got to come off somehow.

EL. Take them off, please.

DAVY. Who! Me?

EL. I'm so drowsy.

DAVY. Poor girl! If I get through this night, it will be a clear case of Heaven's mercy—

NEIL. [*Groans*] Oh, you're coming round now, just when you ain't wanted. What are you doing there?

DAVY. Well, come and look. There, miss, just keep them feet wrapped up, and I'll get some more wood if it takes the roof off the house. [*Exit. Neil groans*]

EL. Is that you, Neil? Are you safe, too?

NEIL. Yes, but don't excite yourself.

EL. I won't—I won't—but—

NEIL. Calm yourself, the peril is over.

EL. Peril! Oh, I remember, I insisted on going into the forest in search of holly berries. Guardy remonstrated. I would not heed him—the snow fell faster and faster, the path became blocked—the horses became restive—and then—and then, all is a dreadful blank.

NEIL. Do try and calm yourself.

EL. Yes, but what will Guardy say, and Mr. Crampton, too?

NEIL. Never fear. They will hunt the forest through to find us. In the meantime, let us thank Heaven that we have been saved from death.

EL. Saved, and by whom?

NEIL. By that hunter—by that—Crockett fellow.

EL. Tell me, Neil, was he not here just now?

NEIL. Yes, he went out a moment since.

EL. I knew it, those tender eyes, that gentle face, that bent over me—it was no dream, then—no dream. [*Re-enter Davy with armful of wood*]

DAVY. There's some wood. Oh, miss, you're all right, aren't you?

EL. Then it was you, really—you whom I have to thank for saving my life?

DAVY. No, miss, he did his part as well as I did. He came in and told me you were out thar freezing. Say, I was a bit savage with you, and I ask your pardon.

NEIL. I'm proud to take it.

DAVY. Miss, he's burning up with the fever—he's a sick man and no wonder.

NEIL. No, it's only a slight ringing in my head.

DAVY. Yes, that's it—that's the fever. Here, let me see if I can't squeeze you out a drop of spirit.

NEIL. No! No!

EL. Do, Neil, to please me.

DAVY. Open your head—thar, don't make up faces—it's good—[*Neil drinks*] Takes the roof off your mouth. Now snooze away.

NEIL. If you require my assistance, you will awake me, won't you?

DAVY. Yes, we couldn't get on without you. Now, snooze away, for you need it bad.

EL. How good you are, Mr. Crockett!

DAVY. Don't say that, miss, for what I did for you I'd have did for any living soul that came to my door in a storm like that. But you are safe, and I thank the Etarnal for that.

EL. How strange we meet again!

DAVY. Yes, 'tis kind of singular.

EL. Is this your hunting lodge?

DAVY. Yes, this is my crib. This is where I come and bunk when I'm out on a long stretch arter game. Miss, here's something belongs to you—[*Hands her book*] You left it at my mother's house—

EL. Oh, *Marmion!*—it's dear Sir Walter's book.

DAVY. Is it? I allowed it was yours.

EL. Yes—I mean—thank you very much.

DAVY. Oh, you're right welcome—what is that, sarmons?—No?—Law, maybe—No? Well, I allowed it was, 'cause that's what lawyer and parson needs.

EL. Yes, and very good reading it must be. But this is lighter.

DAVY. Is it? Yes, that's right, light—I've seen weightier books than that.

EL. No, I mean—this is more interesting.

DAVY. Yes, I allow it must be, if you say so.

EL. Shall I read you something and let you be the judge?

DAVY. Well, if you would, I'd like it right well.

EL. Is he asleep?

DAVY. I hope so. Yes, he's snoring like a bar in midwinter. Miss—are you right comfortable there where you are?

EL. Oh, it's delightfully cozy.

DAVY. Ain't that good to hear you say that!

EL. Now, what shall I read?

DAVY. I don't know. I've no choice.

EL. I know—cut and choose at hazard.

DAVY. Yes, read that—

EL. Ha, ha! Now listen: "Oh! Young Lochinvar," etc. [*Reads first verse of Scott's poem of "Lochinvar"*]

DAVY. Sounds pretty, don't it—goes on jest like music. My, but that's pretty!

EL. "He stayed not for bread—." [*Second verse of "Lochinvar"*]

DAVY. There's a gal in it. Well, it makes it all the prettier. [*Eleanor reads third verse*]

DAVY. [*Interrupting*] Say, miss, this ain't true—what you're reading, is it?

EL. Well, it might be, although such things are rare nowadays. [*Finishes verse*]

DAVY. Yes, I reckon they be—go on, miss—go on!

EL. "Then spoke the bride's father.
    Tread me a measure, said young Lochinvar."

DAVY. A nod's as good as a wink to a blind horse.

EL. Why, how excited you are! Does it please you? You see, we have brought our young knight errant to the test. Father, mother, brother, all the world against him, but the lady's hand is in his own.

DAVY. Well, what did he do?

EL. What would you have done?

DAVY. Me—I—well, go on, let's hear it out.

EL. "One touch to her hand," etc. [*Reads sixth verse*]

DAVY. True blue, and the gal's his—go it, you divil—oh, gal! Well, there's something in this rough breast of mine that leaps at the telling of a yarn like that. There's a fire—a smouldering fire that the breath of your voice has just kindled up into a blaze—a blaze that will sweep me down and leave my life a bed of ashes—of chilled and scattered ashes.

EL. Heavens, what have I done? Sir—Mr. Crockett—Davy—

DAVY. Oh, don't mind me. I ain't fit to breathe the same air with you. You are scholared and dainty, and what am I, nothing but an ignorant backwoodsman, fit only for the forests and the fields where I'm myself hand in hand with nature and her teachings, knowing no better?

EL. Oh, hear me—

DAVY. No, I heard too much of you already. I've seen too much—afore you came. Dod rot me—I've skeered you—Miss, I didn't mean to skeer you. I'm an unlicked cub, but my heart's in the right place, and if ever you want a friend—

EL. A friend, Davy—?

DAVY. Well, you've made a fool of me. You've just gone and forced pesky nonsense out of my mouth, but I only want you to believe that I'm your friend. I'm ready to work for you, to starve for you.—What's that?—

EL. I hear nothing.

DAVY. Don't you? Well, maybe I'm mistaken. [*One howl*] No, thar it is again.

EL. What is it?

DAVY. Keep still and listen. [*Howl again*]

EL. I hear a long, low cry as of some animal in distress.

DAVY. Ah, you hear it then? I was right, wasn't I? [*Howl*] Thar it is again.

EL. What is it?

DAVY. That's wolves.

EL. Wolves—! [*Screams*]

DAVY. Don't be skeered.

EL. But—is there no danger?

DAVY. Ain't I here?

EL. Yes, but they are so dreadfully near.

DAVY. Yes, they tracked you in the snow, and smell blood.

EL. Blood!

DAVY. Take it easy, girl. This door is built of oak, I built it—and—blazes, the bar's gone! [*Warning curtain*]

EL. Gone! [*Wolves howl all around cabin*]

DAVY. Yes, I split it up to warm you and your friend. Rouse him up. The pesky devils is all around the house.

EL. [*Goes to Neil*] Neil—help! [*Wolves throw themselves against door. Bark*]

DAVY. Quick, there, I can't hold the door agin 'em—

NEIL. I tell you, Uncle, if the girl says no, there's an end of it—

EL. My God—he is delirious!

DAVY. What!

EL. 'Tis true, nothing can save us!

DAVY. Yes, it can!

EL. What?

DAVY. The strong arm of a backwoodsman. [*Davy bars door with his arm. The wolves attack the house. Heads seen opening in the hut and under the door*]

TABLEAU

ACT III.

SCENE: *Same. Discovered: Crockett still at the door. Eleanor.*

DAVY. This is getting kind of monotonous, this business is—[*Wolf howls*] Yes, howl away, but you got to scatter at dawn. That dear, blessed girl, she's had a sleep—and that is just as good as rest to me to think she owes her life to me—that will be no more to her after this than the dog at her feet at home —not so much—for he will feel the pressure of her soft white hand in his shaggy coat, and I'll never see her after tonight, never again—I mustn't if I could.

EL. [*Starting up*] Who's there? Who called?

Davy. No one. You must have been dreaming.

El. And have I been sleeping? How selfish, and you have not left that door the livelong night?

Davy. Well, miss, if I had ventured away from this door they'd been among us like a falling hemlock.

El. But you must be dreadfully tired.

Davy. Oh, no, takes more than a handful of wolves to wipe a man out in these parts.

El. But your arm, your poor arms!

Davy. That's right swellish, I must say, as if some rising young blacksmith had been sledging on it all night.

El. Oh, Mr. Crockett—Davy—

Davy. Oh!—my name spoken like that, miss—you ain't crying for me, are you?

El. Yes, look at my tears—my soul is welling through my eyes. This night has shown me all your noble self—your loyalty, your unselfish devotion. I read your nature, as you cannot, for in the greatness of your heart, you depreciate those qualities which in my eyes raise you far above your kind, to where, rugged and simple but still preeminent, you stand a man. Fate seems to have linked our lives, but the world divides us. We must part here, and both must learn to forget.

Davy. Forget! Hold on, miss, I have listened to you as a man dying of thirst listens to the trickling of a stream of water that he can't reach—and though I know there's no hope for me, yet you might have stopped this side of that word forget. Do you think I could forget you? Do you think I could forget the touch of your hand in mine, the sight of your face? You called me a man, and as a man I couldn't forget you if I would, and I wouldn't if I could.

El. Well, at least you will not think me heartless?

Davy. Heartless? When I've seen you cry for me?

El. And since you must remember me, let it be as one who dreaming of what might have been, is aroused at the voice of duty to dream no more. Can you do this and not reproach the dreamer? Brave knight—true friend—may Heaven bless you as I do!

Maj. R. [Without] Hollo—

El. Guardy's voice! [Two shots]

Davy. Take care. Look out. [Two shots]

Oscar. [Without] Hollo—

Davy. There's the other one. [Two shots] Aim low, boys, but slew 'em—do you hear the critters scamper? How I'd like to be among 'em!

MAJ. R. Bravo, lads—they are found—stand by the horses—open the door.

DAVY. Hold on! The door's bolted!

MAJ. R. Why don't you open the door?

DAVY. The bolt is a trifle swelled.

MAJ. R. Confound it! Open the door.

DAVY. 'Tarnal death, hold on! There's a sartin amount of patience required about all these things. Oh, right here near this joint—there she comes, and not an inch to spare. [*Enter Major and Oscar. Davy falls on couch*]

OSCAR. Neil! [*Hears Davy groan*] What is that man doing here?

EL. Look at him and ask. Look at his pale face, his torn and mangled flesh, his brave life's blood freely drained, and for me! Look at all this and then question. Shall I tell you what he has done? He has saved me from a fate too terrible for thought—myself and yonder wretched man—saved us, defended us, stood the livelong night at that door—his strong arm our only salvation, a living barrier between us and death, signing a compact written in his own blood. And for me, for me!

OSCAR. We are losing ground here—[*Goes up*]

MAJ. R. Don't fret, girl. He is only faint from loss of blood.

DAVY. Who's faint? Davy Crockett? It's a—there, don't you worry—I'm worth a dozen dead men yet.

OSCAR. Neil, don't you know me? Why, the boy is seriously ill.

MAJ. R. Oh, Eleanor—

EL. Hush, Guardy—poor Neil!

OSCAR. You remain here and I will summon the servants—he must be removed at once.

MAJ. R. Remove him? Do you want to kill the lad? Let him remain where he is.

OSCAR. Here! Impossible.

DAVY. You're right, Squire. If that boy ventures out in a storm like this, it is more than his life is worth.

OSCAR. But—

DAVY. Well, I reckon I know, don't I? I was raised in these parts and I know the fever when I see it. There's only one thing to be done, and that's got to be done quick.

OMNES. What's that?

DAVY. Well, just cover him up with the skins, build up a blazing fire—pour a horn or two of that liquor down his throat, and wait till I come back.

OSCAR. Where would you go?

DAVY. To the nighest settlement. A short ten miles from here.

EL. For what?

DAVY. For help, for a man what's sick and needs it bad.

EL. Are you mad, to venture out in such a storm, and in your condition? You shall not go.

DAVY. I must, girl—it's duty—duty.

EL. But you could never find the path in such a storm.

DAVY. Oh, yes, I could. I could find the path if the snow stood breast high.

EL. But for my sake, think—it may be death.

DAVY. Well, let it come.

NEIL. Oh, Eleanor! Eleanor!

OSCAR. Do you hear him, girl? Have you no heart?

MAJ. R. Speak to him, Eleanor. It may save his life.

EL. No, no, I cannot.

DAVY. Go to him, girl. There's your place by his side. [*Music, "Annie Laurie"—very soft*] There's a new light dawning on us both. Our ways in life lie different—Yours and his is by the warmth of the firelight, but mine is out thar in the storm fighting for life and breath. It's hard, I know, but I must not shirk my part. Good-bye, girl, I'll never see you again.

EL. Never!

DAVY. How can I, when you belong to him? But don't say you'll forget. And when time has passed, you might waste one thought on Davy Crockett. It's all he asks—it's all he's worth. Good-bye, I'm going out of the Heaven of your life. I'm going out of your sight forever.

EL. No, Davy, you shall not go. [*Warn curtain*]

DAVY. Oh, girl, don't tempt me—don't you see that Satan is tugging at the strings of my wicked, sinful heart, saying Don't go, stay here, let him die?

EL. Die?

DAVY. For he will die afore morning, if I stay, and that will leave you free—free for me to love. That's what is ringing in my brain, and I'm trying to fight it down—I'm trying to do what's right.

EL. Forgive me, Davy. You are right.

DAVY. Then let me "go ahead." [*Exit Davy. Ring down. Music swells*]

TABLEAU

ACT IV.

SCENE: *Interior of Major Royston's mansion. Discovered: Oscar.*

WAT. [*Without*] Take the candles to the supper room. I'll attend to the evergreens myself. [*Enter from C.*]

OSCAR. Ah, Watson, more decorations, eh?

WAT. Yes, for the supper room. The house begins to look like a bazaar or a Christmas fair.

OSCAR. Or a gentleman's mansion decorated for a wedding.

WAT. Yes, sir. I suppose the wedding will follow?

OSCAR. All in good time, my dear friend.

WAT. Well, they will make an uncommon pretty couple—a very pretty couple. [*Exit C.*]

OSCAR. [*Solus*] A pretty couple, yes—and a golden couple—rich—rich—and here the instruments with which I have brought it all about: Royston's I.O.U. on every one of them. And here the master's key of all the forged notes —Ah, Royston, little did you dream twenty years ago the interest I would demand today. Fool, you have sown the wind; now reap the whirlwind! [*Enter Neil from C.*] Ah, the bridegroom-elect, and what a face! Are you to be married or to be hanged?

NEIL. Spare me your—sarcasm—I am unhappy enough without it.

OSCAR. Unhappy, my dear convalescent? Your fever has not quite left you.

NEIL. [*C.*] Ah, it is from the time I contracted that fever that I date my present unhappiness—but my eyes have been opened since. Uncle, I love the girl—yes, love her still, but her heart is not mine—never can be mine. I have known it ever since that night in the forest, and I should be either a fool or a coward to wed with her. [*Enter Major Royston*]

MAJ. R. Neil, have you seen Eleanor?

NEIL. Not within the hour, sir.

MAJ. R. Nor I—she keeps her room with a pertinacity more marked than commendable.

OSCAR. Ah, Major, we have been young ourselves, let us remember that.

MAJ. R. Hypocrite! [*Enter Watson from C.*]

WAT. Squire, the lawyer is below.

MAJ. R. Very well, I will see him in my own room. Crampton, will you join me?

OSCAR. You know, my dear Royston, what a poor head I have for figures, but when the mutual interest of those dear to us is considered—Neil, where are you going?

NEIL. To my own room. Do not be afraid. I'll join you at the proper moment.

MAJ. R. [*Goes up to him*] Come, Neil, rouse yourself. Your dejection will affect your bride.

NEIL. The reproof is deserved, sir. I will try. [*Exit C.*]

OSCAR. Love is a strange disease, my dear Royston.

MAJ. R. True, but shame and the bondage of shame is still stranger.

OSCAR. Why, your abstraction almost equals poor Neil's—but come, the lawyer and the settlements await—[*Exit L.*]

MAJ. R. Heaven forgive me! What a wedding night, and what sad hearts to grace it! [*Exit L. Enter Davy*]

DAVY. So this is her home, and this is her wedding night! I wonder if that man loves the girl as well as I do? I don't think he do—and I don't think he kin. [*Enter Eleanor from door R.*] It's the gal herself, how pretty she do look! Just like a statue done up in real frost. [*Hides behind portrait*]

EL. Robed for the ceremony that links my fate to his! Orange blossoms on the brow, but in the heart what they should have decked me in is black, not white. The flowers should have been dead roses woven in a wreath of cypress.

DAVY. Poor girl, thinking so deep, and she don't seem just happy in her looks, neither!

EL. Oh, Father, you see me here, wayward as of old, and heartsore. If you can see, pity your child and send some kind friend to save me from this bitterness worse than death.

DAVY. [*Coming from behind portrait*] Here, I'm here, heart and hand, ready to serve you.

EL. You, here!

DAVY. I've skeered you agin—but I didn't mean to, 'deed I didn't. My heart got into my throat, and it was them words of yours that put it there, too.

EL. Oh, why have you come, and at such a time? Don't you know this is my wedding night?

DAVY. Well, how could I help knowing it? And I declare to you I never thought to see you again—Ah, I meant every word I said, and I tried dreadful hard to keep my promise, but since I see you first, I haven't been myself at all. I seem to be chained right down to the place where you are, and I can't shake myself clear nohow. Why, miss, for days and days I've hung about here watching the bare walls that held you, and last night I stood under your window from sundown to dawn again, and when the light went out behind your curtain it seemed to me as if the light of my life had gone out with it, for I knew today would give you to another man. Yet I stayed just to get one more look at the sweet face, and then to go away forever.

EL. Where?

DAVY. Well, I don't know where, and I don't care much, for it's all one to me now—but just say one kind word afore I go, will you? Say you forgive me?

EL. Yes, but leave me.

DAVY. I'm going, miss, and I'll never set eyes on you again.

EL. Stay! Don't go! You think me cold, unwomanly—do you think a woman, young, ardent, imaginative, could look on a love like yours unmoved? A love that asks nothing save the privilege of dying at my feet? You think this, you who saved my life, you who—Oh, Heaven, never pausing to look deeper into my heart to read my nature by your own, to see there that I love you—I truly know you for what you are, my hero and my lord—but the confession which should have been my pride is now my shame, for I am bound by honor and duty to another! [*Turning away*]

DAVY. No—no—to me, and to me alone, and by the Etarnal, I'm going to have you!

EL. How can you think to win me?

DAVY. Well! I don't think nothing about it—it's settled down into a matter of the deadest certainty—Yet hold on; can you;—a girl like you—can you think to join hands with an ignorant, backwoodsman like me? I'm just wild to hope it.

EL. Stay! If you can save me from this marriage which fills me with disgust and loathing,—do it, I am yours.

DAVY. Oh, I'll do it! If Satan himself stood there, he shouldn't bar my way out.

EL. Oh, be prudent!

DAVY. Don't worry, I'm only dazed a bit—I'm just dazed with the happiness of this minute—to think that this dear hand I never thought to touch again, to think it belongs to me. Oh, if I go mad, it's your own fault—There, I've given my heart; now let's talk business.

EL. But what plan? What scheme? [*Looking to left door*]

DAVY. Well, I don't know, yet stay—I'll tell you what to do—let the ceremony go on as it's commenced, until the time comes.

EL. And when it comes?

DAVY. Oh, I'll be thar.

EL. May Heaven help you! ·

DAVY. Yes—but Heaven helps the man as helps himself—fair means or foul, I mean to have you now, and the man that comes between us—oh, say it again!

EL. I love you, Davy.

DAVY. Come here—the clouds have passed away and—someone's coming.

EL. Davy—only be sure you are right.

DAVY. And then go ahead. [*Exeunt. Enter Major Royston*]

MAJ. R. [*From L.*] The shame and humiliation of this accursed affair will prove to much for me—tortured by a villain who is ready, nay, eager to proclaim my dishonor to the world, should I dare to thwart him. No—no, I must go on to the end. [*Re-enter Davy*]

DAVY. Very well, I'll see the squire myself.

MAJ. R. He here! Crockett, I'm pleased to see you, but—

DAVY. I know you'd rather have my room than my company, 'cause this is the gal's wedding night.

MAJ. R. Well—

DAVY. Yes, I know—but—she ain't married just yet.

MAJ. R. Well, much as I owe you, much as we all owe you, I must confess your call is a little inopportune. Is your business so very pressing?

DAVY. Yes—Oh, yes!

MAJ. R. Because we might take some other time.

DAVY. No, I don't see how it could be put off—'cause it's got to be done tonight.

MAJ. R. Very well, my lad, speak out and quickly.

DAVY. To tell you the truth, Squire, you can do me a big kind of a service. They tell me you've got a horse yonder, a black stallion that you are willing to back agin anything in the settlement.

MAJ. R. And he deserves it. Devilskin deserves it.

DAVY. Yes, I've seen the horse and I allow I'm a judge of horseflesh—that's why I come to you.

MAJ. R. Well?

DAVY. Well, I've got a little job on a little matter of something I kind of set my heart on. Well, it ain't worth while going into detail, is it?

MAJ. R. No, no, certainly not.

DAVY. No, because you might not see my little game with the same eyes that I do, 'cause I don't mind telling you thar's a gal in it—a pair of eyes I took a fancy to.

MAJ. R. Ho, Ho! A love scrape—oh, you sly dog!

DAVY. Nothing more, Squire, honor bright.

MAJ. R. Oh, don't mistake me. I was young myself once—and not so very long ago.

DAVY. I am right glad to hear that, 'cause you ain't going to be hard on me, are you, Squire?

MAJ. R. No, I admire you all the more. But you're a cunning dog, Crockett—well?

DAVY. Well, Squire, the game I'm going to play is full of danger and full of dare. It may be one man agin a score, and it may be one horse agin the field, and now to make a long story short, I wish you'd lend me that horse, Devilskin. Thar now, it's out.

MAJ. R. The stallion is yours—[*Business*] not as a loan, but as a gift. You saved my Eleanor's life—

DAVY. No, Squire, I wouldn't take your horse as a gift.

MAJ. R. Come, come, I know you are proud, but you shall not refuse him —take the beast and may Heaven prosper you in all you do!

DAVY. Well, that's good of you, Squire, you've floored me.

MAJ. R. Pshaw! Lad, take the horse, and once on his back you may defy pursuit, for he's strung like steel and the wind alone can catch him.

DAVY. Well, Squire, I'll take the horse, but with this special understanding—if ever you have cause to change your mind about me or mine, the bargain is off, and the horse will stand in your stable next morning.

MAJ. R. Oh, no fear of that—no act of yours could ever change my esteem for you.

DAVY. Well, I wouldn't be too sure of that—for this is a rough-and-tumble world and things is putty apt to get mixed, especially when there's a gal—

MAJ. R. Oh, I'll risk it.

DAVY. Well, good night—and give my best wishes to the bride.

MAJ. R. And to the bridegroom-elect, eh?

DAVY. Oh, he'll take care of Number One, I reckon.

MAJ. R. Well, good night, and don't make a mess of it.

DAVY. No, I'll do my part. The rest lies with Devilskin.

MAJ. R. Oh, he'll not fail you. Remember he's strung like steel.

DAVY. Is he? Well, the horse and man are both alike, and the wind alone can catch us. [*Exit*]

MAJ. R. There's a lad of mettle. I wish Neil was a little more like him. Ah, well, we cannot pick and choose in these matters. If we only could— [*Wedding March. Enter Oscar*]

OSCAR. The wedding march—how my pulse keeps time to it, and my heart throbs as if it would burst with the exultant triumph of this moment! [*Enter guests and Eleanor, Neil and Quickwitch from door L.*]

MAJ. R. Welcome all—is everything prepared? [*Go down C.*]

OSCAR. You see, Neil? What think you now? There is your bride,—her fair hand only waiting for the ring.

NEIL. Her hand indeed! Ah, if I but knew her heart were in it!

OSCAR. You talk like a poet or a fool. Come, play the host amongst your guests—your guests and mine. [*Music soft, "Annie Laurie"*]

MAJ. R. Eleanor, you are abstracted. Remember who you are and where you are.

EL. He does not come! My courage begins to fail me.

QUICK. Your signature, sir. [*Neil crosses to table*]

OSCAR. You hear, by a stroke of the pen and she is yours.

NEIL. Look, Uncle, look at her face now.

OSCAR. Fool—ingrate! Have you lost your senses! My hopes, my fortunes all are centered here, fail me and—come, Nephew! [*He signs*] So all is over. Now, Eleanor.

MAJ. R. Come, Eleanor.

OSCAR. The pen, sweet Mistress Eleanor. Only a word—write here—a little word, your name—your signature is all we want. [*Enter Crockett*]

DAVY. Hold on! Stop!

OSCAR. Who said "Stop"?

DAVY. I said "Stop."

OSCAR. And who are you?

DAVY. Davy Crockett—you need not introduce yourself, because I know you and it would only be a waste of time.

MAJ. R. Crockett, why are you here, and what do you want?

DAVY. My bride.

OMNES. His bride?

DAVY. Thar she is, if you don't believe me. Look in her eyes.

OMNES. Eleanor!

DAVY. Come on, let's go on with the marriage—here's everything—here's a lawyer, he's got the document, here's the bride—but thar's a small mistake about the bridegroom—I'm the man, consequently you ain't. Squire, I told you thar was a gal in it, didn't I?

OSCAR. Is this a trick?

MAJ. R. Crockett, leave my house and depend upon it you shall answer to me for this public insult.

DAVY. All right, Squire, I'm your man.

NEIL. Sir!

DAVY. Or yours.

OSCAR. Ha! Ha!

DAVY. Or yours, particularly yours.

MAJ. R. Leave my house, sir, or the servants shall force you out.

DAVY. Force—say, Squire, I want to tell you a story. There was once a game young knight, I think that is what they called him. He was a scout—a trapper, a man who forded rivers in his buckskins with nary a friend but his horse and his rifle. Away he went, caring for nothing, stopping at nothing, until he reached the house that held the gal of his heart. "What do you want here?" says the dad—"I want my bride," says the knight—"Get out," says the

dad—"Whoop," says the knight, "I'm Lochinvar. Who dares to follow?"
[*Runs off with Eleanor*]

OMNES. Stop him! Stop him!

TABLEAU

ACT V.

SCENE: *Interior of Dame Crockett's home. Discovered: Parson and Dame.*

PAR. So, Dame, you've heard nothing from Davy?

DAME. Nothing, Parson, nothing. He's more of a rover than ever. It's a good month since I set eyes on the boy.

PAR. Kind-hearted boy, Dame, but rash, rash to a fault.

DAME. Yes, Parson, he takes arter his father, but such as he is, he is my only one, and my heart gets heavy without him.

PAR. Well, Dame, it's getting late, and I must be going. [*Enter Bob in nightdress*]

DAME. Mercy on us! What's the boy doing out of bed?

PAR. What is it, my little man?

BOB. Has our Davy come yet?

DAME. No, child, why?

BOB. 'Cause I heard him.

DAME. Heard who?

BOB. Heard our Davy a-hollowing just now.

DAME. Oh! Parson! If anything should have happened to our boy!

PAR. Never fear, Dame, he is in good hands, remember that. Go to bed, Bobbie, and if your Uncle Davy comes, you'll see him in the morning.

BOB. He's a-coming now, I tell you, he is—

DAME. How do you know?

BOB. Why, can't you hear him a-hollowing? [*Horse's hoofs*]

DAVY. [*Outside*] Hollo! Hollo!

DAME. I do believe the boy's right. [*At window*]

DAVY. [*Outside*] Hollo! Hollo!

DAME. Yes, that's my boy! [*Taking light. Enter Davy and Eleanor*]

DAME. Marcy on us, who's this?

DAVY. Mr. and Mrs. Davy Crockett.

DAME. Miss Eleanor here, and with you? It's the girl's wedding night!

DAVY. So it is, sure enough.

EL. Oh, madam, don't condemn me.

DAVY. Sit down, you must be pretty well tired out. Mother, I left you single-handed and alone, but I've brought you home a daughter, your son's wife.

DAME. Your wife?

PAR. Marcy preserve us!

DAVY. Leastways, if she ain't my wife just now, she's going to be in considerable less than five minutes. [*Omnes outside—Hello—Hello*]

DAME. What's that? What does it mean? [*Hoofs*]

DAVY. [*Bars door*] It means, Mother, that we're here just in time. Parson, you're a saving angel. Come out with your book and marry us off-hand.

PAR. Eh! What?

DAVY. I know it's a little unregular, but it's our only hope.

PAR. I—I—don't understand?

DAVY. I ain't the least bit particular you should understand, so long as we do! Come now, do it, will you?

PAR. *I certainly will not.*

DAVY. Parson, if you're the man I take you for, you'll show it now. This girl belongs to me, I won her fair, square and legal. I saved her life, when the wolves were howling around her. I took her from the arms of them that are coming to take her from me now, but if a foot dares to cross that threshold, and she's not my wife, you'll see bloodshed.

DAME and PAR. Bloodshed?

DAVY. Mother, give me my rifle!

PAR. *Davy! Davy!*

DAVY. Will you marry us? [*Horse's hoofs swell*]

PAR. I certainly will. [*Takes book out of pocket, amidst noise and confusion at door*] Do you take this man—? [*Noise and confusion stop*] Do you take this woman—? [*Noise still kept up*] notwithstanding the irregularity of the proceeding—[*Noise—confusion—crash, door broken open. Enter Neil, Royston, Crampton*]

DAVY. Mr. and Mrs. Davy Crockett at home until further notice.

CRAM. Scoundrel!

DAVY. Yes, I know your name. You needn't introduce yourself.

MAJ. R. Eleanor, in the name of all the furies, what has *induced* you to take a step like this?

EL. Be patient, Guardy.

MAJ. R. Patience, girl! We are disgraced, ruined!

DAVY. Ruined! Didn't I tell you we were fast married?

OMNES. Married? Impossible!

DAVY. Impossible? Ask Parson!

PAR. Not at all, gentlemen, but a fact. I performed the ceremony myself.

CRAM. Did you dare?

PAR. I did, and am willing to bide the consequences of the act. [*Placing hands in sparring attitude*]

DAVY. Oh, Parson!

PAR. Heaven forgive me!

MAJ. R. Eleanor, in your father's name, I command you to leave that man!

EL. Never!

MAJ. R. I am your guardian.

EL. *He* is my husband.

CRAM. If you be man, tear the girl from *him*.

DAVY. [*Presents rifle*] Eternity is a-yawning for you, if you dare to touch her!

DAME. Stop, son! He is dead and gone that taught you how to kill, but I'm here still to teach you when to spare.

DAVY. I reckon you're right, too, Mother.

CRAM. [*To Neil*] You hear this, and say nothing?

NEIL. Uncle, this violence is shameful, and I am not base enough to be a party to it. [*Crosses to Eleanor*] Eleanor, I have known the truth of this from the first, and had not a *will* stronger than mine compelled me, I should long since have released you from all troth to me. They may divorce you, but from me you have nothing to fear. [*Exit door L.*]

MAJ. R. Eleanor, my girl, this is childish folly. His reckless ardor has excited your fancy, and you believe you love him, but when you find yourself alone amidst ignorance and privation, think of that, my girl, think well of that!

DAVY. It's true, every word he says. 'Tain't too late, take time to think; look about you—this is all I've got to offer you, and you've been used to better.

EL. Used to what? Gaudy jewels that please the eye when the heart is empty? Oh, I have been so lonely amidst all these splendors.

DAVY. But can you give it up, and *all* for me?

EL. I *love* you, Davy.

DAVY. Squire, *hearts* are trumps.

CRAM. If persuasion fails, use force.

MAJ. R. I will use force, as you shall see.

DAVY. Will you? Come on, then! [*Pointing gun*]

DAME. Davy!

DAVY. All right, Mother, put it away.

MAJ. R. Eleanor, my girl, a villain, cold and cruel, for years has held my name and honor in his hands. I have feared him until now, but now I defy him.

CRAM. At last the mask is off. I thank you, Royston, it will make my revenge the more complete. He speaks the truth. Listen, all. This man has been the slave of my caprice, and why not? You and all the world believe him upright and honorable, I, his fate, his nemesis, can *blast* his honor and lay bare his crime. I do it with a breath—I strike the first blow now—here are the proofs of his guilt, read, read—[*Handing Crockett papers*] You will not? Then I pronounce that man a criminal and a forger. [*Davy seizes papers*] Robber, ruffian!

DAVY. Look here, do you know what we do with men like you in these parts, when a man wearing the image of the Almighty Maker shames nature and changes off with the wolf? We of the hills and mountains band ourselves together, and form a court of law where there's mighty little learning, maybe, but where there's a heap of justice, and where a judge sits that renders a sentence—strikes terror to the boldest heart. Do you know his name? It's Lynch—Judge Lynch.

CRAM. Why—what do you mean?

DAVY. I mean business, and damned little of that. Now, what's your game? You're dumb. Well, I allowed you'd be. Squire, hold up your head. We are neither your judges, nor your accusers, but your children and your neighbors. Can you lay any claim to these documents?

MAJ. R. No, they are lawfully his—he holds my notes for large amounts. I am irretrievably in his power.

DAVY. Well, then, they belong to him.

EL. No, no, give them to me.

DAVY. First be sure you're right—then go ahead.

EL. The nature of these notes is best known to you. Make out your claim in full, and my solicitor will cancel all obligation.

MAJ. R. No, Eleanor, no. I cannot consent to this sacrifice. Your fortune is sacred.

EL. My fortune is there. I ask no other.

CRAM. You settle matters very easily, Mrs. Crockett.

DAVY. Eh!

CRAM. There is another debt, one of vengeance. How will you settle that?

EL. That is for you to do—treat it as I do these. Burn it. [*Burns letters*]

DAVY. Now, I allow, that makes him right sick.

CRAM. Royston, we shall meet again—my revenge shall come!

DAVY. Look here, you're a marked man in these parts. Keep a watch over your tongue, for if you don't—

CRAM. Well, if I don't—?

DAVY. Well, private interests must give way to public weal.

CRAM. Ill luck and disappointment on you all!

DAVY. Thank you—same to you!

CRAM. Bah!

DAVY. Yes, that is what the sheep said. [*Bob puts head in door*] Come here, Bob. There she is—there's your new Aunt Crockett.

BOB. Say, Davy!

DAVY. Eh!

BOB. Is she the one what was took out of the cradle?

DAVY. Young man, your mind is wandering—go back to bed and sleep it out. [*Exit Bob*] Mother, that boy's getting a deal too pert. He'll have to be took down. [*Parson rises to go*] Parson, take a chair. Mother, the light in the window has brought me back to my old resting-place.

EL. And me to my new resting place—the heart and home of Davy Crockett. [*Music, "Home Sweet Home"*]

CURTAIN

SAM'L OF POSEN;
Or, THE COMMERCIAL DRUMMER

By George H. Jessop

CAST OF CHARACTERS

Samuel Plastrick

Mr. Winslow

Frank Bronson

Jack Cheviot

Con. Quinn

Mr. Fitzurse

West Point

Folliott Footlight

Uncle Goldstein

Mlle. Celeste

Rebecca

Ellen

Mrs. Mulcahy

ACT I—INTERIOR OF MR. WINSLOW'S JEWELRY STORE.

ACT II—INTERIOR OF PRIVATE OFFICE OF MR. WINSLOW.

ACT III—A BEAUTIFUL PARLOR IN MLLE. CELESTE'S CLUBHOUSE.

ACT IV—GOLDSTEIN'S PAWNBROKER'S SHOP.

ACT I.

SCENE: *Interior of Mr. Winslow's jewelry store with partition to separate office R. Store front with C.D. and two large windows, one on each side. Carpet down, street-scene backing, people occasionally passing. Safe up R., desk down R., counter L. with stools in front of it. Show case back of counter. Lively music at rise. Con. Quinn discovered dusting showcase.*

QUINN. Well, I have everything ready for another day's business. Everything looking clean and neat, as should be. There's piles of dust here every morning. I'm sure I can't see where it all comes from. Well, that's all I have to do; for I sit here all night doing nothing, nothing, but smoking my pipe, and when I get tired of sitting down I walk about the place. I'm sure it's an easy job, and I ought not to complain, but I fancy fault-finding is natural with all of us, to say the least. It's the best-paying job I ever had, and Mr. Winslow is such a fine gentleman. Sure, he would never say a cross word to anyone. But there is one man about the house I don't like, and that is Mr. Winslow's nephew, Frank Bronson. He has such a hangdog look about his eyes. I wouldn't be at all surprised to hear some day that he had run away with some of his uncle's money. At any rate, I wouldn't trust him with my money. [*Enter Jack, C.D., carrying light overcoat on arm*]

JACK. [*Yawns as he enters*] Well, Con, how fares it with you this morning? I'm earlier than usual.

QUINN. Good morning, Master Jack. You are early indeed. You look as if you had been dissipating.

JACK. Yes, dissipating as usual. But I have made up my mind to stop, and I'll give you my word, last night was the last night of carousing for Jack Cheviot.

QUINN. That's right, Master Jack. Give me your hand, for I am glad to hear it. And I hope you will never touch a card again while you live, for don't you know, Master Jack, it's a bad thing to play cards for money? Sure, a fine gentleman like yourself ought not to do it.

JACK. Your sentiments are very true, yet I would not be likely to continue this foolishness, as I have nothing left to play with. In fact, I am so heavily in debt that I don't know what to do. By the way, Quinn, how has Frank been acting towards Uncle, regarding me. Do you know?

QUINN. I don't, Master Jack. I don't.

JACK. [*Half aside*] Somehow I hate to ask Frank for a loan, and still I must, or raise the money on this ring. A present from dear Ella.

QUINN. What was you saying to yourself, Master Jack?

JACK. Oh, I was just thinking of my present condition.

QUINN. Yes, and you were doing your thinking so loud that I caught what you were saying. Now, Master Jack, take my advice and do not do that. Speak to Master Frank, tell him of your resolve, tell him you are going to be a better boy in the future, and I don't think he'll refuse you. If he does, he's no man. [*L.1 E.*]

JACK. You're right, old friend, and I shall follow your advice. [*Shakes hands*]

QUINN. I am glad to hear it, Master Jack. I always try to be your friend, and I always shall be.

JACK. Thank you, Quinn, thank you. [*Crosses to R. Hangs hat and overcoat on hat tree*]

FRANK. [*Enters C.D.*] Good morning, Quinn. [*Sees Jack, who has been standing before hat tree*] Ah! Good morning, Jack, this is rather early for you.

JACK. Yes, it is rather early for me. [*Crosses to back of counter. Frank enters office and sits at desk*]

QUINN. [*To Jack*] I'm sorry, Master Jack. I have no money of my own to let you have, for I would trust you with every cent I have in the world.

JACK. Thank you, Quinn, your kindness is deserving of more appreciation than I can reward you with.

QUINN. [*Putting duster under counter, then crosses to hat tree, takes hat and is about to exit C.D.*] Well, I'll be going after my breakfast. [*To Jack*] I wish you success. [*Pointing to office and exits*]

JACK. Thank you. [*Crosses to office and enters, walks to Frank*] Frank, I don't wish to interrupt you, but will you please turn to my account and let me know how I stand. I would like to ascertain if there is any there; is there any balance in my favor, or to the contrary, if I have overdrawn my monthly compensation.

FRANK. I thought you had something to ask me, being here so early in the morning. Well, Jack, I have been looking over your account just this minute, and find, I am sorry to say, that you have overdrawn to the amount of twenty-five dollars. But why do you ask?

JACK. I will tell you, Frank. Last evening, Dupres, one of my creditors, improved the opportunity to approach me for an old gambling debt, which was contracted some time ago, and he threatened to lay the matter before Uncle unless I settle by ten o'clock this morning.

FRANK. What is the amount of your indebtedness? Is it very large?

JACK. One hundred dollars.

FRANK. Well, that is not so bad as it might be.

JACK. Now then, Frank, since the expression you have just uttered gives me courage, could you oblige me with the required amount? I'll promise to return the money to you as soon as possible.

FRANK. Had you spoken to me about this matter yesterday, I would have considered it a pleasure to accommodate you with any amount, but this morning I am as poor as yourself, Jack. Only last night I made another payment on some property which I purchased some time since, and I am sorry to say, drained my pocketbook dry. But I will speak to Uncle if you like and try and induce him to help you.

JACK. Had I better speak to him myself?

FRANK. As you like, Jack, but if I were in your place I should like someone to pave the way for me. If you will trust me with the matter, I know we will be successful.

JACK. Thank you Frank, I will trust you. [*Exit and crosses behind counter*]

FRANK. Very well. [*After he exits*] Rather a fortunate debt, that, for me, and I would throw a hundred in the street if the amount of that debt were five thousand dollars. Oh, I'll pave the way for you, dear brother! At any rate, I'll get you out of my way.

CELESTE. [*Enters C.D.*] Ze nice morning, Monsieur Jack. You are well zis morning?

JACK. No. Not as yet.

CEL. She is late zis morning. [*Goes up and enters office*] Good morning, Monsieur Frank.

FRANK. Ah, Celeste, good morning. I hope you are well, my darling.

CEL. Oh, yes. I am quite well.

FRANK. I am pleased to hear it.

CEL. I zee the Monsieur Jack come back? Ze grand plan is a failure, Monsieur Frank, ze bad failure.

FRANK. [*After a pause*] No. I rather expected the old man would take him back. He, however, has only taken him back on trial, and we must manage so that the trial is unsatisfactory to the governor. Do you hear? Jack must be gotten out of the way. I'd be a fool, when it is almost as good as settled that I'm to be a partner in this concern, to let my brotherly feeling interfere with my plans for keeping Jack from getting back into the old man's graces.

CEL. Or even let him get ze place. Monsieur hopes to gain the pretty Ellen's affections, bah. You reckon wildly, Monsieur Frank. If you think when ze good fortune comes, you will cast the old love off for ze new, it shall never be, Monsieur Frank Bronson.

FRANK. When will you cease to be foolish, Celeste? Have I not promised you everything when I get the coveted position? Now let me hear no more of this complaining.

CEL. But ze Mlle. Ellen—ze report says zat ze Monsieur Frank pays her ze lover's attention. Poor Jack is no longer allowed zat pleasure. How about zat?

FRANK. Report be hanged! If I do treat the girl courteously, what does it signify? You know it has always been the governor's desire that one of his nephews should marry her; preferably the one he proposes to make his partner. Therefore, you see it is but natural that I should and must for a time devote some attention to her, in order to humor the old man's whim.

CEL. I don't like ze idea. Bye-and-bye ze Monsieur Frank fall in love with ze Ellen's fortune, and ze infatuation for Celeste be a thing of ze past.

FRANK. Bah. No. I have promised to declare our marriage as soon as I am made partner, and I'll do it, if you continue to help me and serve me faithfully. Now, keep your eyes open and go back to your counter. [*Kisses her*]

CEL. Very well, don't you forget ze promise. [*Enters store and crosses to lower end back of counter*]

REBECCA. [*Enters C.D.*] Ah, good morning, Jack. I am late, am I not? [*Goes down to hat tree*]

JACK. Oh, no, plenty of time. Better late than never, you know. [*Laughs. Is at back end of counter*]

CEL. Good morning, Mlle. Rebecca, you are late. [*Business at show case behind counter*]

REB. [*Crosses and goes behind counter*] Ah. Indeed, I'm sorry. Oh, Jack, I nearly forgot to tell you I have seen Miss Ellen this morning. She said she would call after a while.

JACK. Her kindness is a matter of great satisfaction.

REB. She thinks somewhat of giving you a lecture. That would be a pleasure rather than a punishment, would it not?

JACK. [*Before counter*] Yes, for my association with her has always been of the most agreeable nature, and any lecture from her will be prompted by good intentions. [*Smiles*]

REB. I'm sorry, Jack, for I'm afraid it won't suit you. [*Laughs*]

JACK. I hope it will not be as serious as you would have me think. [*Goes down to hat tree and returns, meeting Mr. Fitzurse in C.*]

CEL. [*Calling*] Mlle. Rebecca—

REB. Yes, in a moment. [*Closes case, which she has had open for some time*]

FITZURSE. [*Enters C.D.*] Good morning, ladies. [*Funny bow*] I hope you are in excellent health this morning. [*Have apple peel on coat*]

REB. [*Sarcastically*] Oh, yes.

CEL. [*Very pleasant*] *Bon jour*, Monsieur Fitzurse.

FITZ. Good morning, Jack. How is the state of your health this morning?

JACK. I'm quite well, I thank you.

FITZ. Ah, my boy, you missed it last night at the party! Why didn't you come? Everybody inquired for you. Oh, we had such a splendid time dancing. It was just delightful. Why, you never saw anything to equal it. And do you know, Jack, I made several favorable impressions, and the young ladies asked me to call any time I wanted. Ain't that charming?

JACK. And no doubt you will call often. [*Laughs*]

FITZ. Why, certainly, I don't see how I could stay away, for they are both just as bewitching as they can be. I tell you, Jack, I am enchanted with their beauty and grace. [*Intimating grace in pantomime*] Ah, you should see them.

JACK. I should judge from your marvellous description that the entire occasion was immense.

FITZ. Oh, yes, it was. And I can tell you, Jack, I was the pet of the ladies last night. Yes, I was.

JACK. [*Aside*] How well he feeds on flattery! [*Aloud*] What a point of success you must have reached! But, I say, Fitzurse, what peculiar ornament is that you have on your coat? Are they going to become fashionable? [*Turns. Fitzurse rises and they brush off his coat*]

FITZ. Oh, as I was passing the corner a crowd of horrid loafers who were standing there started to cry as they saw me coming: "Look at him! Ah, there, I wonder whether those are real?" [*Limp, etc.*] So I stopped right before them and told them that they ought to be ashamed of themselves, crying at a gentleman passing by. And when I said "gentleman," one of those horrid creatures hit me right in the neck with a tomato. Wasn't that awful vulgar? I tell you, Jack, I was mad enough to shed tears.

JACK. Well, I suppose you went for them with your cane.

FITZ. Oh, no. I took my departure at once. Do you suppose I would fight with those horrid creatures? Oh, no! [*Looks at Rebecca with eyeglass*] But I say, Jack, who is that young lady back of the counter? She is a beauty, ain't she? What's her name, Jack?

JACK. That is Miss Heyman, and one of the nicest ladies I ever met.

FITZ. She is beautiful, Jack, beautiful. Will you introduce me, Jack? [*Crosses to Celeste before case*]

JACK. Certainly. If you like, with pleasure. [*Crosses to Rebecca, who is at upper end of case*]

FITZ. I would be delighted to make her acquaintance. But wait. I wish to speak to Mlle. Celeste. Mlle. Celeste, I have a solitaire ring here, the stone of which is priceless, but I don't fancy the setting. I wish something new, you understand. Something very fine. [*Hands ring to her*]

CEL. Oh, ze beautiful solitaire, monsieur; oh, ze beautiful. [*Opens showcase, takes out tray to show rings and settings*]

JACK. Mr. Fitzurse, if you please.

FITZ. [*Eyeglass. Looks at Jack*] Ah. Oh, yes, excuse me just a moment, mademoiselle. [*Goes to Jack*]

CEL. Certainly, monsieur. [*Insulted*] Ze big fool!

JACK. Miss Heyman, permit me to introduce my friend, Mr. Fitzurse. [*Walks up and back of counter*]

REB. [*Bows*] Mr. Fitzurse, I am pleased to meet you.

FITZ. I am quite honored, I assure you, Miss Heyman. Beautiful morning, is it not?

REB. Oh, no. [*Laughs*]

FITZ. [*Business of thinking*] Strange answer. Did you say it is not a nice morning?

REB. [*Carelessly*] Oh, yes. Very nice. [*Laughs*]

FITZ. I thought you had misunderstood me. But pardon me, Mlle. Celeste is waiting, I believe. [*Bows himself away and backs into stool*] Oh, dear me!

CEL. Monsieur, here is our assortment, and you will see the new styles. [*Shows tray*]

FITZ. Oh, what beauties! Your assortment makes it difficult to select. I don't know which to take. You will pardon me if I ask Miss Heyman to assist me.

CEL. Certainly. [*Aside*] Ze big fool!

FITZ. Miss Heyman, will you favor me with your good taste?

REB. I'm afraid my choice will not be yours.

FITZ. I would like to wager that it will.

REB. I'm not so sure of that. [*Takes ring from tray*] Now, this would be my fancy.

FITZ. [*Not being suited*] Yes, yes. That's quite nice. [*Aside*] Oh, it's horrid taste!

REB. Do you fancy my choice?

FITZ. Well—Oh, yes—[*Aside*] I'll change the order tomorrow.

CEL. Will monsieur have that one? [*Points to ring*]

FITZ. [*Aside*] I do hate to insult a lady. [*Aloud*] Yes. I will have it like that.

CEL. Very well, monsieur. [*Whispers to Frank*] Whenever you can.

FITZ. Miss Heyman, I am extremely obliged to you for your kindness.

REB. You are very welcome.

FITZ. By the way, Miss Heyman, what is being played at the opera tonight? Do you know?

REB. *Carmen*, I think.

FITZ. Ah, indeed. I love *Carmen*. I think the music grand. [*Business*]

REB. Yes, the music is quite good, but I fancy other operas better. [*Comes down to end of showcase after Samuel comes down*]

SAMUEL. [*Outside*] All right, Mr. Schwimelhumer, I'll see you further. [*Enter C.D.*] You want to buy some shoulder-braces? Three pair for a dollar.

FITZ. No, sir. I don't care for any.

SAM. Well, everybody knows his business best. If you want to buy any Boston garters, two pair for a quarter. They have brass buckles and attach at both ends. They never break to pieces. [*Business*] You want to buy?

FITZ. I don't care for them.

SAM. You don't want them? Everybody wants them. Everybody wears them. How do you keep your stockings up without garters?

FITZ. I don't wish for any, I tell you.

SAM. Well, everybody knows his business best. Would you like some rolled plate collar buttons? I'll sell you three for ten cents.

FITZ. No, I don't wear them.

SAM. Don't wear them? How do you keep your shirt on without collar buttons?

FITZ. You are a horrid fellow.

SAM. A horrid fellow? "New est mis och vecht." Can't I sell you some patent suspenders with double end nickle buckles and brass pulleys on both sides? Made of the best India rubber? I tell you, you can go out and shovel dirt from morning to night with these suspenders. Two pair for a half a dollar.

FITZ. [*Aside*] I'll buy them to get rid of the fellow. [*Gives money to Samuel*]

SAM. And I'll stick to him till I have got his money.

FITZ. Let me have them.

SAM. [*Aside*] Everybody knows his business best. [*Aloud*] Thank you. For a half a dollar you've got a bargain. [*Aside*] They cost me a dollar a dozen. [*Enter Quinn*]

FITZ. [*To Quinn*] Here. I will make you a present of them.

QUINN. [*Takes suspenders*] I thank you, sir. [*Bows; goes down R.*]

SAM. You want to buy some socks with double heels and double toes, warranted not to rip or tear? The longer you wear them, the thicker they get. Four pairs for half a dollar.

QUINN. No, I have all the socks I want.

SAM. I'll give you ten cents for those suspenders.

QUINN. I think you're too sharp.

SAM. How do you know? I pay half a dollar a dozen for a dozen of the same.

QUINN. If that's the case, you can have them. [*Hands them to him*]

SAM. For nothing?

QUINN. For ten cents.

SAM. [*Gives money. Aside*] I bet I made money on dem shoulder braces. [*Aloud*] Here. I will give you these. [*Hands him collar buttons. Quinn about to take them*] For ten cents. Do you smoke?

QUINN. [*Business of accepting a cigar*] I do, sometimes.

SAM. Well, here is a match.

QUINN. You'll die with brain fever. [*Retires up*]

SAM. How do you know? [*Down stage*]

FITZ. Well, Mlle. Celeste, do not disappoint me. Miss Heyman, *au revoir*. [*Business with umbrella and exit C.D. Frank enters store; crosses to front of showcase; converses with Celeste. Rebecca comes down to Samuel at exit of Fitzurse; looks over lace on tray*]

SAM. Miss, ain't you a yrhdum inne von unsure lustre?

REB. Yes, I'm a Jewess.

Sam. Ich habe gedacht. Wie heissen Sie? Was ist Ihr nahme, wann ich Sie fragen darf?

REB. My name? Rebecca Heyman.

SAM. Rebecca Heyman?

REB. My uncle keeps a broker shop on Tenth Street.

SAM. What? You are Isaac Heyman's niece? Then you are from Posen, too?

REB. Yes. I was born in Posen and lived there until I was twelve years old.

SAM. Then you must know some of my people in Posen. You know Sam'l Plastrick?

REB. Yes, I knew him very well.

SAM. Vell, dat's my fadder und Ihr unkle kenne ich sehr goot, und sie sind sie, nighte?

REB. Then you know my uncle?

SAM. Do I know him? Er ist doch ein sehr guter freund von mein fatter. Wir sind susammen gegangen zu die selben schule. [*This means, translated, "He is a very good friend of my father's. They went together to the same school."*]

REB. Uncle will be pleased to have you call.

SAM. Oh, I was in his store several times. But see here, Rebecca. I would like a situation in this house. I used to vas in the jewelry business in Posen.

REB. Indeed, I wish you could get a position here, for then you could come with me at night and I would not be afraid.

SAM. I'll take you home half a dozen times every night, if you get me the job.

REB. [*Laughs*] Mr. Plastrick, how do you sell this? [*Handling lace*]

SAM. Don't buy it. It's all Moch shoven. Job lot. Vot I buy at auction for a matsia.

REB. [*Laughs*] Now, if you like, I will introduce you to Mr. Cheviot, one of Mr. Winslow's nephews. [*Calling*] Mr. Cheviot!

JACK. Yes. [*Comes down*]

REB. Mr. Cheviot, allow me to present Mr. Plastrick, a friend of mine. [*Goes back of counter*]

SAM. [*Shakes hands*] I am glad to meet you.

JACK. It's a mutual pleasure, I assure you. [*Surprised*] Why, you are the same young man I met in the street, the other day, when I had the misfortune of being upset in my buggy! Besides, to lose my ring, which you found and returned to me, for which allow me to thank you again, and I hope some time in the future I will be able to do something for you in return.

SAM. I was just speaking to Rebecca this minute. I told her I would like a position in this place. I know I could make money for the firm.

JACK. Upon the arrival of Mr. Winslow I shall consider it a matter of duty to address him in your behalf. If you will call again I will offer you the advantage of an introduction.

SAM. Thank you, Mr. Cheviot. [*Shakes hands*] You're a dandy. [*Goes up to Rebecca*] If I get the job, I'll take you home half a dozen times every night. [*Exit C.D.*]

JACK. Very well.

FRANK. [*Sarcastically*] A friend of yours, I believe.

JACK. He is an honest and industrious young fellow, and I am proud of him as a friend. [*Enter Mr. Winslow C.D.*]

FRANK. Good morning, Uncle.

WINSLOW. Good morning, Frank. [*To others*] Good morning. [*Enters office, takes off hat and sits at desk. Calls Frank*]

FRANK.   Yes, sir. [*Enters office. Jack and Rebecca up at upper end of case, behind counter. Celeste at lower end of case*]

WIN. [*Laughing*]   Has Jack said anything about my reproaching him last night?

FRANK.   Not anything. But I thought he was to leave us.

WIN.   My nature forbids me acting hastily, and upon reflection I have concluded to give the boy another chance.

FRANK.   Jack, then, does not seem to improve any. Upon my arrival here this morning he requested me to advance him one hundred dollars to liquidate a gambling debt. Now, such actions cannot become profitable to you and I think you ought to bring him to such a point that he will cease his desire to contract debts—especially debts of such a nature.

WIN.   Say to Jack that I would like to see him.

FRANK.   Yes, sir. [*Enters store. To Jack*] Uncle wishes to see you in the office. [*Crosses to front of case, lower end, and whispers to Celeste*]

JACK. [*Crosses and enters office*]   Uncle, I have been requested to attend your presence.

WIN.   Jack, I understand that you are in need of a hundred dollars.

JACK.   I am. And to be honest with you, Uncle, to pay a gambling debt which I contracted some time ago. I have ceased this folly and with your kind assistance I shall be a better man in the future.

WIN.   Jack, your promises are like piecrust—easily broken. [*Laughs*] My boy, if you will continue this foolishness it will ruin your prospects forever, and for your own good I must refuse you any assistance. [*Jack bows and exits; meets Ellen who enters C.D.*]

ELLEN.   Why, Jack, you look so troubled. What's the matter?

JACK.   Oh, nothing. Only a blessing from uncle.

ELL.   Well, I am really disappointed, for I myself came here on a lecture tour.

JACK.   You have? Then proceed, for I might as well cure my sickness with one good dose as to lick the spoon and trust to luck.

ELL. [*Laughs*]   Well, Jack, I will have pity on you and postpone the lecture until some future time.

JACK.   Thanks for your consideration. I fear you are too kind. [*Smiles*]

ELL.   But, for not calling on me last night I shall never forgive you. [*Going toward office door*]

JACK.   Oh, yes, you will. You wouldn't be so unkind. [*Crosses to Rebecca; up before case*]

ELL.   You deserve a severe scolding. [*Enters office*] Guardy, here is a note for you. [*Hands letter*]

WIN. Thanks, Ellen. I am glad you have come, as I have something to say to you.

ELL. Indeed?

WIN. Ellen, my child, I am very much afraid you will have to postpone your marriage with Jack.

ELL. But why, Guardy?

WIN. He is too wild, and reports speak very badly of him. Ellen, my child, I fear Jack gambles.

ELL. That report, I think, originated with some wicked-minded person. I will never believe that of Jack.

WIN. It would certainly enrich no one to speak adversely to his interests.

ELL. Well, Guardy, I am willing to take my chances with Jack, unless it is proven to you that reports speak correctly. But please don't lose any sleep over it, Guardy. [*Kisses his forehead and crosses to Rebecca*]

SAM. [*Enter C.D.*] I said I would be back in half an hour. What do you think of my suit? It is the one I wear when I go to Sunday school. What do you think of the hat? It is one I brought over from Posen.

REB. [*Comes down when Sam'l enters*] You look very well.

SAM. I look like a regular dude. Has the governor come in yet?

REB. Yes. Mr. Winslow is in the office and Mr. Cheviot is waiting for you, I think.

SAM. Well, I'll go and mind his business. [*Goes up*] I come back for instructions.

JACK. So I see. Just a moment. [*Enters office; closes door. Sam'l follows him and has business of having nose pinched by door. Then follows Jack in office*] Uncle, here is a young gentleman in search of employment. He is of Hebrew type. After what has happened, I don't know what weight my words have with you, but I will say this for the young man: he is honest, trustworthy and industrious. He is the same person who found my ring and returned it to me.

WIN. I don't know as we have an opening for the young man at present.

SAM. [*Has been listening at door*] I don't get the job!

WIN. But show him in.

JACK. Very well. [*Opens door; speaks to Sam'l*] Mr. Winslow will see you. Step in. [*Crosses to Ellen; whispers to her and when Frank is called in by Winslow he goes down to lower end of case and takes ring from it*]

SAM. Mr. Winslow, I believe. I come to see if you want any help about the store. Miss Rebecca will recommend me, and as there is no harm in asking, I came in to see you.

WIN. Oh, no harm done. You say you know Rebecca?

SAM. Yes, and I know all her people in Posen.

WIN. Well, I would like to accommodate you, but what can you do?

SAM. I don't know so much about that until I try. I think I could do a great many things, because I used to was in the jewelry business in Posen.

WIN. Indeed? But what were you last employed in?

SAM. You mean, what am I doing now? I'm in the go-as-you-please business.

WIN. What business, did you say?

SAM. I sell shoulder-braces, roll-plate collar buttons, Boston garters and sox that never rip nor tear.

WIN. I see you have been in the mercantile business.

SAM. I guess that's what they call it. Now, Mr. Winslow, I should like to start with you for a small salary.

WIN. Very sensible. What is your name, did you say?

SAM. Samuel Plastrick, and I come from Posen, Germany.

WIN. Well, Mr. Plastrick, I'll give you a trial as stock clerk.

SAM. You'll find me a regular stock clerk in half an hour. [*Aside*] I'll own this business in a year!

WIN. [*Goes to door*] Frank, you may show this gentleman his work as stock clerk.

FRANK. Yes, sir. This way, if you please. [*Crosses to L.I.E.*]

JACK. [*Coming down*] Frank—one moment. I wish to speak to Mr. Plastrick.

FRANK. Very well. [*Returns up stage*]

JACK. [*In undertone*] Mr. Plastrick. [*Takes him aside*] I would like you to take this ring to Rebecca's uncle and get me a hundred dollars on it for a month. I must have the money.

SAM. I'm always open for business. [*About to go up*]

CEL. Help—help—Mon Dieu—Monsieur Fitzurse's ring is gone from the showcase!

FRANK. [*To Sam'l*] Stop! You stop right there.

SAM. Wie-heiszt? [*"What do you mean?"*]

WIN. [*Enters from office*] What is it?

CEL. Ze solitaire—ze priceless Fitzurse's solitaire ring is gone from ze showcase! It was here not five minutes ago.

WIN. Who has been here since then?

FRANK. I saw that dutiful nephew of yours remove something from the showcase and give it to that man.

JACK. Stop! I placed my own ring in that box. [*Points to one in Sam'l's hand*] If it is not there now the rings have been changed.

WIN. Jack, my boy, I fear you are in a fix.

REB. No—he is not. I saw that woman [*Points to Celeste*] change the rings.

WIN. What was your object in this foul attempt?

CEL. Ze object—I will tell you ze object, monsieur. Jack Cheviot was my lover and he refused to marry me, so I sought a glorious revenge. As I have failed—I will go. [*Exit C.D.*]

WIN. Jack, you may consider yourself discharged. Rebecca, you and Sam'l may also go.

SAM. I had a job for half an hour.

ACT II.

SCENE: *Interior of Mr. Winslow's private office. Door R. and L.3., entrance. Desk opposite R.1. Entrance. Table and two chairs opposite L.1.E. Carpet down. Scene boxed. A safe below 1.2.E. Hat tree against flat R. At rise Rebecca is discovered seated at desk.*

QUINN. [*Enters at rise—L.3.E.—Crosses to Rebecca*] A letter for Miss Rebecca from your friend—to judge from the handwriting. Oh, now, you need not be ashamed of it. Sure, he is a smart bit of a man and can sell anything that has ever been invented. Will you read to me what's in the letter? [*Laughs and crosses to L.1.E.*] Never mind, Miss Rebecca, he's smart bit of a man and it's a fine husband he'll make you. [*Exit laughing*]

REB. He is always teasing me about Sam'l. [*Looks at letter*] From Sam'l, sure enough. [*Opens and reads:*] "Grand Rapids, Mich.—May the first. My Darling Achen Rebecca—Your welcome letter just received, from which I see that you have had the good fortune of receiving a promotion, and I hope you will be pleased with the position as bookkeeper. I am indeed very sorry to hear that things have taken such a bad turn with our friend, Jack Cheviot. Will do all I can to help him when I get home, which may be the fourth." [*Spoken*] Why, this is the fourth, so he will be home today. [*Reads:*] "Hoping that I will find you in good health and spirits, I am, yours truly, Samuel Plastrick. S.O. Somebody's Orphan" [*Speaks*] Every time I receive a letter from Sam'l it reminds me of the morning he entered the employment of Mr. Winslow, and I shall never forget the look on his face when he thought himself discharged about fifteen minutes after he had been engaged.

QUINN. [*Enter L.3.E., ledger in hand. Crosses to Rebecca*] Miss Rebecca, I was told to bring this to you. [*Hands her ledger*] Well, will you tell me what he said in the letter? [*Laughs and crosses L.1.E.*] Never mind, he's the smartest bit of a drummer on the road. [*Exit*]

REB. [*Gets up—has right hand on desk*]   I wonder what train he's coming on?

SAM. [*Enter L.U.E. Rushes to Rebecca and kisses her*]   Always on the lightning express.

REB. [*Turns*]   Oh, Sam'l! [*Throws arms about him*]

SAM.   Oh, Rebecca! [*Patting her on back*] Once more for the cigars. [*Embrace again*] Well, Rebecca, how was business while I was gone?

REB. [*Mad*]   Of course, it must be business the very first thing!

SAM.   Business before pleasure, Rebecca. But how have you been since I was gone? [*Patting her on back. She is pouting—has back turned*] I nearly forgot—I must go downstairs.

REB.   Oh, I'm not mad, Sam'l.

SAM. [*Business*]   Oh, I thought you were. [*Arm about her*] Now, tell me how you have been since I saw you last.

REB.   Oh, I have been very well, with the exception of a slight cold.

SAM.   Why didn't you use a mustard plaster? Or some of that patent medicine I used to peddle around the country? It will break up your cold in half an hour.

REB.   I shall try some the next time I have a cold, just to please you.

SAM.   That's right, Rebecca—but be sure and not take too much, for too much is worse than none.

REB.   Oh, I believe you, but tell me, did you have a pleasant trip?

SAM.   Oh, I had a splendid trip and I had lots of fun. Last Sunday I stopped at the Moulton House in Grand Rapids, and do you know the house is full of widows?

REB.   What?

SAM. [*Eye business*]   I mean the hotel is full of windows what you look out of and—

REB.   Oh.

SAM.   And I had a beautiful corner front room with widows—I mean windows. You see, Rebecca, I always get the word mixed—from which I could see way far out to where they turn the street cars around to make the horses look fresh, and guess who I met there, Rebecca?

REB.   I can't Sam'l—how could I?

SAM.   I was just going to tell you. I met that Schismine Greenfelder from New York. I was just going to ask him to pay the ten dollars he owes your uncle, when he told me he wanted to buy a necklace. I sold him a ten dollar necklace for twenty dollars and now I am going to give your uncle his money. A new way to collect old debts.

REB. That is indeed a new way.

SAM. By the way, Rebecca, where does Jack keep himself?

REB. I don't know. I met him in the street this morning, but he never noticed me—poor fellow. He looked so worried and broken hearted.

SAM. I'm afraid it ain't all worry that affects him.

REB. What else can it be?

SAM. Gin cocktails, schnapps—

REB. You don't think there is any truth about Jack frequenting Celeste's gambling house, do you?

SAM. At first I didn't, but now I am certain he does.

REB. But, oh Sam, how could a nice moral young man like you know anything about such places? Just explain that.

SAM. [*Whistles; walks to L.; thinks. Aside*] I have it! [*Aloud*] Oh, well, Rebecca, you see we business men find out such things by hearsay.

REB. Oh, if that is the case, you are excusable.

SAM. Everybody knows his business best.

REB. But, Sam'l, I'm afraid you commercial travellers are sometimes very naughty.

SAM. Rebecca—the drummer is the most innocent man on the road. [*Looking at her—smiling, etc.*] But say, Rebecca, how do you like my new suit? Isn't it a dandy?

REB. Yes, indeed. It must have cost you considerable.

SAM. Not a cent. [*Takes her aside*] That's extra baggage.

REB. Why, what do you mean?

SAM. I charge it to the firm as overweight of trunks. [*Puts arm about her*] But, say, Rebecca—

REB. Well, what is it? I'm all attention.

SAM. While out on my last trip I made up my mind to get married.

REB. [*Smiles*] Yes?

SAM. Yes, and she's the nicest girl that ever stood in overshoes.

REB. [*Mad*] Indeed? [*Takes his arm from about her*] Well, then, just go and place your arm around her.

SAM. But, say, Rebecca—

REB. Don't speak to me again.

SAM. Why, Rebecca! It's you I mean.

REB. Me? Oh, Sammie! [*Throws arms about him*]

Sam. I knew that was just the way she was going to refuse me. Well—what do you say?

[*Song introduced here—"Take me, Sammy dear" sung by Rebecca*]

Sam. [*Kisses her*]   That seals the bargain.

Win. [*Enter L.3.E.*]   And a good bargain, Mr. Plastrick.

Sam. [*Hands in vest armholes; walks to L., whistling*]   I sold myself, and without opening my sample trunk.

Win. Yes, and you need not be ashamed of it.

Sam. [*Aside*]   The drummer is ashamed of nothing!

Win. For Miss Rebecca will make you a good wife, and any young man could feel proud of her as a wife.

Sam. Take a cigar, Mr. Winslow? [*Smiles*]

Win. [*Takes cigar; lights it; seated L. of table L.2.*]   Be seated, Mr. Plastrick [*Points to chair R.*] I have something to tell you of importance.

Sam. [*Sits*]   I'll bet a half a dollar it's about extra baggage.

Win. I have an important errand for you to fulfil.

Sam. [*Aside*]   The baggage account will stand increasing.

Win. I would like you to go to New York, Mr. Plastrick, and deliver those diamonds to Mrs. Fairchilds, which I imported for her at a cost of ten thousand dollars. I could send them by express, but fearing for their safety, and knowing you to be perfectly honest, I will trust you with their care.

Sam. Thank you, Mr. Winslow. When will I start?

Win. At six o'clock this evening. [*Rises*]   Now, if you will do this as you should, I will give you a lift when you and Rebecca go to housekeeping. [*Business, laughs and goes up L.3.E.*] When you are ready, you can come for the casket, and don't forget to be very careful of yourself. [*Exits after Sam'l's speech*]

Sam. [*Shows revolver*]   It is a rainy day when I get left. Rebecca, my credit is good at this house.

Reb. Yes, but I don't like it a bit that you should go out again so soon.

Sam. Business is business, Rebecca. And now I must go and see that my trunks are sent to the depot.

Reb. Don't stay long.

Sam. [*Kisses her*]   I'll be back in half an hour. [*Exit L.3.E.*]

Reb. What a change in circumstances from eight months ago, when Sam was but a stock clerk, and today Mr. Winslow trusts him with ten thousand dollars' worth of diamonds. I'm sure it pays to be honest.

Frank. [*Enters R.3.E.*]   Miss Rebecca, I have been requested to ask you to stop downstairs, a lady friend awaits you.

WIN. [*Enter L.1.E.*] Frank, I have concluded to establish Filkins in your position, and hence ask you to withdraw any further claim upon it. [*Sits*]

FRANK. [*Aside*] Damnation! I never expected this. [*Aloud*] Be it so. I am somewhat surprised; I will no doubt be able to find an opening somewhere else.

WIN. Any such calculation on your part will be unnecessary. I intend to make you my pardner shortly.

FRANK. Thank you, most generous uncle! I fear I do not deserve such kindly treatment.

WIN. [*Laughs*] Maybe not. Now, regarding Ellen. She still declares that she will never marry you, but will cling fervently to the remembrance of Jack until he himself proves himself a traitor, in confessing his love for her, which, rumor says, he has already given to Celeste.

FRANK. There has been no lack of effort on my part to secure her affections.

WIN. Within the peculiarity of her actions there is a good deal of shrewdness. She knows what interest she possesses in my business, and if her love for Jack is not entirely erased and they are married, I must accept him against all odds as my partner.

FRANK. Suppose that we could demonstrate to her the deception that Jack is practising, would she believe it?

WIN. That is a matter to be tested.

FRANK. The old adage that seeing is believing can certainly be applied in this case. Ask her to allow you to escort her to Madame Celeste's and to give her an opportunity to observe Jack as he sits enveloped in deep study over his vocation.

WIN. A most excellent plan, I think, and this very day after she has made up her disguise I will go with her. About what time had I better go?

FRANK. At about eight o'clock this evening would be the most suitable time, I think.

WIN. I think your plan will succeed. [*Enter Ellen L.3.E.*] And here is Ellen. You come, my child, at a most opportune time. My nephew and I were just comparing issues over a subject that should interest you.

ELL. Indeed, Guardy, and what may it be?

WIN. Our conversation refers to Jack.

ELL. Has he been here?

WIN. No. And his presence here is not desirable.

ELL. I hope you have not allowed your credulity to be imposed upon?

WIN. Not at all, my child. But where there is smoke there must be fire. Now, I am going to be liberal with you, and we will investigate this matter together, in order that we may ascertain the truth. [*Rises*] Now, for the present I must leave you in company with Frank, who can detail to you what has been said and acted upon. [*Exit R.3.E.*]

ELL.   Well, Mr. Bronson, what has been said about your brother, Jack?

FRANK.   The stories about my brother, I am sorry to say, are so numerous that I could not repeat them.

ELL.   Yes, and I know many of them to be lies.

FRANK.   No doubt of that, and, being his brother, I sincerely hope so.

ELL.   Mr. Bronson, I do not think it right in you to boast of your brotherly love for Jack, for I believe, and have reasons to think, that some of the stories afloat regarding poor Jack are your own inventions.

FRANK. [*Surprised*]   My inventions?

ELL.   Yes, your inventions.

FRANK.   You wrong me. Be that as it may, but did not mademoiselle herself say that Jack was her lover?

ELL.   She did, but I do not believe her. But had she said the same of you, I could believe it.

FRANK.   Then you wrong me grossly, Miss Ellen.

ELL.   Indeed!

FRANK.   Yes, you misjudge me awfully. And I would not incur any further dislike from you by making the slightest effort to prove his infidelity.

ELL.   Ah! Then you were to prove his infidelity?

FRANK.   Not I. It was Uncle's desire that you should go with him, and should you go with him, I hope as a brother should that the proper evidence will not convict him.

ELL.   I shall go to satisfy my guardian of Jack's innocence. [*Gets up and goes to R.3.E.*]

FRANK. [*Aside*]   Victory is mine! [*Aloud*] Miss Ellen, I beg of you stay and give me an opportunity to right myself in your eyes. I know that you have misjudged me in the past, and I suppose because of my professed love for you; but I hope you will believe me when I say it was no fault of mine, for I love both you and Jack so well that I should have forever remained silent, and after this I shall become perfectly heedless to any solicitations on the part of Uncle.

ELL.   Perhaps, Mr. Bronson, I have been hasty in forming an opinion, and if I have wronged you in the past I crave your forgiveness. [*Offers hand*]

FRANK. [*Takes her hand*]   Forgive you? With all my heart. And I hope you will regard me differently in the future.

ELL.   I shall, Mr. Bronson. [*Bows and exits L.3.E.*]

FRANK. [*Aside*] Frank Bronson, success will crown your efforts in the future! [*Enter Rebecca, R.3.E. To Rebecca*] The lady was a friend of yours, was she not? [*Exit R.3.E. After Rebecca's speech*]

REB. Yes, a very intimate one. [*Sits at desk*]

SAM. [*Enters just in time to see Frank exit; kicks at him*] Du ecklicher schimmel—I feel a monumental—

REB. Why, Sam, what kept you so long?

SAM. Business, Rebecca, business. I just sold a customer of mine a bill of machshoves—and when he came to the door here I heard Bronson speaking to Mr. Winslow, so I waited on the outside, and, what do you think, Rebecca? Mr. Winslow is going to take Miss Ellen to Mlle. Celeste tonight, so she may see for herself that Jack goes there.

REB. Oh, Sam, this must not be. If she finds Jack there, it will be the breaking of the last chance for him in her favor.

SAM. Well, they're not going to find him there, because I'm going around to Celeste and tell her of the trick Bronson is going to play on her. It's a frosty day when Sammy goes back on a friend.

REB. But Sam, you should not go to that place without me. For I could not think of trusting you in the society of a fascinating woman like Celeste.

SAM. Rebecca—you think I'm a masher? What do you want at a club house? You don't know a red from a white. Besides, it's enough if one in a family plays Keno. Well—now—I came nearly forgetting the diamonds.

REB. I don't think you are a bit nice—now there. [*Pouting*]

ELL. [*Enters L.3.E.*] Why, Miss Rebecca, haven't you gone home yet? You are late for Saturday.

REB. I should go presently. I am waiting for Mr. Plastrick's return.

ELL. Then Mr. Plastrick has returned from his trip?

REB. He came home this afternoon.

ELL. Did he know or speak of any news regarding Jack?

REB. [*Aside*] What will I say? [*Aloud*] No, he said nothing to me about Mr. Cheviot.

ELL. I suppose he has not had time to see Jack yet?

REB. Maybe not. If he had, I think he would have spoken of him. [*Exit R.3.E. Ellen goes up and takes hat from rack; puts it on; screams when Sam'l kisses her. Turns as he enters*]

SAM. [*Enters R.3.E.*] Now, Rebecca, don't be mad. [*Steps behind Ellen and kisses her. Quinn enters with duster in hand L.3.E., followed by Frank, who stands in door. Rebecca and Winslow enter R.3.E.*]

PICTURE

ACT III.

SCENE: *Parlor in Mlle. Celeste's house (club), richly furnished. Has large window C. (bay) backed by garden. Boxed scene. Carpet down and bric-a-brac about stage. Celeste discovered at table L.C. Door bell rings when curtain rises.*

CEL. [*Calling*]   West Point.

WEST POINT. [*Enters R.1.E.*]   Mademoiselle? [*Bows*]

CEL.   Someone is at ze door. Go and see who it is. [*West Point goes L.3.E., reenters*]

W. P.   Mr. Bronson.

CEL.   Show him in. You know Monsieur Bronson is always welcome. [*Exit West Point and returns at once, bowing Mr. Bronson in. To West Point*] You may be wanted in ze card room. [*West Point bows and exit L.1.E.*]

FRANK. [*Comes down and meets Celeste C.*]   My darling Celeste! [*They embrace*] You are growing prettier every day in your new home. This is an elegant establishment, Celeste, and you must be proud of it.

CEL.   I have ze pride and you reap ze profit.

FRANK.   I have paid the last˜ mortgage on the place, and from today it shall be yours alone, so you may enjoy the profit as well as the pride. Now, my dear Celeste, I shall ask something of you in return. Old Winslow desires to know of Jack's visits here, and proofs of this will secure my partnership. This must be given to him, and once done I will claim you before the world as my wife.

CEL.   You swear you will do zis?

FRANK.   I do, Celeste, I do.

CEL.   Zen ze gladness comes to me, Monsieur Frank. Ze joy of my life will be complete, but Monsieur Jack has never been here.

FRANK.   Oh, that can easily be arranged. I will send Jack a message, telling him that I must see him on business of great importance. I'll sign the message A. J. Webster, and Jack will be sure to come, as Webster is his friend.

CEL.   I will make ze arrangements with Monsieur Webster. Will you come with Monsieur Winslow?

FRANK.   No, Winslow is not to know that I am arranging for his admission here tonight. Now, Celeste, it may be possible that Sam intends coming here to forewarn Jack. See that he does not.

CEL.   I will do as you say, Monsieur.

FRANK. The old gentleman has ordered Sam off to New York with a diamond necklace worth at least ten thousand dollars, which he is to deliver to a party there. If he should come here, it is likely that he will have this necklace in some inside pocket. [*With a smile*] A word to the wise is sufficient. [*Smiles*] Celeste, you are not slow to comprehend.

CEL. Ten thousand dollars! [*Rubbing hands*] Zat is ze grand—ze magnificent—ten thousand dollars—I will see zat it never leaves the house if he comes here. I can fix it. Ze glass of drugged wine, or ze drugged cigar, will make him go to sleep. And zen my work will be easy.

FRANK. You are right, Celeste. But see that the Governor sees Jack, and the more embarrassing the situation he is in when discovered, the better it will be for our purpose.

CEL. I comprehend ze plan. Ze magnificent plan.

FRANK. Well, my darling Celeste. I must be leaving you. [*They kiss*] I will see you again before morning. [*Noise heard off R.1.E. as if men were disputing*]

CEL. [*Starts at noise*] What can zat noise be? [*Rushes off R.1.E.*]

FRANK. How my love urges her on! This fickle woman Celeste will purloin the jewels and be imprisoned. My rival Jack will become a thing of the past, and as for Samuel, [*Laughs*] he will go into the next bankrupt stock to make up a full dozen. [*Exits L.1.E. Enter Celeste and West Point R.1.E.*]

W. P. [*As they enter*] Well, Mademoiselle, I cannot help it if Mr. Webster will get mad because he drinks more than he is willing to pay for. You see, he gave me a five-dollar note to take out what he owed, and when I gave him his change he said I must be mistaken. Now, Mademoiselle, I never make mistakes. I always know what a gentleman has called for. I have a great noodle. [*Puts his finger to his head*]

CEL. If zat is ze case, Monsieur Webster must pay at the time he gets ze cigar or ze wine. [*Doorbell rings. West Point turns and walks quickly to R.1.E.*]

W. P. Mademoiselle.

CEL. West Point, go to ze door. [*He exits L.3.E. Celeste seated at table L.C. West Point enters, bowing in Jack*]

JACK. Good evening, Mlle. Celeste.

CEL. Good evening, Monsieur Cheviot. Are you well zis evening?

JACK. [*Somewhat coldly*] Yes, thank you. Where will I find my friend, Mr. Webster?

CEL. Your friend Mr. Webster is in ze card room. [*Points off R.1.E.*]

JACK. Thank you. [*Crosses to R.1.E. Bows to her, smiles sarcastically, and exits*]

CEL. I nearly forgot ze wine—and ze cigar. [*Calls West Point. West Point enters R.1.E.*]

W. P. Mademoiselle, at your service.

CEL. West Point, go in my room and get ze box of ze small cigars. You will find zem on ze table. And get some wine, in ze bottle. [*Points to table up C.*]

W.P. Yes, Mademoiselle, I will do so. [*Goes to table and takes tray with bottles and exits L.1.E.*]

CEL. I must get ze powder to drug ze wine. [*Exit R. Enter West Point, filler and box of cigars on tray, which he places on table up C.*]

W.P. [*Showing box of cigars, holding them up*] The result of science. One continuous rock-ballasted Havana wrapper and dust-filler can pull two hundred pounds of live frame through six passenger and two baggage cars without stopping. I took a trip with one of these the other day. We had a nice time—but bless the coming person—for there is going to be an episode. [*Enter Celeste with small package in her hand*]

CEL. Have you filled ze bottle?

W.P. Yes, Mademoiselle. [*Aside after having glanced at package in Celeste's hand*] More episodes. [*Doorbell rings. He turns, goes toward R. 1.E.*]

CEL. West Point.

W.P. Mademoiselle?

CEL. See who is at ze door. [*He exits L.1.E. Celeste puts powder in bottle*] Monsieur Plastick may come now. [*Enter West Point*]

W.P. Mr. Plastrick, or some such name.

CEL. Show him in and let ze Monsieur be seated at ze table. [*Pointing to bottle L. going towards R.1.E.*] I will return shortly and see Monsieur Cheviot. [*Aside*] I'll see that Jack is safe. [*Exit R.1.E., West Point bowing to Sam'l, who enters*]

W.P. Be seated, Mr. Rolstron, Mlle. Celeste will see you directly.

CEL. Mr. Plastick, if you please. Say, how is business?

W.P. Very good this evening. All the rooms are full.

SAM. [*Aside*] I guess he ain't far from it. [*Aloud*] You are doing a good business here every evening, ain't you?

W.P. Yes, sir—pretty fair.

SAM. Say, young man, ain't your name West Point?

W.P. Yes, sir—it is.

SAM. I thought I remembered you. [*They shake hands*] Tell me who owns this place?

W.P. I don't know, sir.

SAM. [*Gives coin*] Now, tell me. Don't Bronson own this place?

W.P. Yes, sir—Mr. Bronson and Mlle. Celeste, as I understand it.

SAM. [*Aside*] I thought the gentleman had an interest in here. [*Aloud*] Say, West Point, how much does he pay you a week for your services.

W.P. I decline to answer, sir.

SAM. You what? [*Looks at him astonished*]

W.P. I decline to answer.

SAM. Oh, I forgot. [*Takes another coin from pocket, gives it*]

W.P. Five dollars a week—board and extras.

SAM. [*Hands him coin*] Here is more extras. [*He looks at it as if ashamed to take it*] Don't be foolish—take it. [*Aside*] Centennial medals a dollar a cross. [*Hands him another coin*] So du canst du Shabes damit machen. [*Starts to go R.3.E.*]

W.P. I was requested to have you wait here.

SAM. I just want to go in and see a friend of mine. [*Going*]

W.P. See here, sir—I can't let you go in there without permission from Mademoiselle.

SAM. You don't tell me. [*Gives coin*] What do you say?

W.P. You may go. [*Sam'l exits R.1.E. West Point comes down-stage*] I don't know, but it seems funny that everyone talks about drummers being so sharp, and always having an eye like the eagle bird. So far as I am concerned I think that some of them are too thick-headed for any smartness. Why, every time that I said no to that fellow, he produced just like a hen laying eggs. [*Starts to go L. when he drops coin; picks it up, bites it and discovers it to be bad*] The drummer is a smart man after all. [*Enter Sam'l R.3.E.*]

SAM. I wonder where Jack is? [*Sees West Point, takes coin from pocket and holds it up*] Here, West Point.

W.P. No, thanks, you are too generous.

SAM. [*Coming down*] But this is a good one.

W.P. [*Takes coin, looks at it, bows to Sam'l, crosses to R.*] Thank you, sir. [*Exits R.1.E. Enter Celeste R.1.E., is very friendly*]

CEL. Ah, good evening, Monsieur Plastrick. [*Extending hand*]

SAM. Good evening, Mademoiselle. [*They shake hands*]

CEL. Won't you be seated at ze table here, while I get ze wine and cigars?

SAM. [*Sits at table R.*] I don't care if I do.

CEL. [*Goes to table up C., brings down tray with glasses and box of cigars*] Monsieur, have some wine. It is excellent.

SAM. No, thank you, I just had a whiskey sour.

CEL. Well, you will smoke ze nice Havana? [*Handing him box over table*]

SAM. I don't care if I do. These French people always smoke good cigars.

CEL. It gives me ze great pleasure to see ze monsieur. How is ze Mam'-selle Rebecca? Why did you not bring her to spend ze evening? I would like to have her call. I am always so lonesome.

SAM. Rebecca has got the lumbago in her head. But if you are lonesome, why don't you take a hand at poker for pastime?

CEL. Ah, monsieur knows ze secret?

SAM. [*Aside*] She thinks I'm a sucker. [*Aloud*] I never knew it was a secret.

CEL. Oh, it's kept very private. You find ze good cigar is ze imported one.

SAM. That's first-rate. By the way, a friend of mine down on Broadway manufactures imported cigars. [*Blows smoke from cigar*]—for seven dollars a thousand if you return the stamps and the boxes.

CEL. [*Very pleasant*] That's very cheap, indeed. Now, won't you try some of ze wine? Come—just to please me—a little drop.

SAM. [*Aside*] If Rebecca saw that, she would pull all the hair out of my head. [*Aloud*] But I might as well be sociable as not. [*Both drink*]

CEL. Well, what is ze news at ze store?

SAM. The latest is that Mr. Bronson is about to marry Miss Ellen.

CEL. What is that you say? Monsieur Bronson marry Ellen? Zat cannot be. You are mistaken, Monsieur Plastrick.

SAM. The drummer never makes mistakes. Listen, Mr. Winslow and Ellen are coming here this evening, and if they find Jack here, the girl will marry Frank Bronson, and he'll become partner in the business.

CEL. [*Madly*] Never—never! [*Drags dagger from bosom of dress*] I will drive this to his black heart first.

SAM. Don't you do it, it's too much trouble. He ain't worth it. You just tell Mr. Winslow that Jack has never been here. That is enough. Then the young lady will refuse to marry Bronson, do you see?

CEL. Yes, I comprehend ze plan. Ze grand one, and I think I will do it. But I must consider it first, to see if it is possible zat he has deceived me. [*Puts hand to forehead, as if in thought*]

SAM. What room is Jack in?

CEL. Monsieur Jack has not come yet zis evening.

SAM. [*Blowing as if warm*] It's awful warm here. Couldn't you kindly open the window. [*Cigar drops from hand as he falls back in chair asleep*]

W.P. [*Just as Sam'l falls asleep, West Point is about to step in door R.3.E. Sees Sam'l and laughs*] The gentleman has reached his destination.

CEL. [*Goes up stage towards window, watching Sam'l. Does not open window, but approaches him on tiptoe, looks into his face*] Monsieur feels the fresh air coming in? [*Aside softly*] He is asleep. [*Goes up and looks off R.3.E. to see if she is watched, comes down*] Ze drug works capital. [*Looks off R. and L. entrances; approaches Sam'l*] There is no one watching me. Now I will get the diamonds. The ten thousand dollars diamonds. [*Kneels by his side; is about to put hand inside coat pocket; starts as if she heard a noise; gets up; comes to R.1.E.*] It was nothing, only imagination. [*Goes back to Sam'l, goes through coat pocket first, then cautiously his vest; puts hand into inside pocket and takes casket from it. Gets up with a start; trembles and conceals casket; recovers herself*] I HAVE ZEM! [*Looks at Sam'l; opens casket; comes down stage, looking at diamonds*] Ah ze magnificent—ze beautiful! I shall wear zem when I go back to La Belle France. [*Closes casket. Frank has been watching her from L.3.E.*]

FRANK. And it is thus you have sold your liberty! [*She turns frightened*]

CEL. Monsieur—how you frightened me! I was not expecting you.

FRANK. Hunters often surprise the game. You have been trapped. Henceforth you are nothing to me, and if you ever dare to trouble me, I will hand you over to the law.

CEL. What is zis you say? You betray me, your wife—who would steal for her husband? [*Points to him*]

FRANK. No, I'll tell you the truth. You are no wife of mine. The marriage was but a sham to satisfy your scruples.

CEL. Monsieur Bronson, you are ze coward!

FRANK. [*Laughs*] And the time has come for an understanding. You my wife—absurd!

CEL. [*Goes to him and looks him in the face*] You forget, monsieur, the ceremony was performed in France, and before ze witnesses. And according to ze law of zat country, you are my husband.

FRANK. And you forget that the witnesses were friends of mine.

CEL. Then I will have ze satisfaction zat you will marry me before you leave zis house. [*Takes dagger and raises it over him*] Or I will kill you!

FRANK. Don't be a fool. Keep your stolen prize, and keep your mouth closed, and you will be let alone. Well, I will leave you now. [*Turns to R., goes up*]

CEL. [*Stands before him with drawn dagger*] Not before you make me your wife. Then you may go. [*Pointing to door L.2.E. Frank laughs and starts to go. She tries to prevent him, when he catches her by the wrists and throws her. She is about to strike him with dagger when he catches her wrists again. They struggle down stage, she trying to stab him, but he in turn turns the knife against herself, she sinks down on her knees—she rises —turns, swoons, and falls into his L. arm. He gently lets her down*]

FRANK. [*Feels her pulse—astonished*] Dead! The devil! I didn't mean to kill her. I must get out of this before I am discovered! [*Goes down C. and picks up diamonds which Celeste had dropped*] And while going there is one important thing I must not forget. [*Shows casket and exits L.1.E. Enter Mr. Winslow and Ellen, L.3.E.*]

WIN. [*Sees her; starts*] What's this? By my faith, Ellen, there has been murder committed here! Quick—Help! Help! [*Enter West Point and Jack from R.3.E., and Frank from L.1.E.*]

W.P. Mademoiselle! Dead! [*As he rushes and kneels beside her*]

JACK. [*Picks up knife*] Yes, murdered!

WIN. [*Sees Sam'l*] And Sam'l here!

FRANK. Could he have done this?

W.P. No, for he has been asleep for the last half hour.

JACK. [*To Frank*] This looks like your work, and if you were not my brother I should denounce you as the murderer! [*Sam'l wakes up, looks about—sees his vest open. Funny business feeling for the diamonds*]

ACT IV.

Rebecca discovered seated L., knitting or sewing. Uncle Goldstein asleep in chair R., with newspaper in his hand at rise.

REB. Uncle! [*Uncle Goldstein snores*] Uncle, are you asleep?

UNCLE GOLDSTEIN. [*Wakes up suddenly*] No.

REB. Give me some money for dinner.

UNCLE G. [*Snores*] I'm asleep. [*Snores*]

REB. Uncle.

UNCLE G. Well, what is it?

REB. Give me the money.

UNCLE G. How much do you want?

REB. Three dollars will do, I think.

UNCLE G. Three dollars for one dinner!

REB. Why, yes.

UNCLE G. Rebecca, come here! [*Takes money from vest pocket*] Here's a quarter; go and buy some cheese sandwiches.

REB. [*Has money in her hand*] Cheese sandwiches won't do for dinner today, Uncle.

UNCLE G. Why not?

REB. Because Sammy is coming for dinner.

UNCLE G. Rebecca, if he eats a three-dollar dinner, he'll suffer with the dyspepsia for a week.

REB. Then, too, Uncle, this is Yuntuff.

UNCLE G. So it is, I forgot about it. Here is three dollars, and it's all the money I've got. [*Gives money. Rebecca is about to exit L.1.E.*] Rebecca, come here, give me back the quarter I gave you for the sandwiches.

REB. Oh, yes. [*Gives him back money*]

UNCLE G. I never pay three dollars and a quarter for a three-dollar dinner. [*Goes back of counter; Rebecca exits; returns at once with hat on. Enter Footlight from C.D.*]

UNCLE G. [*Puts L. hand in back pocket*] Hello. [*Takes bill from pocket*] I'm worth two dollars more than I thought.

FOOTLIGHT. Good morning, sir. [*Bows to Rebecca*] How fares the goodness of the morning with you?

UNCLE G. How are you, Rebecca? Der seed aus ware er maschuker.

FOOT. Could I see the young gentleman?

UNCLE G. He is out walking for a dollar and a half.

FOOT. Ah—he is not in, you say? I regret this exceedingly, for he knows me well.

UNCLE G. You look like you have been here before.

FOOT. Oh, yes—I have known the young man for an extended time.

UNCLE G. He's been busted before.

FOOT. I suppose you are his substitute?

UNCLE G. [*Reaches for package*] Let's see what kind of a tute.

FOOT. I said you were his auxiliary, you are taking the young man's place while he is out.

UNCLE G. Now I understand. I thought first you were a musician, and had a tute you wanted to put up.

FOOT. No, sir—I am not a musician. I'm an actor.

UNCLE G. A what? An actor?

FOOT. Yes, most reverend senior, that's where I hold my cruel grip.

UNCLE G. [*Aside*] I said he was crazy.

FOOT. This package contains some very valuable wardrobe, on which I would like to secure the loan of five dollars. [*Uncle Goldstein opens package. Business of showing it to Rebecca.*] Can we use that? And how is that? How much do you want on the stuff?

FOOT. What I said.

UNCLE G. What did you say? I don't hear very well at times.

FOOT. Five elegant cases. [*Rubbing hands*]

UNCLE G. Rebecca, get the gentleman five matchcases.

FOOT. No, no, no! Lucre, piasters, boodle money, five dollars.

UNCLE G. Five dollars? Why, they are all old!

FOOT. Humph! You don't understand, then, that age has the tendency to enhance the value of such chattels as these. Why, sir, these were once the property of the illustrious Forrest, and should bring back to everyone such memories of his genius that nothing but a fabulous sum should touch them. Any actor would give you five dollars for them, while I only ask the loan of five paltry dollars.

UNCLE G. I don't want them for five dollars.

FOOT. [*Taking stage*] Ye Gods and little fishes! [*Business*] You will then insist in heaping such humility upon me! [*In emotion*] I pray you give me three dollars. [*Going towards counter*]

UNCLE G. I'll give you two dollars less fifty cents. [*Business*]

FOOT. Ye Gods and Hebrew mathematicians! [*Shaking head*] And Greece must bend her knees in suppliance to your intriguing power! You would stoop to such a paltry sum as this. Why, perchance you should meet the right man within only a day's travel. He would feed upon the opportunity to give you twenty times as much.

UNCLE G. I won't give any more.

FOOT. [*Taking corner L.*] Then if you will grind me down to starvation, take the consequences upon your own head. [*Draws sword from under cloak. Makes rush for Uncle Goldstein*] How now!

UNCLE G. [*Gets under counter*] Look out! Don't get mad!

FOOT. Nay, nay—I am not mad. But thou art so mysterious. Thy very manner and laugh is so full of tissue that I cannot fathom the worth of thy seeming nature. I will subdue this sudden burst of passion, or else the wasp may sting me, and I would make more food for the vultures of the air. Why, sir, with the keen edge of this noble steel, I have severed in twain the diabolical systems of monopolies [*Business with sword*], given wings to visions of ecstasy, [*with emotion*] and have oft-times caused the scanty means at home [*with emotion*] to be replenished. I am a Democrat from the Second Ward, and for years have assisted in having bills passed, but never yet have I succeeded in putting the fourth wall of generosity before a pawnbroker's shop. [*Throws sword on counter*] Now, how much will you give?

UNCLE G. Two dollars full, not a cent more!

Foot. Let me clutch them ere I go for a haircut. Avaunt, bright shekels, and quit my sight. There is no speculation in the brightness thou dost glare with. But hold, the sum will not buy many chips, so be careful, Horatio, but fail to spend thee now. [*Looks at money*] No, for in the bright lexicon of youth, there is no such word as fail. Ha, I go, for the doleful bell of bygone days invites me. [*Business*] And yet a voice from the rear seems to whisper, "Here is not Duncan," for it is a knell that summons to heaven or to hell. Avaunt: For when gaunt wolves meet lions in the track, I'll rend the rugged rocks asunder. Adieu; Adieu. [*Exits C.D.*]

Uncle G. Rebecca, that fellow is a good actor, I have seen him play that fellow what says "Friends, Romans, Countrymen. Lend me your ear for half an hour." You know what I mean.

Reb. Yes, you mean Mark Anthony in *Julius Caesar*.

Uncle G. That's the fellow. But business is awful dull this morning. It's just like Yuntoff.

Reb. Well, Uncle, it's early yet. You can't tell how it will be before night. It may be better this afternoon.

Uncle G. Yes, wie heisst. I don't believe it. When it starts so dull, it stays dull all day, I think we'll mark the goods down.

Reb. [*Laughs*] Just like you, Uncle! If business is dull for a day you mark the goods down. Then if I should happen to make a sale tomorrow, at today's prices, you'd say, "Rebecca, you sold them too cheap."

Uncle G. Yes, wie heisst. [*Boys appear at C.D.*] Say, boys, get away from the doors! You'll get them full of cobwebs.

Boys. [*Outside*] Ah, you old Sheeny!

Uncle G. Rebecca, get me some hot water to throw on the loafers. [*The boys disappear*] Never mind, Rebecca. They are gone.

Reb. If you wouldn't take notice of them, they would go just as soon.

Uncle G. Yes, wie heisst. I don't want to hide the store front. Rebecca, now you mark that lot of goods that came in yesterday. I'll call off the numbers.

Reb. Why, Sam did mark them yesterday.

Uncle G. So he did. I forgot. From my memorandum. But we want to check the memorandum from the bill now. [*Has two documents, gives her one*]

Reb. Oh, I understand you now. You just want to compare the invoice with the memorandum. Is that it?

Uncle G. That's it, Rebecca.

Reb. Well, you call the number and the price from the invoice, and I will check them off the memorandum.

UNCLE G. Are you ready, Rebecca?

REB. Proceed.

UNCLE G. Number four thousand three hundred odd nothing and six, one dozen plain beaver coats, fifty-seven dollars a dozen.

REB. Yes.

UNCLE G. Number five hundred six thousand seven odd nothing and two, one dozen of diagonal dress goods, fifty-six dollars and fifty-six cents.

REB. Yes.

UNCLE G. Number nine thousand six hundred and twenty-one—one lot of—one lot of hogskin. [*Rebecca laughs*] What is that? I can't make it out. Rebecca, you see what he's got here. [*Handing bill to her, who reads*]

REB. One lot of Hogan's best jean pants, eighteen dollars a dozen.

UNCLE G. [*Takes memorandum*] Oh, that is that quarter of a dozen. A job lot. I tell you, Rebecca, that is a bargain. I didn't want the pants, but I bought them because they were cheap. I tell you, those are good ones. [*Gets pants and shows them to her*] They are all big ones. You won't have any trouble with the fit. [*Lays pants on table*]

REB. Very well. Proceed, Uncle.

UNCLE G. One lot of boys' Reymour jackets. Six dollars a dozen. That's all. [*Takes bill from her, puts it in pocket, and goes back of counter*]

SAM. [*Enters C.D.*] Good morning, Uncle.

UNCLE G. Good morning, Samuel.

SAM. Good morning, Rebecca, how is business? [*Goes down and shakes hands*]

REB. It was very dull, indeed. Uncle wants to mark down his stock. But why must it always be business first thing?

SAM. Business before pleasure, Rebecca. [*Puts arm around her*] But how are you anyhow?

REB. Oh, I'm very well.

SAM. By the way, Rebecca, I saw Mr. Winslow, and—

UNCLE G. [*Behind counter*] Sam'l.

SAM. Just a moment and I'll tell you all about it, Rebecca. [*Goes to counter*] Well—?

UNCLE G. Sam'l, there's a fellow that owes me a dollar and a quarter. If you will stay here, I will go and see him.

SAM. All right, Uncle. [*Goes L. to Rebecca*] Now, don't stay long, Uncle, because we always feel so lonesome when you are gone.

UNCLE G. [*Going to door*] I won't be long. [*Exit C.D.*]

SAM. Now, Rebecca, I'm going to talk business to you. [*Gets chair and sits R. of her*] I'm going to tell you all about the town we are going to live in after we are married. It is a town I discovered while I was out on my last trip. It's full of Germans and Yiddish people. I know you would like the place.

REB. What's the name of the town?

SAM. Milwaukee, Wisconsin.

REB. Oh, I know the place very well. I've been there on a visit. I have an aunt living in Milwaukee.

SAM. You don't tell me! Do you like it there?

REB. Oh, yes, indeed. I think it a nice clean city.

SAM. Well, I am glad you like it, because I thought of going there to open the three-ball business, Rebecca.

REB. But what about your seeing Mr. Winslow? Does he still think it was Jack who stole the diamonds?

SAM. I think he does.

REB. Well, I rather think that myself.

SAM. You do? Well, I don't. And I wouldn't if all the farmhouses would turn into brownstone fronts. And then I be darned if I'd believe it.

REB. I hope you think rightly.

SAM. Well, I'll soon clear up the entire matter, for I've got a new idea.

REB. What is your idea?

SAM. I'll tell you.

REB. Yes?

SAM. Next week.

REB. Come, do tell me now.

SAM. I might as well advertise it in the newspaper.

REB. [*Angrily*] Sam, I don't think you love me at all.

SAM. Oh, yes I do. [*Kisses her*] That proves it.

UNCLE G. [*Enters C.D.*] That is how lonesome they are when I am gone.

SAM. [*They are surprised at his entrance*] Rebecca has got something in her eye. [*To Uncle*] Well, how is it?

UNCLE G. I got a dollar and a quarter. Now if you stay here, Sam'l, I will go after another fellow.

SAM. But, very well, Uncle. But business is awful dull.

UNCLE G. The letter-carrier just gave me a letter. [*Looks through his vest pockets for glasses*] I wonder where my glasses are? [*Has glasses on*]

SAM. I'll sell you a new pair for a dollar and a half.

UNCLE G. Never mind, I'll find my old ones. [*Goes to desk looking for glasses*] I can't find those eyes of mine. Here, Sam'l, you see what it is. [*Hands him letter*]

SAM. [*Aside—starts*] Frank Bronson's handwriting! I wonder what he wants. [*Opens letter and reads, aside*] "Mr. Isaac Goldstein, being pushed for cash, would like to ask you for a small loan. I have some very valuable diamonds which I will give as security. Please call at once. Respectfully, Mrs. Dalton, 1010 Poplar St." [*Speaks*] I'll just have Mrs. F. Dalton. [*Comes down from behind counter*]

UNCLE G. I can't find—[*Discovers glasses on his forehead*] Well, well, there they are! What is it, Sam'l? Let me try and read it. [*Tries to take letter from Sam'l, who folds it up*]

SAM. It's only a price list from Rosen, in New York.

UNCLE G. [*Disappointed*] Is that all? [*Takes stick and hat, and exits C.D.*]

REB. I came near forgetting the roast I had in the oven for dinner. You will excuse me, Sam? [*Exit L.1.*]

SAM. Why, certainly! [*After her exit*] Now for Frank Bronson's diamonds. [*Goes to desk and writes*] "Philadelphia, June 1, 1854. Mrs. Dalton, In reply to your favor, will say that I am pleased to give you the loan you ask for, but must ask you to call on me. Yours in hock, Isaac Goldstein. P.S. Please call between eleven and twelve o'clock." [*Folds letter—puts it in envelope and addresses it*] I guess that will do. [*Enter West Point C.D.*] Hello, West Point, glad to see you!

W.P. Good morning, Mr. Sam'l. I have brought you the document you wanted. [*Hands document with red seal*] The last words spoken by poor Mlle. Celeste, stating that she received her death at the hands of Frank Bronson.

SAM. [*Opens letter and document*] And witnessed by you and A. J. Webster. West Point, you should have delivered this to the proper authorities long before this.

W.P. No doubt, and it was my intention to do so, but I feared Frank Bronson's vengeance.

SAM. The sheriff will hang them both when he gets his hands on them. Now, Mr. West Point, I would like you to call on Mr. Winslow and ask him to come here with Miss Ellen as soon as possible.

W.P. Very well, Mr. Sam'l.

SAM. And then find Jack Cheviot, and bring him here and lose as little time as you can.

W.P. All right, sir.

SAM. [*Hands him letter*] By the way, West Point, give this to a messenger boy while you are out, and have it delivered at once.

W.P. All right, Mr. Sam'l. [*Exit C.D. Enter Mrs. Mulcahey C.D.*]

Mrs. Mulcahey. Good morning to you, sir.

Sam. What can I do for you?

Mrs. M. I came in to get two dollars on this shawl.

Sam. [*Opens shawl and looks at it*] That's an awful poor shawl, and some of the fringe is worn off of it, too.

Mrs. M. Faith, I know there is. My baby cut it off with the scissors.

Sam. It's a bad thing to let babies play with scissors.

Mrs. M. So it is, sir—so it is.

Sam. That shawl is awful poor.

Mrs. M. Faith, I paid eight dollars for the shawl when I bought it.

Sam. But it's a long time since that shawl was bought.

Mrs. M. Not so very long, now.

Sam. Well, it's old enough to be worn out. I'll give you half a dollar.

Mrs. M. Oh sir, I must have two dollars, for I need the money very bad.

Sam. It ain't worth two dollars.

Mrs. M. Well, I suppose if you can't give it I must go elsewhere, because I must have the money to buy some medicine for my poor sick child, and bread for myself and the other children, for I can't work and leave the sick child at home.

Sam. Where is your husband—why can't he work?

Mrs. M. [*Crying*] Sure and I wouldn't be pawning me shawl if he was living. He's been dead for the last two years and I've been wearing out washboards ever since, and, faith, the youngest of fourteen children is sick and I want money on the shawl now to get the childer food and nourishment. Faith, I wish I had been born a grasshopper.

Sam. [*Takes money from pocket and gives her two dollars*] Here. [*Hands her money*] Let me have your basket for a moment. [*Crosses to L. E. and calls Rebecca. Rebecca enters L.1.*]

Reb. Did you call?

Sam. Rebecca, die frau hat a grosses schlimaell. Go and get her something to eat, for her children. [*Aside*] A true Hebrew never goes back on the widows and orphans! [*Reenter Rebecca with basket*]

Reb. Here, Sam'l. [*Handing him basket*]

Sam. [*Takes basket, puts shawl in it and covers it with paper—fringe of shawl must show—hands basket to Mrs. Mulcahey*] Now, you take this home and give your children a Jewish picnic.

Mrs. M. Faith, sir, you've made a mistake, you've given me back my shawl.

Sam. That's all right, wrap the baby up in it.

Mrs. M. You may want it for your own?

SAM. Rebecca, do you want it?

REB. Sam'l!

SAM. No—Rebecca don't want it.

MRS. M. Well, the Lord bless you both! [*Exit C.D.*]

SAM. But not with twins! Good-bye.

REB. Sam'l, what time have you?

SAM. Twenty minutes after eleven.

REB. So late! Then I must go and set the table for dinner.

SAM. And I must play your uncle. [*Puts on long coat, beard and hat to impersonate Uncle Goldstein*] Now I am ready for business. [*Enter Frank Bronson in disguise*] And not any too soon, for here is my man now.

FRANK. Good morning.

SAM. Good morning. What can I do for you, my friend?

FRANK. I came in to see if I could sell you some diamonds.

SAM. Are they your own property?

FRANK. Why, certainly they are my own.

SAM. [*Aside*] You lie!

FRANK. At least, they belong to my wife. But here. [*Shows letter*] She gives me the right to dispose of them.

SAM. Are they nice ones?

FRANK. Yes. Gems of almost peerless value.

SAM. They may be too high for me.

FRANK. [*Takes small case of diamonds from pocket*] You see, our circumstances are such that I must take a loan, or dispose of them at a very low price. I am the husband of Mrs. Dalton, who wrote you this morning.

SAM. [*Aside*] How you can lie! [*Aloud*] Oh, are you Mr. Dalton? [*Business. Shakes hands*] I am glad to meet you. Have you the diamonds with you?

FRANK. Yes, I have them here. [*Opens case and hands them to Sam'l*] And they are the real gems.

SAM. Why, they are beauties! How much do you want for them, Mr. Dalton?

FRANK. Oh, they are worth fully ten thousand dollars.

SAM. [*Has them in hand*] And can you trust me with them? Thank you, more than I'd trust you with.

FRANK. Sir, what do you mean? [*Enter Winslow, Ellen, Jack, West Point and Rebecca L.1.E.*]

SAM. [*Throws off disguise*] I mean, Frank Bronson, that you are a scoundrel!

FRANK. [*Crosses to L.*] What's that? [*Takes pistol from pocket*]

SAM. Yes, and here are the proofs. [*Points two large revolvers at Frank, which he takes from under the counter*] Now, just hand that revolver to Rebecca. [*Frank is about to do so*] To shoot you with. [*Frank hesitates*] Go ahead—[*Frank does so*] For these ain't loaded. [*Laughs. Frank makes rush at Sam'l, who grabs gun from back of counter*] But this is. [*Rebecca points butt of revolver at Frank and muzzle to herself—Mr. Winslow comes down*] Mr. Winslow, here are the diamonds, and here is the thief! [*Points at Frank*]—and murderer of his own wife.

FRANK. You lie!

SAM. I do generally—to sell goods always—but not this time. [*Holding up Celeste's confession*]

WIN. [*Tears beard from Frank's face and throws it aside*] Bronson, you are a scoundrel of the blackest dye—a murderer. [*Showing document, which he has taken from Sam'l*] I would be acting legally to hand you over to the authorities, but for relations' sake, and for the desire to have no further disgrace, I will give you one day to get out of reach of the authorities. If found upon American soil after tomorrow night, you shall suffer the full penalty of the law.

FRANK. [*Goes to door*] I go, but my curse remains with you! [*Exit C.D.*]

SAM. That's it—sneak! [*Crosses to Rebecca L.*] I said I will clear up the whole business pretty soon.

REB. So you did.

WIN. Mr. Plastrick, my gratitude cannot be expressed in words, but shall be proven in act. I shall give you a start in business for yourself. As for Jack, he is my future partner, and Ellen shall be his wife.

SAM. Thank you, Mr. Winslow.

JACK. Sam, you have made a new life for me, and have given me a world of happiness. [*Embraces Ellen*]

SAM. Now, as you are all happy, Rebecca and I will be married, and if any of our friends in front wish to buy diamonds, call on Sam'l Plastrick and he will sell you some as large as this, [*Holding up big piece of cut glass*] for half a dollar.

Jack and Ellen R.   Winslow C.   Sam'l and Rebecca L.   West Point

CURTAIN

OUR BOARDING HOUSE

By Leonard Grover

CAST OF CHARACTERS

Colonel M. T. Elevator, *A commercial exchange operator*

Professor Gregarious Gillypod, *Inventor of the flying machine*

Joseph Fioretti, *Our last new boarder*

Walter Dalrymple, *Possessed of means and desirious of speculating*

Mrs. Dalrymple, *Walter's mother*

Matthew Eligible, *Dealer in corner lots and given to flirtation*

Dr. Shouter, *Manufacturer of patent medicine*

Tim, *A "hackman"*

Alonzo, *A colored servant*

Postman

Beatrice Manheim, *A teacher at the Conservatory, our interesting boarder*

Florence, *Her little child, our pet*

Mrs. Violet Eligible, *Our society boarder*

Mrs. Marie Colville, *Mistress of our boarding house*

Clarence Dexter

Betty, *Our maid of all work*

Jack Hardy, *A detective*

Boy with fiddle

Annie

SYNOPSIS
ACT I.

Scene 1: *Carpet down; small card table against flat L. with dinner bell on it. Doorbell to ring, L. Feather duster for Betty. Seven letters for prompter. Slips*

of newspaper in Shouter letter. Newspaper for Elevator. Lots of parcels and newspaper for Gillypod. Burned cork for Alonzo.
SCENE 2: *Large dinner table C. and eight chairs. Dinner set for eight persons, handsomely set on table. Castor—plates—cups—saucers—small covered table L.C. Decanter and glasses, etc.*

ACT II.

Sofa R. Curtains on L. door, handsome set, table and chairs L. Books—vase of flowers on table—bottle and glasses R.2.E. Jewel case and ring for Manheim. Gun—crash ready. Dinner bell for Betty.

ACT III.

SCENE 1: *Baize down, two garden chairs. Six cigars for characters. Tin money for Gillypod. Guitar and sheet of music R. Stick of candy.*

ACT IV.

Lake, represented by baize. Leave carpet down.
SCENE 3: *Table and chairs R. and L. Handsome. Handcuffs and pistol for Hardy.*

SCENE PLOT

ACT I.

SCENE 1. Chambers in 1 groove.
SCENE 2. Chamber in 3.

ACT II.

SCENE 1. C.D. Fancy—door open—balustrade cross backed by garden in 4. Set doors R. and L.3.E.

ACT III.

SCENE 1. Garden in 4.

ACT IV.

SCENE 1. Landscape. In 4.
SCENE 2. C.D. Fancy chamber. Doors practical, 3 and 4, backed by interior.

ACT I.

SCENE 1: *Plain chamber in 2. Set door R.1.E. Double door L.2.E. Balustrade and candelabra R.2.E. Hatrack with looking glass at back L.C. Betty discovered at rise, dusting.*

BETTY. Slave, slave from morning till night! Oh, dear, this is a nice place I've got into! I think I am going to leave it. Missus don't make Alonzo answer the bell [*Goes to D.L.*] Oh, there are the advertising circulars again. It's all I can do to keep the house from being overrun with them. [*Picks up one and reads*] "Mrs. Farnshaw," that's the milliner, "plumbs herself off scene"—. Oh, she plumbs herself—what's this? "Dr. Shouter's anti-bilious —calis—calis—." So Shouter is at it again, is he? Cures everything—I wonder if he cures a board-bill? [*Reads*] "New York Mammoth colus"—that makes the second circus I've missed this summer. Now I give warning, if I don't get to this very next circus that comes along—[*Bell rings*]

MRS. C. [*Outside*] Betty!

BETTY. M'am?

MRS. C. There's the bell.

BETTY. I hear it, m'am. [*Opens D.L. Enter postman*] Oh, it's the new postman!

POST. [*Gives letters*] Clarence Dexter; [*one*] Miss Annie Colville; [*one*] Dr. Shouter; [*one*] Mrs. Matthew Eligible; [*two*] Colonel M. T. Elevator; [*three*] Gilly—Golly, got anybody here by the name of Gillop Sisows?

BETTY. Oh, Gillypod!

POST. Yes, that's it. There you are! [*Gives one. Exit L.D.*]

BETTY. [*Puts letters on hatrack*] There are never any for me, of course. [*Bell rings*]

MRS. C. [*Outside*] Betty!

BETTY. M'am?

MRS. C. There's the bell.

BETTY. I hear it, m'am. Do you think I'm deaf? [*Aside. Goes to D.L. Enter Dr. Shouter, hangs hat on rack, sees letters*]

DR. S. Letters! Let me see: "Dr. Shouter," that's me. [*Opens letter which has an advertisement enclosed*] Yes, here it is, my advertisement. [*Reads ad*] "Wanted, a party with $2,000 capital to engage with the advertiser in the manufacturing of a staple article realizing 100 per cent per month." Two hundred per cent, that's more like it. What more staple article than Dr. Shouter's Anti-bilious Calesfonical Mixture? [*Reads letter*] "Answer to the —enclosed advertisement. See you at half-past seven this evening." Good— ah—half-past seven—That will be as soon as dinner is over. I must hurry up. [*Exits upstairs. Bell rings*]

MRS. C. [*Outside*] Betty!

BETTY. M'am?

MRS. C. There's the bell.

BETTY. I hear it, m'am. [*Goes to D. Enter Dexter*]

DEX. Good evening, Betty. This is awful warm weather, almost hot enough to make custard of a fellow's brains, you know.

BETTY. Then it will never trouble you.

DEX. That's good, Betty. That's if I was an egg, I'd cook.

BETTY. Bless you, they don't cook bad ones!

DEX. Bad what?

BETTY. Bad eggs.

DEX. Betty, you are improving. Any letters?

BETTY. Yes, here's one. [*Hands letter*]

DEX. Is dinner ready?

BETTY. You'll hear the bell.

DEX. Thank you. [*Reads letter*] Damnation! Tailor wants money; can't have it, positively. [*Exits upstairs*]

BETTY. He's a good-hearted dunce, and he does wear such lovely neck-ties! Now, why shouldn't he fall in love with me? There is nothing so strange in that. There was a fine young gentleman who married the poor servant girl in *The Black Hand, or the Red Avenger.* [*Bell rings. Betty admits Colonel Elevator*]

COL. Betty, any letters for M. T. Elevator.

BETTY. Yes, three.

COL. Let me have them. [*Takes letters*] Colonel M. T. Elevator, Colonel M. T. Elevator, Colonel M. T. Elevator. "Ground your bait and fly your hook, catch a sucker with a worm and an eel with a bob." Make no mistake, these are answers to my advertisement in the *Tribune.* [*Draws paper from pocket and reads*] "A party with $5,000 capital can have a magnificent oppor-tunity by associating himself with a sterling business man with large but insufficient means for the enterprise"—that's me. Now we shall have the necessary spondulix. Betty, is dinner ready?

BETTY. Not yet, sir.

COL. No, punctuality is not a virtue usually to be found in a boarding house, but always will remain the motto of Colonel M. T. Elevator. Make no mistake. [*Exits upstairs*]

BETTY. I hope he does get the spondulix. I don't know of anyone who wants it more. If he gets rich I'll marry him. [*Bell rings*]

MRS. C. Betty!

BETTY. M'am?

MRS. C. [*Outside*] There's the bell.

BETTY. I hear it, m'am. [*Opens door*] So that's you, Mr. Gillypod?

PROF. [*Outside*] Yes, 'tis I, Professor Gregarious Gillypod. Betty, relieve me of these super-in-cumber-ences before they fall off. [*Throws parcels one by one. Betty catches them*] There's my block work mortar, my net work, the parachute, the quill toothpicks and the hydrogen generator. Now, then, I am at your service. [*Enters. He has several small rubber balloons*]

BETTY. Oh, Mr. Gillypod, what are you going to do with these things?

PROF. That, Betty, is a model of my new airship, which is destined to cleave the ambient space with the velocity of the carrier pigeon, with my wings gently flapping, with my floating parachute extended, and my fish-tail steering apparatus, I shall fly with the speed of a comet.

BETTY. What! Are you going to fly these things? [*Slapping parcels*]

PROF. Gently, gently, Betty, with your fairy-like fingers. That's a glass co-do-dimn.

BETTY. A what? I—me—

PROF. A cododimn, an instrument to indicate the atmospheric density all the way to vacuum.

BETTY. So you think you will fly, sir?

PROF. Think I shall fly? I know I shall fly. While others have failed, miserably failed, I shall succeed.

BETTY. And you are going to make a flying machine out of these things?

PROF. A model only. [*Takes her arm*] In the still calm hours of the night, have you never felt a yearning for the clouds?

BETTY. Never!

PROF. Have you never felt a boundless desire to fly?

BETTY. Not when my board-bill was paid.

PROF. Pshaw! Why should I waste words in explaining to you the difference between those blundering inventions of others and my perfections? Why should I explain to you that while they are massive and sphere-shaped, I am tall. While they thunder on without a steering apparatus or power to guide, at the mercy of every wind, I with parachute extended with hydrogen and fish-tail [*Betty laughs*] female, whyfore this merriment?

BETTY. Because you end with such a fishy tail.

PROF. A waste of genius upon the desert air.

BETTY. Did you never fail, sir?

PROF. .Sixteen times. The sixteenth time was a highly successful failure. I am waiting the event—of—in fact, of capital. I have inserted an advertisement in the *Tribune* [*takes paper from pocket and reads*] "Wanted, a party with $2,000 to engage with the advertiser to complete an invention which will assure boundless wealth. Address Professor Gregarious Gillypod, Bon Ton Boarding House, Wabash Avenue."

BETTY. Well, there are two letters for you.

PROF. Two hundred letters for me! I mean $2,000 letters for me, ah—at last my fondest hopes are to be realized. At last, already I begin to feel myself flying. [*Waves his hands. Betty bites his finger*] Oh, Betty, what are you doing?

BETTY. I was only clipping one of your pinions, to see how you would fly lopsided.

PROF. Help me up with the parcels, Betty. [*She loads him with parcels*]

BETTY. I am going to advertise, too, sir.

PROF. You, Betty?

BETTY. Yes. "Wanted a $10,000 husband by a party of large but not quick enough capital who is ready to jump at the offer."

PROF. Betty, you are—[*Exits upstairs. Bell rings*]

MRS. C. Betty!

BETTY. M'am?

MRS. C. There's the bell.

BETTY. I hear it, m'am. [*Goes to door. Enter Walter and Mrs. Dalrymple*]

WALT. Is this the Bon Ton Boarding House?

BETTY. Yes, sir.

MRS. D. What rooms have you?

BETTY. Front parlor, bed room, green furniture, lace curtains, alcove. First floor back, red furniture, brussels carpet, two closets. Hall chamber, plain furniture, ingrain carpet, one gas burner, no closet, with the privilege of putting trunks in bathroom.

MRS. C. [*Outside*] Betty!

BETTY. M'am?

MRS. C. What are you doing?

BETTY. Showing the rooms, m'am.

MRS. C. I'll be down in a moment.

BETTY. All right, m'am. Please to take seats in the reception room a moment. [*Exits R.1E.*]

Mrs. D. Walter, what is the meaning of this sudden determination you have taken to leave the comfortable rooms at the hotel, to subject yourself to the inconveniences of a boarding house?

Walt. I will tell you, mother. You know, I am desirous of investing capital in some paying enterprise. Well, this morning, three advertisements gave the Bon Ton Boarding House as the address. I do not wish to go into anything blindly, so I made up my mind to come here and live amongst them before investing.

Mrs. D. Do you not fear the society you will come in contact with?

Walt. No, the Bon Ton Boarding House is renowned for its respectability. Our friends the Eligibles board here. [*Enter Mrs. Colville downstairs*]

Mrs. C. You wish to engage board?

Mrs. D. If you please.

Mrs. C. We set a very good table, if I do say myself; dinner at six, luncheon at one. This young gentleman looks as if he were a good deal of a gore man.

Mrs. D. [*Aside*] A gore man? What does she mean by that?

Walt. Evidently a gourmand. I have heard that Mrs. Colville is rather eccentric in her vocabulary.

Mrs. D. Quite so, it seems.

Mrs. C. [*Calling upstairs*] Betty!

Betty. M'am?

Mrs. C. Is that lilac chamber ready?

Betty. In a minute.

Mrs. C. You will excuse the confusion; Professor Gillypod has been using the room to construct some sort of an apparatus, and I am afraid it is in a state of arnica.

Mrs. D. A state of arnica!

Walt. She evidently means a state of anarchy.

Mrs. C. You will please walk upstairs? [*They go up, Mrs. Colville following*] You will excuse her appearance. It is very hard to keep servants in order. Not that my servants are any worse than any other people's servants. [*Bell rings*] Betty!

Betty. [*Enters*] M'am?

Mrs. C. There's the bell. [*Exits upstairs*]

Betty. I hear it, m'am. [*Goes to D.*]

Tim. [*Outside*] Ask the gentleman if I am to stay down here or bring up the trunks. Sure, three dollars is not enough to bring up four big trunks. If I had known it I would not have taken the job.

BETTY. [*Closes door*] Stay where you are. [*Dusting and singing*]
"Oh, there was Napoleon Bonaparte, he had ten thousand men,
He led them up the hill, and he led them down again,
When they were up they were up, and when they were down, they were
    down,
And when they were in the middle they were neither up nor down."
MRS. C. [*Outside*] Stop that noise!
BETTY. Yes, m'am. [*Enter Tim with trunk D.L.*]
TIM. Sure, man, there are four big trunks, and I only get three dollars
for the job. It's not enough.
BETTY. Oh, don't be so fresh.
MRS. C. [*Outside*] Betty!
BETTY. M'am?
TIM. Haven't ye got a nager about the house?
BETTY. Alonzo! [*Enter Alonzo R.1.E.*] Help the man with the trunks.
[*Pushes Tim off*]
AL. I came here to wait on table; I don't carry no Irishman's trunks.
[*Tim and Alonzo carry four trunks upstairs, then they exit, after which
Betty calls dinner, takes large bell from corner, rings, and exits R.1.E.*]

SCENE 2: *Dining room—box scene—doors R. and L.U. Sideboard at back.—
Large table C. Seats for Mrs. Colville, Colonel Elevator, Professor Gillypod,
Dexter, Mr. Eligible, Violet, Annie seated—Betty waiting—Alonzo at side-
board.*

BETTY. [*To Professor Gillypod*] Boiled whitefish, roast beef, chicken pie
—and mutton hash.
PROF. Yes.
BETTY. Which?
PROF. What?
BETTY. Boiled whitefish—roast beef—chicken pie, etc.
PROF. Bring it all.
ELIG. How is the grain market, Colonel Elevator?
COL. Looks like another corner in Spring. Over two and a half cents raise.
DR. S. Two cents and a half!
MRS. C. Betty! Claret for Mr. and Mrs. Eligible.
BETTY. Claret.
DR. S. Why, that makes over a million!
COL. Over a million. Over a million, make no mistake.
MRS. C. Betty, Colonel Elevator's decanter of brandy.
BETTY. Alonzo! Brandy.

Mrs. C. [*To Annie*] What will you have, my dear?

Annie. A piece of fish, m'am.

Prof. Where's Mrs. Manheim?

Col. Yes, where's the charming widow?

Mrs. C. Beatrice has not returned from her music lesson yet.

Vio. Our table loses its brightest ornament when she is away.

Col. You are complimentary, my dear, but I quite agree with you.

Vio. Well, you need not say so.

Betty. The new boarders, m'am. [*Enter Walter and Mrs. Dalrymple R.*]

Mrs. C. Take these seats, please. [*Betty places chairs*] Mr. and Mrs. Dalrymple, our new boarders. [*All bow*] Mr. Dexter, Colonel Elevator.

Elig. [*Rising*] Why, Walter, how do you do?

Walt. I am delighted, and how is Violet?

Vio. Well, thank you, Mr. Dalrymple, I am so glad you are to be here with us. We have a lady friend that you will be pleased to meet; Mrs. Beatrice Manheim, a young widow just from the East.

Col. And as good as gold.

Elig. And pretty! Look out for your heart, Walter!

Col. Yes, she's awfully pretty—and holds a corner on eyes, make no mistake.

Mrs. D. Then she is exclusive?

Vio. Oh, very.

Mrs. D. Wealthy, I suppose?

Vio. No, she is a music teacher.

Mrs. D. Oh!

Vio. You will like her when you come to know her.

Betty. Here she comes now. [*Enter Beatrice and Florence R.*]

Mrs. C. Mr. and Mrs. Dalrymple, Mrs. Manheim.

Mrs. D. I am glad to make your acquaintance, Mrs. Manheim. I hope we shall be friends.

Bea. I shall be very happy, I have so few friends. I hope to see many pleasant hours with you and your husband.

Mrs. D. My son, Mrs. Manheim. [*Beatrice and Walter bow*]

Elig. Mrs. Dalrymple, will you and Walter join us in a glass of claret?

Vio. Won't you, Beatrice dear?

Walt. I wonder which are my adventures?

Col. This corner in Spring offers a better chance to make a fortune than at any time during the last ten years.

Prof. You think so?

Col. Yes, farmers expect its cowboy merchants will hold back for higher prices. With the facilities at my command I might make a walkover the sharks, if I had a little capital.

Walt. That's one, evidently.

Elig. I think that real estate offers some good opportunities.

Dr. S. Yes, that is very true. Real estate may go up, it may go down, the grain market may go up—

Col. May go up? It will go up, make no mistake.

Dr. S. And it may go down.

Col. Never! never!

Dr. S. A better field for capital is in the manufacturing of a staple article, where profits are enormous and the market is always on your hands.

Dex. One of your patent medicines, for instance?

Dr. S. What more staple article than Dr. Shouter's Anti-bilious Calesfonical Mixture?

Prof. My dear Shouter, you have discussed the case well. Wheat may go up and it may go down, corner lots may go up and they may go down. But as to your patent mixture, although I have no doubt they are excellent humbugs, you don't seem to make them go down with the people. [*All laugh*]

Dr. S. That's where the capital comes in.

Prof. The proper sphere of capital is in assisting the inventor, benefiting the unborn, and pocketing the dividends of a cornice on Mr. Pullman. While you will flounder on the face of the earth anxiously watching for fluctuations in front feet and early garden scenes—[*Colonel Elevator whispers in ear*] I mean cabbage—[*Colonel Elevator whispers*] I mean beets—[*Same business*] that is to say, wheat. [*Rises. Colonel Elevator pulls back his chair*] The noble inventor will soon soar above you on the pious philosophy, with parachute extended and hydrogen quill erect and with fish-tail—

Betty. Boiled whitefish, roast beef, chicken pie, and mutton hash. [*Professor Gillypod sits on floor. Colonel Elevator and Dexter assist him to rise. He accuses one of them of pulling him down*]

Walt. This, beyond doubt, is the third.

Mrs. C. Mr. Eligible, did I tell you I had another new boarder, an Italian gentleman just from New York, very wealthy, and thinks of investing in real estate?

Elig. Indeed! I shall be able to offer him some rare bargains.

Flor. Oh, ma'am, I saw a bad man today.

Walt. I hope not as bad a man to little children as I saw today.

Vio. Who was it?

WALT. A gentleman who was remarkable for a light pair of cassimere pants, today got off a State Street car. A little newsboy, scarcely larger than your little girl, came towards him to sell him a paper, when in his eager haste he stumbled and fell into the mud, scattering his papers and ruining his wares and, worse for him, scattering a few drops of mud upon the cassimere of the gentleman. He, instead of commiserating the greater misfortune of the boy, fell to swearing in Italian and with his cane administered several sharp blows upon the shoulders of the little fellow. The whole affair transpired so quick, that none of us could interfere, but upon the cries of "Shame!" from some of the bystanders, he desisted.

ALL. Shame, shame!

WALT. From a bystander I learned the gentleman's name was—

BETTY. [*Announces*] Mr. Fioretti, ma'am. [*Enter Fioretti, R.*]

WALT. The very man.

FLOR. Oh, mama, there's the bad man. [*Beatrice turns and faces him*]

FIO. [*Looking at Beatrice*] Madam Colville, I think I have the pleasure to be acquainted with one of your boarders; if I am not mistaken, madam—

BEA. [*Rising angrily*] Sir! my name is Beatrice Manheim.

FIO. [*Bowing*] Madam Beatrice Manheim.

BETTY. Boiled whitefish, roast beef, chicken pie—mutton hash—

ACT II.

SCENE 1: *Parlor scene. Door C., R. and L. Window R.3.E. Door L.2.E. Elegant furniture. Table and chairs R. and L. Decanter and wine glasses. Book of drawings on L. table. Eligible discovered at back of L. table. Annie seated R. of L. table. Both looking over book.*

ELIG. My dear Annie, you have no cause to doubt my affection. It is sincere, I assure you.

ANNIE. And yet you wouldn't want your wife to know about it?

ELIG. You see, my wife wouldn't appreciate this thing in the proper light, so we'll leave her out of the question.

ANNIE. How happy I would be were I in her place.

ELIG. Happy! why of course we would be! We'd do nothing but make love all day long. Where did your mother procure this copy of Hogarth? It is an excellent copy.

ANNIE. Oh, never mind Hogarth.

ELIG. The Rake's Progress.

ANNIE. Look at yourself.

ELIG. How madly he is making love! Some other man's wife, I'll be bound.

ANNIE. Do you think he loves her much?

ELIG. Oh, very much, indeed.

ANNIE. Then it is some other man's wife.

ELIG. If I thought some other man was making love to my wife—

ANNIE. What would you do?

ELIG. Wring his neck.

ANNIE. Yet you are another woman's husband and insist on making love to me.

ELIG. That's a very different matter. Besides, our love is platonic.

ANNIE. [*Rises and crosses R.*]   But I am determined it shall end here and forever.

ELIG. By all means. Oh, by the bye, Annie, as I was passing Mayor's to-day I saw in the window the handsomest little diamond ring in the world. I want you to wear it as a good-bye memento.

ANNIE. You are not going away?

ELIG. No, but you will wear it as a token of past and gone love—platonic, of course.

ANNIE. I should cherish it dearly, but I can't receive it! I'm afraid it's improper. Only think of my receiving a present from a married man! What would ma say?

ELIG. You can say it came from a school friend, or a cousin. Mothers are so soft, you know.

ANNIE. But you can't cousin mother.

ELIG. Oh, nonsense. I fly, and get one kiss before I go.

ANNIE. I'm afraid it wouldn't be proper.

ELIG. A sort of brotherly love.

ANNIE. I wish you were my brother. [*He kisses her*]

ELIG. I wish I was. Well, good-bye till I come back. [*Exits C.D.L.*]

ANNIE. [*After he's gone*]   Oh, it's improper. I wish I had someone to advise me. [*Enter Mrs. Dalrymple R.D.C.*]

MRS. D. Ah, Annie, studying?

ANNIE. Oh, Mrs. Dalrymple, tell me, would it be improper for a lady to receive a present from a married man?

MRS. D. That depends upon the age of the lady. There would be no impropriety in your mother receiving such a present.

ANNIE. The lady is much younger, but the gentleman has a brotherly love for her.

Mrs. D. Tell the young lady to beware of the married gentleman who professes brotherly love. If it should be good for her to receive the gift, the wife should present it.

Annie. The young lady will not receive it.

Mrs. D. Poor Annie, just from boarding school, her head full of men, of course! Can it be for her the present was intended? Who knows what this may lead to. We shall see. [*Exit D.L. Enter Fioretti and Violet R.C. They sit R. and L. of R. table*]

Fio. Angelic, accept my devotion! Never mind your husband. The love of Fioretti is worth ten thousand husbands.

Vio. See here, Fioretti, I don't object to flirting. I rather like it. But when you say, "Don't mind your husband," I *do* mind him, I think a great deal of him. In fact, I rather prefer him to you.

Fio. Ah, my bella, you know not what a passion I dote upon you!

Vio. I don't object to you—but don't dote too much.

Fio. You will let me present you with a little present, a souvenir of affection?

Vio. What kind of a present?

Fio. A ring.

Vio. That depends altogether upon the character of the ring.

Fio. It shall be a diamond.

Vio. Your taste is excellent.

Fio. I fly to procure it.

Vio. Stay! Diamonds are very difficult to refuse, but I am afraid I shall have to deny myself the pleasure of wearing yours. My husband is not the least bit jealous, but he could scarcely fail to remark so prominent an article of Violet's as a diamond ring upon my finger.

Fio. Tell him it came from your sister, your cousin. Husbands are blind.

Vio. Perhaps so, but I shall never deceive him.

Fio. He deceives you every day.

Vio. [*Crosses to L.*] It is false!

Fio. It is true.

Vio. I'd just like to catch him at it!

Fio. You keep your eyes open! He makes love to the little school girl, Annie.

Vio. I'll not believe it. And as for her, the little beggar—

Fio. Disgraceful!

Vio. I'd give the world to know if this was true.

Fio. Good, she is jealous! She is in my power, sure. My triumph is certain.
[*Exits C.D. Enter Beatrice R.1.E.*]

Vio. Oh, Beatrice, I am so glad you have come. I want to ask your advice.

Bea. Violet, what is it that troubles you?

Vio. I have received a piece of information which—pshaw—I don't believe it.

Bea. What is it you have heard?

Vio. Fioretti gave me a hint.

Bea. Fioretti! I have watched with concern your growing intimacy with that man. Avoid him, he is a bold, bad man.

Vio. [*Aside*] He is no worse than the rest, I fancy. [*Aloud*] I thank you for your warning. I will avoid him. [*Aside*] I knew it wasn't true, but I'll watch. [*Exit D.L.*]

Bea. Poor Violet, surrounded by all that could make her happy, and borrowing trouble for herself! What would she do if she had passed through the terrible ordeal in which I have been tried? Sorrow chasteneth the soul as fire refines the gold. [*Plays mournful air. Walter, C.D., crosses to R. of her, leans on piano*]

Walt. Beatrice, alone?

Bea. Yes, alone, with my own sad thoughts, the memory of the past.

Walt. Can you not forget the past in the brightness of the present?

Bea. Yes, my present was bright, was happy, until he came.

Walt. What dark spell of magic does this strange man exercise over you?

Bea. Do not ask me to unravel my past life to you.

Walt. I thought you respected and esteemed me. I have sometimes thought you entertained a warmer feeling for me. You cannot have failed to notice that I have learned to love you?

Bea. [*Comes D.R.*] Oh—no—no—we say those words, "It can never be, let us forget that they were ever spoken."

Walt. Am I, then, unworthy of your love?

Bea. Oh, no. You are a pure and high-minded gentleman. Both you and your mother have been very kind to me, and I have been happy in your friendship. Had I known you years ago, I might—no—no—what am I saying? We can never be more to each other than we are at the present moment. [*Going to D.R., Walter delays her by a motion*]

Walt. Stay, Beatrice! You cannot refuse to listen to me, when I tell you that without you I can never know happiness!

Bea. Then I see how it is. This dear house where all have been so kind to me, can be my home no longer. My child and I will go alone. [*Crosses to R.*]

Walt. Nay, Beatrice! If we must part, I will go.

Bea. No, I cannot permit that. When I am gone, I will be free at last from the presence of that bold, bad man.

WALT. But I shall see you again?

BEA. I shall not depart without saying good-bye to all. [*Gives hand to Walter. He kisses it. Exits R.D.*]

WALT. I was premature. She must love another. No: there has been nothing in her past life to warrant it. [*Sits at table R. Enter Dr. Shouter*]

DR. S. Ah, Mr. Dalrymple, my dear boy! I'm delighted to find you alone. [*Takes chair*] I must explain more fully that little matter.

WALT. I'm not in very good humor for business, but proceed.

DR. S. My Anti-bilious Mixture is made of jalup, rhubarb, molasses, and mayweed. It can be made for two and a half cents, a bottle included. Sells readily for a dollar.

WALT. Oh, there's no lack of readiness about the seller. But the buyer—

DR. S. It's an excellent blood purifier.

WALT. And if I let you have the money?

DR. S. [*Shaking his hand*] You will make me the happiest man in the world.

WALT. Well, you shall have my decision in the morning.

DR. S. In the morning. [*Rising*] In the morning. [*Exits C.D.*]

WALT. So a little money will make him happy. We shall see, when he gets it. [*Enter Colonel Elevator C.D.*]

COL. Ah, Mr. Dalrymple, my dear boy, alone! [*Takes chair*] A glorious opportunity—a clean give-away—the market brightens. On, ye braves, never give it up, never! I've got it dead to rights. Five thousand dollars does it. The next forty-eight hours tells the story. We divvy a cool $20,000.

WALT. I never applied the $20,000 to our moments. I thought your $5,000 remarkably cool.

COL. Cool! Oh, you mean my style? Rather fresh, eh? But how do you jump? Is it a chicken?

WALT. And if you get this money?

COL. Oh, if I get the pewter, we divvy the rate. Bet your life I'm square. Why, it'll make me happier than a three-year-old heifer in a clover patch. I'll marry the widow, go to Saratoga or Long Branch for a honeymoon.

WALT. Marry the widow?

COL. Marry the widow. Bet your last quarter she is an A-1 creature, accomplished, like a house afire, or she wouldn't go for the colonel.

WALT. And are you engaged?

COL. She may speak for herself. I am, you may bet your boots.

WALT. Well, I shall decide upon the matter in the morning.

COL. In the morning, very well. But make it early. I shall buy 20,000 bushels on the Street before the Board opens, slick as a bantam rooster, or a

June bug, make no mistake. [*Goes to C., then returns*] I say, you are not going to throw any money away on that Gillypod, are you, or old Shouter? If you do, you'll quit losers. Shouter is a chump.

WALT. A what?

COL. A chump, a regular chump. His Anti-bilious what-you-call-it is N.G. Why don't he cure himself? I tell you, he was bilious as a spavined turkey a week before Thanksgiving.

WALT. And Gillypod?

COL. That old flying-machine? You let him get into you for a couple of thousands and he'll show you how to fly, make no mistake. He means well, but don't you trust him! [*Exits C.D.1.*]

WALT. Can Beatrice have engaged herself to such a man? No, I'll not believe it! [*Crosses and sits at table. Enter Gillypod C.D.*]

PROF. Ah, Dalrymple, my dear boy, alone. [*Takes chair*] Are you prepared to become the benefactor of your race?

WALT. Oh, the invention, the airship?

PROF. The greatest in the world. Oh, fly with me to my cloud-clad home, where the eagle dare not climb! I observed last night that you did not catch the distinction between the flitting parachute and—

WALT. Oh, yes, I understood you perfectly.

PROF. You see, by generating the extremities we procure a saltpeter class of concrete gases and—

WALT. Oh, yes, I see!

PROF. Absorbing, as it were, the center-currents—

WALT. Precisely.

PROF. And elevating by means of hydrogen—

WALT. Quite so.

PROF. Quite so.

WALT. And the sum you mentioned will quite suffice for the experiment?

PROF. Amply! Amply!

WALT. And may I ask what you propose doing with your share of the profits?

PROF. My dear boy, I don't mind telling you in confidence, it is my intention to marry the charming widow, Mrs. Manheim, and spend the remainder of my days in doing deeds of charity.

WALT. Marry Mrs. Manheim?

PROF. Exactly.

WALT. Are you engaged?

PROF. Not exactly. Next thing to it.

WALT. You proposed?

PROF. Oh, yes, I proposed and she treated me very politely. She said "No" with a great deal of grace.

WALT. Suppose she would again say No?

PROF. Then I should surely have her.

WALT. How so?

PROF. Because two negatives are equal to an affirmative.

WALT. Well, I shall decide upon the matter in the morning.

PROF. [*Shakes his hand*] I wish to make an early experiment of the Co-dedimn. [*Exits C.*]

WALT. [*Crosses to R.*] So they are both going to marry her? Well, we shall see! [*Enter Dexter C.D.*]

DEX. Ah, Dalrymple, my dear boy, so glad to find you alone. I want you to do me a great favor.

WALT. What is it, a patent-medicine?

DEX. No, damn it, no!

WALT. A corner in the grain market?

DEX. No, no.

WALT. An invention?

DEX. No, by Jerusalem! I don't want to borrow any money.

WALT. You relieve me.

DEX. No, I'm pretty well fixed for money. That is, I would be, if my damn tailor wasn't always short. The fact is, my dear boy, I'm in love.

WALT. You surprise me.

DEX. Yes, I am, and I don't mind telling you who it is. It's Mrs. Manheim.

WALT. Mrs. Manheim! Great Heavens, another!

DEX. And I want you to speak to her for me. I can't, you know, I'm so infernal spooney. She likes you, you have a mother.

WALT. It is impossible for me to be of the slightest assistance to you in this matter, so I beg you will say nothing more about it. [*Exit C.D.*]

DEX. Oh, but you might, you know. When a fellow is spooney he is completely demoralized. He is, by Jupiter! [*Runs into Eligible, who enters C.D.*] Oh, I beg your pardon. [*Exits C.D.*]

ELIG. I have the ring, all right, if little Annie would only pop in. As the French fellow says, Play diamonds if you would win women. [*Goes to C.D.*] Ah, there she is now. She's coming this way. I thought the ring would fetch her! [*Comes down R. Enter Violet C.D.*] My wife! [*Puts ring in his overcoat pocket*] How do you do, my dear?

VIO. Are you going upstairs, Matthew?

ELIG. No, dear. You see, I'm just a trifle tired. Would you mind taking up my hat and coat? [*Gives them to her*]

VIO. Certainly. [*Goes up to C.D.*]

ELIG. There's a dear. I'll be up presently. [*Discovers he has left ring in coat*] Oh, my dear, my handkerchief, if you please. [*Violet hands it to him*] My dear, you needn't mind taking up my coat.

VIO. Oh, it's no trouble at all. [*Starts to go*]

ELIG. I may want to go out.

VIO. It's nearly dinner time, and you can't go out. There, now.

ELIG. My cigarette case, dear. I'll just have time for a smoke.

VIO. I'll get it for you.

ELIG. [*Nervously*] No, let me! I won't trouble you. [*Tries to get at coat. She prevents him*]

VIO. I insist upon it! [*Takes out jewel case, ring, both down stage*] What's that?

ELIG. That!

VIO. Yes, that!

ELIG. Oh, that in your hand?

VIO. Yes, that in my hand!

ELIG. Why, that's my tobacco box!

VIO. [*Puts it to her nose*] Why, it don't smell like tobacco.

ELIG. No, you see, it's a new one.

VIO. It looks like a jewel case.

ELIG. Oh, not at all.

VIO. I am going to open it.

ELIG. No, don't dear, I beg of you!

VIO. I shall.

ELIG. Be careful, you'll break it. Let me show you how.

VIO. I can do it. [*Opens it*]

ELIG. There, you've done it.

VIO. Why, it's a diamond ring!

ELIG. Of course it is, my dear. You always spoil everything. In time you should have known all about it.

VIO. I am determined to know all about it.

ELIG. I see you are.

VIO. [*Reading inscription*] "With my best love." What does that mean, sir?

ELIG. Why, don't you see, my dear? It is a ring that Walter gave to me to give to you. [*Mrs. Dalrymple enters C.D.*] There's Mrs. Dalrymple. Come now, be sensible. He gave the ring to me to give to you, to give to somebody else, don't you understand?

VIO. Who did Walter want you to give the ring to?

MRS. D. What is it that my son wants to present in such a round-about way?

VIO. This diamond ring.

MRS. D. Indeed, and to whom?

VIO. Yes, to whom?

ELIG. You see, Walter wanted me to give that ring to my wife, for her to give to—to Beatrice. Don't you see, as though it came from herself. He was afraid she would refuse to accept it if he offered it himself.

VIO. And so she would! [*Enter Walter D.C. down L.*] Walter, here is the ring you wished me to give to Beatrice.

WALT. Ring? What ring?

ELIG. [*Signalling him*] Why, you don't mean to say you have changed your mind?

WALT. And what was my mind?

ELIG. Why, you know, you wanted me to give the ring to my wife to have her give it to Beatrice as her own gift, you know.

WALT. [*Realizing position*] Oh, that ring. Of course, where is it?

VIO. [*Gives him case*] Here, Walter.

WALT. It's very pretty. Why, it's a diamond.

ELIG. [*Signalling*] Of course it's a diamond.

WALT. I didn't look at it so closely before, yes—yes.

ELIG. Yes, yes. [*Attempts to take it*]

WALT. [*Preventing him*] Yes, yes.

ELIG. [*Disappointed*] Yes, yes.

WALT. Violet, you will please give this to Beatrice, and please don't mention me as the donor. [*Beatrice passes through room*]

VIO. There she goes now. I'll give it to her at once. [*Goes off C.D., followed by Eligible. Business and exit. Eligible comes D.*]

ELIG. Oh, damn it! [*Exit quick C.D. Walter comes down laughing*]

MRS. D. My son, I know it was not you that sent the ring, and I know for whom it was intended.

WALT. Surely not for Beatrice?

MRS. D. No, but let the secret rest with me for the present. It is a sad affair. We must try and avert the consequences of this evil step. When men engage in unworthy objects towards our sex, exposure and disgrace is sure to follow. [*They exit R. Enter Betty and Fioretti C.D. and R.*]

FIO. Betty, will you please tell Madam Manheim, if she is not busy, to come down and make herself agreeable, you understand?

BETTY. Oh, yes, I'm to tell Madam Manheim if she is not busy to come down and make herself agreeable.

FIO. No, no, you little goose.

BETTY. I'm not a little goose.

FIO. [*Patting her under chin*] No, you are not a goose, you are a little duck, eh? Tell Madam Manheim I would like to see her in the parlor.

BETTY. Certainly. I will of course. [*Exit D.R.*]

BEA. [*Enters D.R.*] Why have you sent for me?

FIO. I want you to assist me.

BEA. What right have you to expect aid from me?

FIO. I do not wish to call ze bad names with you. Do you know your position in this house? You are respected by everybody. I have to speak but one word to cast you out, an object of contempt and humiliation. You have a proud spirit. You will spare yourself the humiliation. You will resist me, eh?

BEA. What is it you require?

FIO. I love Madam Eligible. [*Beatrice starts*] She loves me in return. Her husband loves another.

BEA. 'Tis false.

FIO. 'Tis true. I see you have already censured her against me.

BEA. Villain, I have.

FIO. I expect you to withdraw your advice and what is more, I expect you to assist me with ze good word. She is your friend, she confides in you, you will tell her what I wish.

BEA. Where will all this end.

FIO. We will leave the city together.

BEA. Monster, I did not dream to what depths your villainy could descend! But I will expose and denounce you. You shall feel a husband's vengeance. There is at least one in this house who will resent the shame you put upon me.

FIO. You mean, Mr. W. Dalrymple? [*She starts*] You see, I keep my eyes open. Do you want him to know your past life?

BEA. Oh, Heavens!

FIO. And more, think of your child! I have the power by law to appoint a guardian and take her away from you.

BEA. Oh, this is cruel, cruel.

FIO. But it is ze law. You will assist?

BEA. Never! Never! I will die first! [*Crosses to R. He catches her by arm*]

Fio. Male witch, you defy me, Fioretti! [*Throws her from him. Violet laughs outside*] The company approaches. I will denounce you before them.

Bea. [*At C.D.*] Those who come this way are my friends. Breathe a word of aught against me to them at your peril! [*Exit C.D.*]

Fio. Mister Walter Dalrymple, your reputation is safe for the present. Safe for ze present, Madam Manheim. [*Exit C.D. Enter Violet, Walter, Eligible D.R.*]

Walt. Did you present the ring to Beatrice?

Vio. [*At table R.*] Yes, Walter.

Walt. And what did she say?

Vio. She was absolutely sentimental, as usual.

Elig. [*Seated*] Decidedly sensible, I should say.

Vio. Beatrice is one of those dear good souls that one seldom meets with except in novels or on the stage. She said the ring did not become one in her position, but she was grateful to my kind heart for thinking of her, and would I be good enough to wear it for her?

Elig. Which you were good enough to kindly consent to do.

Vio. I could not refuse such a glorious chance, so I immediately closed with her offer. [*Shows ring*] Here it is.

Walt. Well since my poor ring—[*Aside*] our poor ring—has passed through so many hands, you are to wear it at last.

Vio. Yes, Walter, and Beatrice is to look at it.

Walt. Well, since Beatrice can't wear it, I am very glad that you can. But I say, Matthew, we will never present a ring in such a round-about manner again.

Elig. No, I'll be hanged if I do!

Walt. And, furthermore, we will neither of us ever give or receive a present to or from any person who ought not to give or receive it, and Violet shall wear the ring as a compact.

Vio. [*Kisses ring*] I will, Walter.

Walt. And now I want you both to do me a favor.

Both. What is it, Walter?

Walt. I know what rascals you both are at practical jokes.

Elig. It's Violet.

Vio. No, it's Matthew.

Walt. Two of my speculators have told me they are going to marry Mrs. Manheim as soon as they have made their fortunes out of my money, which, of course, they will immediately proceed to do.

Elig. Of course.

Walt. Now, as she can't marry both of them—

Vio. Not very well.

Elig. Not in this State!

Walt. And I don't think she cares for either. I don't like to hear the lady's name so much spoken of.

Vio. Who are the gentlemen?

Walt. Colonel Elevator and Professor Gillypod.

Elig. What? Make no mistake. And the balloon man.

Walt. Now, I want you to continue some harmless joke upon the rascals which will give us all a hearty laugh and end this stupid nonsense.

Elig. Old Elevator is fair game.

Vio. I say, Matthew, I'll make love to old Gillypod, and make him wild.

Walt. Excellent.

Elig. She can do it, she's a terrible flirt.

Walt. I'll leave it all in your hands. [*Exit C.D.*]

Elig. Let me see, what shall I do.

Vio. What shall we do? Be quick. Here comes Colonel Elevator. [*Enter Colonel Elevator D.L.*]

Elig. Colonel Elevator!

Col. Sir!

Elig. I desire a few words with you.

Col. Name your place and state your time, and Colonel M. T. Elevator will get out of bed to enjoy the sport, make no mistake.

Elig. I understand you are a military man.

Col. Yes, sir, I served with the gallant Ninth at Sumter during the glorious campaign of the three months' call, and smelt blood, sir—smelt blood!

Elig. Then we can easily arrange this little affair.

Col. What little affair?

Elig. I understand, sir, that you have been very particular in your attentions to my wife.

Col. Who says so? It's a lie, a base fabrication. The man that says that, tell him my name is Colonel M. T. Elevator. Make no mistake.

Elig. The man that does that must meet me with pistols.

Col. What's that? Do you mean to say that I—?

Elig. You did!

Col. I never! I never! Mrs. Eligible, I appeal to you. Have I not always had the highest regard for you? [*Eligible starts towards him*] Polite regard, polite regard! Colonel M. T. Elevator is always the highest-toned gentleman, make no mistake. Mrs. Eligible, did I ever smile at you, did I ever wink at you, did I ever look at you?

Vio. No, Matthew, I can't say that Colonel Elevator has ever been very particular in his attentions towards me. [*To Eligible*] I believe you were informed so, were you not?

Elig. Yes, m'am, and by a gentleman.

Col. A gentleman! What gentleman? Show him to me!

Vio. I believe it was Professor Gillypod who told you, was it not, Matthew?

Elig. Yes, sir, I was told so by Professor Gillypod.

Col. Gillypod! Where is he? Let me get at him! I'll cut him up, I'll kick him from the attic to the street door and back to the attic. [*Crosses to C.*]

Vio. and Elig. My dear sir! [*Trying to pacify him*]

Col. Don't talk to me, but give me Gillypod. I will toy with him as the wounded panther toys with its prey—I will have his crimson life stream— was it for such as he that I served my country's army? Forgive me, Gillypod —more I ask not—[*Rushes off C.D. Eligible and Violet convulsed*]

Vio. Here comes Gillypod. [*They become serious. Enter Professor Gillypod D.L.*]

Prof. Did some one call me?

Elig. Yes, Colonel Elevator. He's in a terrible rage.

Prof. Drunk again, I suppose. [*Puts leg on table*]

Elig. Don't trifle at such a moment, sir. He is enraged with you. He swears to kick you.

Prof. I won't let him. I'll apologize.

Elig. He even threatened to take your life.

Vio. Oh, conceal yourself, for my sake!

Prof. I'll conceal myself for my own sake. But where shall I hide?

Vio. There is that closet.

Prof. That will do. [*Drinks wine*] I say, Eligible, you wouldn't stand by and see me murdered in cold blood would you?

Elig. He is in such a rage, he might murder us all.

Prof. Oh, Lord! [*Opens closet*] Here is a double-barrelled gun, I will defend my life.

Elig. To the last extremity! [*Strikes attitude*]

Vio. There he comes! [*Professor Gillypod steps into closet. Pokes his head out*]

Prof. Is he gone?

Vio. That was a false alarm. I hear him pounding upstairs. You may come out. [*Eligible stamps his feet. Professor Gillypod falls on his knees to Violet*]

Prof. Save me, save me!

ELIG. You needn't be alarmed. He isn't here yet.

PROF. [*Takes more wine*] Oh, my poor nerves.

ELIG. That's right! It will put courage into you.

PROF. It does put courage into me. I'll have his gore. [*Goes to C.D. taking decanter with him*]

COL. [*Outside*] Where is he? Where is Professor Gillypod? [*Professor Gillypod rushes into closet. Colonel Elevator enters D.C., raving*] Give me Gillypod! Let me see the man who dares trifle with the honor of Colonel M. T. Elevator! Oh, give him to me alive! [*Sees Professor Gillypod's hat on table*] Oh, he has been here! If I had him here I'd serve him as I do this hat. [*Throws hat on floor, stamps and kicks it, is about to put his foot on it again, Professor Gillypod comes out of closet with his coat off. Comes down. Colonel Elevator stands for an instant with his foot raised*] So, sir, you have—

PROF. No, sir, I have not.

COL. The presence of this lady protects you, sir.

VIO. Oh, don't let me be in the way, sir.

PROF. Pooh, Pooh, sir!

COL. What?

PROF. Pooh, Pooh, sir!

COL. If you dare to "Pooh, Pooh" to me, sir—[*Makes a kick*]

PROF. You will kick me, sir, kick me as you would my hat, a hat which I revere—go on, sir, I defy you, sir, go on, sir, I defy you to kick. You are a braggart and a coward! Come on!

COL. No, sir, I decline to sully my hand or foot on such as you. Blood alone shall wipe out this insult. You shall meet me, sir, with pistols.

PROF. Pistols! Guns, sir, double-barrelled guns! [*Goes into closet*]

COL. What does he mean?

ELIG. He has a double-barrelled gun in the closet. Try and save yourself. [*Professor Gillypod comes down with gun, points at Colonel Elevator, who gives a yell, and rushes off D.L., followed by Professor Gillypod, Eligible and Violet laugh. Everybody enters from all entrances, all talking*]

MRS. C. What is the meaning of this disturbance in my house?

ELIG. Nothing. Only Professor Gillypod and Colonel Elevator are chasing each other about the house.

VIO. And crushing each other's hats.

WALT. [*To Eligible*] I hope you haven't been too severe?

ELIG. Have no fear, it's all over now. [*Enter Betty C.D.*]

BETTY. Oh, ma'am, Professor Gillypod and Colonel Elevator are playing the old cat in the kitchen. The Professor is chasing the Colonel around the dining room with a gun, breaking all the crockery. [*Crash heard. Colonel rushes past C.D., screaming, followed by Professor Gillypod. Ladies scream all through this business. Colonel Elevator rushes on R.3.E., looks around, conceals himself behind chair which he places L. Professor Gillypod enters from window, looks around, Mrs. Colville and Annie scream and faint. Ladies scream. Walter, Eligible and Violet laugh. Professor Gillypod discovers Colonel Elevator and stands on chair. Snaps gun at him and strikes attitude]*

PROF. I give you your life.

ELIG. Colonel Elevator, is your honor satisfied?

COL. It is perfectly satisfied.

ELIG. Then we will all be friends.

COL. Friends! Never! Mrs. Colville, my room is empty this day week.

MRS. C. Thank Heavens! *[Betty comes on, rings dinner-bell]* Dinner! *[Exit everybody except Professor Gillypod and Colonel Elevator. Professor Gillypod goes to C.D. then turns and looks severely at Colonel Elevator]*

PROF. Elevator!

COL. No, no!

PROF. *[Throws away gun and extends hand to Colonel Elevator]*

COL. Gillypod! *[Takes hand]* Friends!

PROF. Brother! *[They embrace, go upstage as—]*

ACT III.

SCENE 1: *A garden. House at back R. with porch and steps in 1, with gate in C. Grass mats and rustic seats about stage. Fioretti, Dexter, Eligible, Violet, Colonel Elevator, Professor Gillypod discovered about stage.*

DEX. It presents the most glorious opportunity for a young man of any place upon the globe. Look at the streets.

COL. Look at the buildings.

DEX. The finest in the world.

COL. Look at her boulevards.

PROF. Look at her mud.

DEX. It has the finest harbors.

COL. The largest firms.

DEX. The handsomest theaters.

VIO. The prettiest women.

EVERYBODY. In the world.

FIO. Vat is ze paradise of which you are speaking?

EVERYBODY. Chicago!

Dr. S. [*Rising*] Why, ladies and gentlemen, I have stood upon this very spot and have seen wolves and prairie chickens.

Everybody. Sit down! Sit down!

Dr. S. I say I have seen the wolves.

Col. Never saw a wolf in my life.

Dr. S. There are the finest opportunities for investing capital; for aiding the manufacturers in preparing a staple article.

Prof. Aiding the investor?

Col. And business men are getting up a corner in Spring. [*Mrs. Dalrymple, Mrs. Colville and Annie enter and sit C.*]

Mrs. D. I cannot agree with you, sir. I maintain that the promise of capital is to aid manufacturers.

Dr. S. Hear! Hear!

Mrs. D. To encourage the inventor.

Prof. Hear! Hear!

Mrs. D. But not to place a forced value upon any commodity, nor to make a barter of the necessity of mankind.

Col. Hear! Hear!

Mrs. C. That's just what my husband used to say when he was alive. The grain market was his greatest diversion.

Annie. Aversion, mamma.

Mrs. C. Yes, he was a government gouger.

Annie. A government gouger!

Mrs. C. Yes, a whiskey squirmasher.

Annie. Mother means a government gauger. Papa belonged to the revenue department.

Mrs. C. Yes, he belonged to the ravenous department. He gouged so much, he spoiled his complexion.

Elig. I don't wonder at it.

Mrs. C. Annie used to say, when she was a little girl, she was going to Heaven to meet her papa. How will you know him, dear, amongst all those people there, said I? Why, mamma, I look for an angel with a red nose.

Prof. A seraphic cherubim.

Mrs. C. He was a very ary-dit man.

Prof. An air-tight man?

Annie. Mother means erudite—learned.

Mrs. C. He used to say that all those vegetables which are farmasie—

Prof. How far in Asia?

Annie. Farinaceous, mamma.

Mrs. C. Yes, I mean all those that belong to the flowery kingdom—

ELIG. That's some distance in Asia.

MRS. C. Should be better employed than in distilling poison in the human system.

MRS. D. I quite agree with him there.

MRS. C. He ruined his health by application to business—he and two other adventures of the government.

ANNIE. Examiners, mamma.

MRS. C. Yes, all belonging to the revenous department were taken with the pulveranium complaint, [*Dr. Shouter laughs*] and the government removed them.

DR. S. That was a sufficient ground for a divorce, madam.

MRS. C. Lord sakes we never thought of those things in my days.

DR. S. [*To Mrs. Colville*] We are going for a stroll by the lake. Will you accompany us? Accept my arm. [*They exit R.U.E. Professor Gillypod puts his feet in Colonel Elevator's lap, who shoves them off. They both jump up and strike pugilistic attitude, then shake hands and embrace and sit down again*]

COL. They never had any of the modern improvements in Mrs. Colville's days. If a fellow got hitched to the traces, he had no way of kicking over.

MRS. D. And it was right. I believe marriage to be the holiest duty to which woman may devote herself.

FIO. But, Mrs. Dalrymple, when husband and wife cannot live happy together, you will excuse a divorce.

MRS. D. No, I hold in abhorrence an institution which may make any virtuous wife tremble for the safety of her household, and which sets at naught the holiest traditions of our race.

FIO. But there may be causes. [*Looks around*] Where is Madam Manheim?

MRS. D. She is attending the examination of her class at the conservatory.

VIO. Oh, yes, I had forgotten. I hope she will succeed.

ANNIE. I am afraid it will be difficult, with such favorite teachers as are in the conservatory.

VIO. Here she comes, now. [*Enters L.U.E. Beatrice followed by Walter, who leads Florence and carries a guitar and music, which he puts on chair. All rise—the ladies kiss Florence. Fioretti crosses to L. at back*]

MRS. D. Have you succeeded, Beatrice?

BEA. Better than I had ever hoped. [*Sits L. of Violet*]

WALT. In the words of Wentworth, she has won her prize.

PROF. In the language of the exultant peasantry; huzzah, huzzah!

BEA. Yes, my class took the first prize for superior execution, and Florence has won the junior medal. My position at the conservatory is now secure.

ANNIE. Let me see, Florence! [*Florence crosses to her and shows medal around her neck*] Who is the greatest little woman in the world today?

FLOR. My mamma.

VIO. [*To Beatrice*] We feared for you.

BEA. Oh, I was dreadfully nervous, but my class behaved admirably—I was afraid Florence would give me some trouble, but her fingers worked as though they were enchanted.

WALT. More power to her fingers.

ELIG. [*At back*] Come, Walter, for a stroll and a smoke. [*They bow to the ladies and exit R.U.E. Colonel Elevator puts his feet on Professor Gillypod's lap and Professor Gillypod raises his pants at bottom and burns his leg with a cigar. Colonel Elevator jumps up quickly, then business as before*]

COL. Remember, we are friends.

PROF. Brother! [*Exit, arm in arm R.U.E.*]

FIO. [*Sitting at L. of Mrs. Dalrymple*] Madam Dalrymple, you said just now before Madam Manheim arrived zot you abhor ze devorce woman.

MRS. D. I said nothing about a divorced woman, I believe it is the duty of both man and wife to observe well the temperament and the habits of the other before marriage.

FIO. But it is so easy to make a mistake, eh?

MRS. D. The past is the only guarantee for the future. A prudent, virtuous life in the past argues well for the future.

FIO. But this city has no past! It is a community made up of people of every land.

MRS. D. Here where no one can speak with certainty of the past; strangers are admitted upon a sort of probation.

VIO. Fioretti, you may consider yourself under probation.

FIO. Certainly, certainly. [*To Mrs. Dalrymple*] But there are women we meet every day whose past has been a life of shame, a history of reproach. She may have a respectable passport of a black dress and, when rich, gain her entrance into good society.

MRS. D. Real characters are sometimes represented in the same person, but it is impossible to long conceal the imposition, as they are sure to meet some former neighbor.

FIO. Then it is ze duty of such a neighbor to expose ze history of such an imposter.

MRS. D. Undoubtedly, if it be of guilt, but we make a distinction between a desire to serve society and the qualifications of malice.

Fio. But how is ze distinction to be made? [*Beatrice, who has become agitated, starts up with a little cry*]

Vio. What is it, Beatrice, are you ill?

Fio. [*Offering his arm*] Allow me to offer you my assistance, Madam Manheim. [*She turns from him*]

Mrs. D. We had better go into the house, Beatrice.

Bea. Thank you, I shall feel better presently. [*Exits with Violet into house*]

Mrs. D. [*Following*] Poor Beatrice, the excitement of the examination has overcome her.

Fio. You think her success is certain?

Mrs. D. [*Turning upon him*] I hope so, for she deserves it.

Fio. Why do you think so?

Mrs. D. Because a woman who labors for her own support and that of another should command the respect and good word from everybody, especially if she is a widow. [*Exit from house*]

Fio. [*Solus*] A widow—her widowhood—we will see. I will tell her story to Madam Colville, who keeps such a respectable boarding house. We will make it very warm for you, Madam Manheim. [*Exit R.U.E. Professor Gillypod and Florence enter same time and come down C.*]

Prof. Florence, my little dear, how would you like to have me for a papa?

Flor. Oh, I hate papas. Come and play peep-a-boo.

Prof. Infant, this mighty brain of mine is stirred with great and colossal projects. It is fired by tender passions. It cannot descend to peep-a-boo. Here is some candy.

Flor. [*Jumping up and down*] Oh, thank you.

Prof. And here is another. [*Searches his pockets, Florence holds her hands*] No, I haven't another. Run and tell your angelic mother what a good man I am. How good I am to little children.

Flor. [*Runs to house, turns on steps*] Then, will you play peep-a-boo?

Prof. Then I will answer your tender age with peep-a-boo. [*Exit Florence into house*] Declare myself—I must propose this very day. The brilliant future of the Empress of the Air awaits her. I will address her in burning words—my burning words fail me. Ah, I have it, she is fond of music. The musical catalogue will furnish me with all the words and musical terms. I will engage an orchestra to accompany me. I will address her in slow music. This guitar, her guitar, will receive my vows. [*Places guitar on stool in front of railing*] Let me rehearse, angelic creature, plunk—plunk—plunk—plunk—plunk—List to my burning vows of love. Ph—ph—ph—ph—behold me at thy feet, there's where I kneel. [*Reads from catalogue*] "Dulcemo, quarto,

We meet by chance in the usual way. Will you love me then as now, when the band begins to play?" Plunk—ph—ph—ph—[*Enter Florence from house*]

FLOR. Peep-a-boo.

PROF. Little blue-eyed darling, will you please waltz up the passage and leave me to my musical exercise? [*She exits R.U.E.*] You called me sweet and tender names. It's funny when you feel that way. When my dream of love is o'er, then you'll remember me. Am I not fondly thine own? Oh, pshaw, I can't make love to a guitar. It gives me an inspiration. [*Enter Betty from house*] Ah, Betty, the sight of a petticoat inspires me! [*Goes up, takes her by the hand and brings her down C.*] List, list, oh list!

BETTY. Well, you needn't take a lady's arm off.

PROF. To you will I address my burning words of love. [*Kneels at her feet*] Behold, at thy feet.

BETTY. Oh, Mr. Gillypod, I thought this of a good many, but I never thought it of you.

PROF. [*Reading*] "Beneath the moon's pale ray we sat by the river, you and I."

BETTY. What river?

PROF. The Swanee River.

BETTY. I never saw the Swanee River in all my life.

PROF. Oh, whisper what thou feelest! "The Boy with the Auburn Hair, His Heart was true to Paul, plump—plump—plump—"

BETTY. Oh, Mr. Gillypod!

PROF. Don't call me Gillypod. [*Reads*] "Call me sweet names. Call me a bird." [*Betty sits on his knee and puts her arm around his neck*]

BETTY. This is so sudden.

PROF. Yes, it's rather sudden.

BETTY. [*Patting his face*] And will you always be good to me? [*Enter Florence R., and points at them*]

FLOR. Peep-a-boo.

PROF. Florence, dear, will you run and tell your mother what a good man I am?

BETTY. What does her mother want to know about it for?

PROF. Because I love her mother to the depths of destruction.

BETTY. And all you have been saying to me—?

PROF. I was rehearsing my passionate avowal from this music catalogue.

BETTY. Thank Heaven, I didn't believe in it! But you needn't trouble yourself.

PROF. Do you think she loves another?

BETTY. If she loves another, and I think she does, you may make up your mind it ain't you. [*Goes up to the house and turns on step*]

PROF. Plunk—plunk—plunk—

BETTY. Why, she wouldn't look at such a thing as you, the boy with yellow hair, his eyes were soft as steel plunk—plunk—[*Exit into house*]

PROF. [*Reads*] "Where are now the hopes I cherished?" [*Enter Florence R.U.E.*]

FLOR. Come, play peep-a-boo. [*Exit R.*]

PROF. Alas, nothing now remains for me but peep-a-boo. [*Reads*] "The heart bowed down with weight and woe—" [*Florence calls peep-a-boo. Exit Professor Gillypod R.U.E. Enter Fioretti and Mrs. Colville same entrance*]

MRS. C. My dear Mr. Fioretti, I am surprised and sorry at what you have told me.

FIO. But it is ze truth.

MRS. C. I can scarcely believe it.

FIO. Ask her yourself.

MRS. C. I hope you won't mention this to anybody.

FIO. I shall use all discretion, Madam.

MRS. C. Now, I am very sorry for what has happened, but for all our sakes, for my own daughter's sake, she must go—[*Enter Annie and Florence R.U.E. Fioretti sits R.*]

FLOR. Peep-a-boo, Annie!

ANNIE. Back already, mamma?

MRS. C. Yes, my dear.

FIO. We walked faster than you and got here before you. [*Enter Beatrice from house*]

MRS. C. Ah, my dear Beatrice, they tell me you have been ill. Are you better now?

BEA. Yes, thank you.

MRS. C. I am glad to hear it, dear. Are you well enough to hear some bad news?

BEA. Bad news? Oh, not now—now—now!

MRS. C. But tell me, is what Mr. Fioretti has been telling me true? [*Beatrice starts and covers her face*] I see that it is. Oh, Beatrice, my child I am very sorry, but you understand.

BEA. Yes, I will go at once, but please don't say anything more.

MRS. C. I shall not breathe a word of it not even to my daughter.

FLOR. Play peep-a-boo, Annie.

ANNIE. After tea, darling.

Bea. Come, Florence, we must go away from here. [*Florence runs to her. As they go up, enter Walter, Violet and Eligible R.U.E., meeting them*]

Fio. What, Mrs. Manheim is not going to leave us?

Walt. Beatrice going to leave us?

Vio. Beatrice, dear, where are you going?

Bea. Where, I know not! [*She faints and falls. Walter catches her. Florence bends over her*]

ACT IV.

Scene 1: *Same as Act II. Walter discovered seated at table R. Mrs. Colville, Fioretti, Dexter at table L. At rise, enter Violet R.U.E.*

Walt. How is Beatrice now?

Vio. Much better, although she is still hysterical.

Walt. May I see her?

Vio. Certainly, she is getting up. She is talking of leaving us. We must persuade her to remain.

Walt. You will remain with her.

Vio. It is not necessary. Your mother is with her. You must take her for a drive, Walter. [*Exit Walter R.2.E.*]

Mrs. C. I am so glad she is better, poor thing. A trip in the country will do her a great deal of good.

Fio. Yes, a trip in ze country will do her so much good!

Dex. Why, she ain't going away is she?

Mrs. C. No, but she has overtaxed herself. A little recreation would be so pleasant for her.

Fio. Yes, and how lucky it is for her, her vacation comes just at this time, so she can go to the country.

Dex. I shall have to follow her in my dogcart. [*Enter Mrs. Dalrymple and Florence R.2.E.*]

Mrs. C. How is she now?

Mrs. D. Much better. I am going to take her for a drive.

Dex. I wish I had arranged to offer her my dogcart. With her in my dogcart, I'd pass everything on the road, by Jupiter.

Mrs. C. We are going for a stroll.

Fio. Allow me to offer you my services, ladies.

Mrs. C. With pleasure. Won't you join us, Mr. Dexter?

Dex. No, thank you; I'm going to drive.

Vio. Beatrice is talking of leaving us. We must keep her here amongst friends. She will enjoy herself so much better than among strangers.

Mrs. C. Poor thing, she has overtaxed herself. A trip to the country would be such a benefit to her.

Fio. I agree with you, Madam, a trip in ze country will benefit her. [*Exit with Mrs. Colville and Violet C.D.*]

Dex. Mrs. Dalrymple, may I speak to you a moment?

Mrs. D. Certainly. Florence, dear, you may run out and play.

Flor. But you will come too, Auntie?

Mrs. D. Yes, dear. [*Exit Florence C.D.*]

Dex. Mrs. Dalrymple, the short acquaintance I have had with you will scarcely warrant the great favor I am going to ask of you.

Mrs. D. Tell me how I can be of any service to you.

Dex. Well, you see, since I left college, where I did not distinguish myself, I have had nothing to do to occupy my mind, but one thing.

Mrs. D. And what was that, pray?

Dex. I fell in love.

Mrs. D. You don't say!

Dex. Jolly, wasn't it?

Mrs. D. Have you been in love often?

Dex. Over a hundred times. I used to do nothing else but fall in love. I used to go all around to the different boarding houses and fall in love with everybody, and have no end of funny adventures, so at last I came here.

Mrs. D. I never observed anything particularly lovelorn or foolish in your conduct here. Surely, as you grow older you will outgrow this folly.

Dex. Bless you, the older I get, the more I do it. I am regularly in love. Head over heels in love this time. Odd, isn't it? Here we have been in the same house for over two months and no one knows who it is. Who do you think it is?

Mrs. D. I cannot guess. I never thought of you very particular in your attentions to anyone. I always thought you an unoffending, well-meaning young man.

Dex. I am glad you think well of me. I want everyone to think well of me now.

Mrs. D. Always conduct yourself uprightly in your own conscience, and the good opinions are—sure to follow.

Dex. Well, I don't mind letting you know. It's Mrs. Manheim.

Mrs. D. Mrs. Manheim! She is young, and a widow. She might be induced to marry again. Why don't you propose to her?

Dex. That's what I want to do. I can't know, I am so spooney, I can't open my mouth to say a word.

Mrs. D. Really, I can't see where I can be of any service to you.

DEX. Now, don't say you won't. I'll esteem it a great favor. Bless you, I can't say good morning to her without dropping my hat and cane. But, oh, I do love her! And she can't do better—No, I don't mean that; I mean—I mean, I have a house on Michigan Avenue, and a team that beats anything on the road. The house is a double front, with two bay windows, and I do love her to distraction.

MRS. D. Well, if you have a sincere affection for her, I see no reason why I should not communicate your wishes.

DEX. It will do no harm. Perhaps she likes me. She may be spooney on me. I hope she is. Tell her I love her and mean to be a father to her out and out.

MRS. D. I will speak to her. After that she is free to do as she thinks best.

DEX. See her tonight, if you can. I shan't sleep until after I have heard from her. [*Exit C.D. followed by Mrs. Dalrymple. As soon as off enter Walter and Beatrice R.2.E. Walter assists her to a chair*]

WALT. Dear Beatrice, why should we part? Why must you leave us?

BEA. Do not ask me, Walter. I have no explanation to offer. There is no appeal against fate. We must shake hands and part.

WALT. Beatrice, I have imagined I read in your eyes that I was not indifferent to you. Then if you care for me, if my peace and happiness are aught to you, remain here, happy in the love of my mother and myself, and be my wife.

BEA. Walter, my eyes told you truly you are not indifferent to me, and your peace and happiness are as dear to me as that of my own child, but I cannot be—we can never marry.

WALT. And why is it? Because of a promise made to your husband?

BEA. No, it is a regard for the living, not for the dead, which compels me to refuse. There is a bar between us. Do not seek to know it.

WALT. Beatrice, I do not fear to know your past life.

BEA. But *I* fear to have you know it. I have too much respect for your honor, and that of your noble mother, who has been such a dear kind friend to me, to allow anyone, much less myself, to bring a stain upon it.

WALT. Your love could be no stain, Beatrice. Do you think so meanly of me as to believe I could look down upon your profession?

BEA. No, I was not thinking of that. I have no false pride about me. I am proud to be able to earn my own bread. But it can never be. I must go from here, and at once.

WALT. Believe me, Beatrice, it is not alone my love that speaks. It is my good sense. It is my confidence in you. I can never be happy but with you. Where you go, I will go. I can believe no more of your past.

BEA. You say this out of the generosity of your noble heart, but I cannot allow the warmth of your love to ensnare you into a marriage with one who, if the truth were known, you would loath and despise. I cannot see lowered with shame the gray hairs of her whom you so nobly love; your mother.

WALT. My mother thinks and believes but in me; she knows your sensitive and delicate nature too well to believe ill of you.

BEA. But there are those who would tell her—who—

WALT. You mean Mr. Joseph Fioretti?

BEA. Alas! Base, black-hearted man as he is, yes!

WALT. Mr. Fioretti will never say anything against my wife.

BEA. But the world will. Society will close its doors against us.

WALT. [*Embracing her*] My wife shall be my world, my society.

BEA. Oh, Walter, this is noble! If a life of devotion can repay you for the generous sacrifice—

WALT. You will be my wife?

BEA. [*Disengaging herself*] Oh, not so fast! I must see your mother and ask her consent.

WALT. Which I am sure she will give. Let us go together.

BEA. No, I must go alone. I go to reveal to her the story of my past life.

WALT. And if she consents?

BEA. Then, Walter, we will be man and wife. [*Exit R.2.E.*]

WALT. Poor girl, how she has suffered! It shall be my task to make up for all the misery of her past life. [*Exit L.U. Enter Colonel Elevator C.D.*]

COL. The time has come, Colonel. Control your feelings. The accomplished widow is about to leave us. I must propose to her at once. Now if she only sees this thing in the right light, I'll try a thirty days' call on her, stand a cent and a half raise, and make her Mrs. Colonel M. T. Elevator, slickery than a slippery alum bark down a boy's throat. Make no mistake. Here she comes. [*Strikes attitude. Enter Beatrice R.2.E.*]

BEA. It is strange I cannot find her. She promised to meet me here. Colonel Elevator, have you seen Mrs. Dalrymple?

COL. She is in the garden, but pause—pause—I beseech you, listen. They say you are about to leave our boarding house. What is it without you? I say, what is it? Slicker than a setting he— No, I mean you are our pride and star, our pearl without price, you shine like a fresh water mackerel—[*She starts to go*] Listen! Listen to me, who is up to all the tricks of the market like a jersey eel, you bet your boots!

BEA. [*Indignantly*] Colonel Elevator!

COL. Listen to one who adores you—to me.

BEA. Colonel Elevator, did you say you had seen Mrs. Dalrymple?

Col. She is in the garden. [*Aside*] She won't have it. [*To her*] Yet, pause, oh, tarry a little bit. Listen to one who is preparing at this moment to—[*She gives him a look*] Go right out. [*Exit R.2.E. Enter Mrs. Dalrymple and Florence C.D.*]

Bea. Oh, Mrs. Dalrymple, I have been looking for you!

Mrs. D. And I for you. I desire a few moments' conversation with you.

Bea. Florence, please run out and play with your ball. [*Exit Florence C.D. They sit C.*]

Mrs. D. It is touching. A proposal of marriage.

Bea. Then he has told you all?

Mrs. D. You know who it is?

Bea. Yes.

Mrs. D. And you love him?

Bea. Yes.

Mrs. D. Then I cannot see why it shouldn't be considered favorably.

Bea. He must first know my past life.

Mrs. D. Surely there has been nothing concealed?

Bea. It is my wish there should be nothing concealed. I will tell it all to you and you must judge between us.

Mrs. D. Go on.

Bea. My name is Beatrice Manheim.

Mrs. D. I know, Mrs. Beatrice Manheim.

Bea. *Miss* Beatrice Manheim.

Mrs. D. I cannot understand you! Then your—?

Bea. We were never married.

Mrs. D. Oh, Beatrice, I never dreamed of this! You have surprised and wounded me!

Bea. [*Rises*] I knew I should. I was fearful that I would offend you and that you would decide against me. Farewell on my last fond hope of happiness.

Mrs. D. Stay, Beatrice. I cannot believe so ill of you. You must have loved the father of your child dearly—

Bea. I did not love him.

Mrs. D. Did not love him?

Bea. No, I grew to hate him.

Mrs. D. Then there was deceit? Your face, your tone. Come, sit by me and tell me all. [*They sit*]

Bea. I am a German girl by birth. My parents were poor. They taught me music. When I was fifteen years old a lady took me to her house. There I was treated with respect by everyone in the family. I acquired a good education. When I had lived with her two years my benefactor died and I returned to my old life of drudgery. Some time after, a man whom I had met in society as an equal made a proposition of marriage to me. My life at home had never been a happy one, and in order to better my condition I accepted. We were married and lived together two years. My husband soon became cold, insolent, and cruel. Soon after our child was born he informed me that the ceremony had been performed by his own brother, who was neither a magistrate nor a clergyman. Hence the marriage was illegal. I begged and pleaded for the sake of our child to have a proper ceremony performed. But he was obdurate. His name was Fioretti.

Mrs. D. Not the man who is in this house?

Bea. No, his name was William Fioretti. He is now dead, but the man who drove me from my home, the man who denied me the rights and the name of wife, who even threatened to take my child from me, her mother, was Joseph Fioretti, who performed the mock ceremony.

Mrs. D. Beatrice, you are a deeply injured woman. Society, it is true, has false convictions, and does not discriminate. Henceforth my house shall be your home. You shall be to us a daughter.

Bea. And you give your consent to our union?

Mrs. D. With all my heart. Here he comes. Leave us alone until I have spoken to him. [Exit Beatrice R.2.E. Enter Walter L.2.E., and Dexter, C.D.]

Mrs. D. Walter, my son, will you leave us alone for a few moments? I have some communication to make to Mr. Dexter.

Walt. Certainly, Mother.

Dex. Yes, Walter, it is about Beatrice. You would not help a fellow, you know, so I went to your mother and she has been such a good kind friend to a fellow that I can never repay her. And if my photograph would be an object, I'll have an impression taken in my new spring suit, I will, by Jerusalem!

Walt. Mother, is this true?

Mrs. D. It is, my son. They both love each other dearly.

Dex. By jove, I knew it! I felt it in my boots. I am so happy! Do you hear, Walter? Congratulate a fellow, can't you?

Walt. Again, I ask is this true?

Mrs. D. It is, Walter. But there are private circumstances which this gentleman must hear alone.

Walt. Certainly, Mother. [Exit L.3.E.]

Mrs. D. I am going to tell you Beatrice's past life.

Dex. Oh, darn it! Don't. I don't want to hear anything about her past life.

Mrs. D. But it is necessary you should hear it. Her child has no father.

Dex. I know that, I'm to be its father, you know!

Mrs. D. I mean she never had a father.

Dex. Oh, come, now. She must have had a father!

Mrs. D. I mean that Beatrice was never married.

Dex. Oh, Lord! Oh, Lord! What have I done? Of course, a fellow must be allowed to withdraw.

Mrs. D. But she was deceived, betrayed by a mock marriage!

Dex. Oh, yes, that's bad, very bad! But the fellows at the club will give me no end of guy. I'll have to leave town!

Mrs. D. Then marry her, and take her with you.

Dex. I am very sorry, you know. But then, I can't, I really can't.

Mrs. D. You do not know her. She has told me her story, and I must say that she is one of the best and purest women I have ever known.

Dex. I am very sorry, and all that, you know. I think a great deal of her. I'm awfully out about it, and if I should be found in the lake, you will not tell what it is for.

Mrs. D. [Turning on him] She is too good for you!

Dex. Oh, yes, that's it. She is too good for me!

Mrs. D. What she could see in you to win a heart like hers, I don't see.

Dex. It was the team. None of them can withstand the team.

Mrs. D. Believing you to be an honest and upright man, I have told you her secret, her secret, mind you. And if you dare to trifle with it I have a son who—

Dex. Oh, no, never, upon my honor, never thought of such a thing! I think a good deal of her yet. [Enter Walter. When Dexter sees him he exits C.D. Enter Beatrice R.3.E.]

Mrs. D. Beatrice, I have seen him. Think no more of him, he is unworthy of your love.

Bea. He has retracted his promise?

Mrs. D. Yes.

Bea. Alas! I feared it would be. I have no hope of happiness left. Good-bye, dear friend, good-bye!

Mrs. D. Stay, Beatrice, you shall come and live with us. Our home shall be yours.

Walt. Mother, there seems to be some terrible mistake here. Whose suit is it you have just withdrawn?

Mrs. D. Mr. Dexter's.

Bea. Mr. Dexter's!

WALT. I knew there was a mistake. Mother! Beatrice came to you to ask consent to *our* marriage, and the man who loves her truly and dearly. [*Crosses to Beatrice*]

MRS. D. [*Weeping*] My son! my son!

WALT. Mother, you will not refuse your consent! I know your heart, your high and sensitive nature which shudders at the thought of calumny, but you have heard her story. You know her true good heart, that has borne her up through all these trials. You said your home should be hers.

MRS. D. My son! my son!

WALT. I tell you, Mother, I shall marry Beatrice whether you give your consent or not.

BEA. No, Walter, we must part! Your mother refuses her consent. I cannot part mother and son.

WALT. Do you hear, Mother? Do you love us?

MRS. D. [*Going to him and embracing*] Walter, did you ever doubt my love?

WALT. Never, Mother, never!

MRS. D. Take him, Beatrice. [*Putting their hands together*] Love him always, for my sake.

CLOSE IN

SCENE 2: *Street in front of boarding-house. Enter Eligible, Violet, Colonel Elevator and Annie, Dr. Shouter and Mrs. Colville R. Professor Gillypod following, carrying camp chair.*

VIO. It's a lovely evening.

COL. So it is, soft and clear. Soft as a mellow peach, make no mistake.

ANNIE. The sunset on the lake was lovely.

EVERYBODY. So it was.

ANNIE. The gorgeous clouds piled in large masses of gold and silver.

COL. Chaotic masses.

EVERYBODY. Yes, yes.

ANNIE. The fairy-like refulgence of the glimmering shew—

COL. The glimmering shew.

VIO. What is a glimmering shew?

COL. What is a glimmering shew?

ANNIE. Oh, it's, you know, the last rays of dying sun kissing each laughing ripple.

MRS. C. And goodness gracious me, the smell—

ANNIE. Oh, it was lovely!

Col. What? The smell? No, I don't mean that. It's equal to Saratoga.

Vio. Better than Long Branch.

Dr. S. Finest in the world, best markets.

Prof. For horns.

Everybody. For what?

Prof. For horns! Every man, woman and child who has the good fortune to make this paradise his home, must begin early and practise late, blowing his horn. [*Sound of horn*]

Elig. Whew! There comes a breeze. We are going to have a storm. Let's go in. I'm for a game of whist. Who's with me?

Everybody. I am! [*Exit all but Professor Gillypod in house*]

Prof. I'll stay and finish my cigar. [*Sits on camp stool. Enter boy with fiddle*]

Boy. Music! [*Enter Betty with broom, and drives him off*]

Betty. Here, you, get out of this!

Prof. Betty, let the festive youth spiel.

Betty. It's not a festive youth. He's a stolen slave.

Prof. A stolen what, Betty?

Betty. A stolen slave—stolen from his home and sold for nothing. He has a master who beats him with a big whip. I shouldn't wonder if he was that fellow around the corner with that harp.

Prof. If he comes this way, I'll ask him.

Betty. Don't Mr. Gillypod, don't. He's got a big knife. They all have knives.

Prof. And we've got a big-sized boot.

Betty. And I've got a big-sized broom and if he comes around here with his tawny—tawny—I'll show him! [*Exit L.*]

Prof. It looks as though we win. Well, Dalrymple is a perfect gentleman. Lent me that little amount in the most gentlemanly manner. And Mrs. Manheim. Oh, if I had only got my airship done in time, it might have been the saddest words of tongue or pen. I wish it were. I bet pretty girls don't wait for balloon ships. That Fioretti is a real rascal—sneers whenever Beatrice's name is mentioned. When I take my first trip across the lake I'll write him to come, and when I want to lighten the ballast, I'll pitch him overboard. [*Sound of wind*] Whew! I guess we are going to have a storm. In the words of the immortal Tom Hood, "Who comes here." [*Enter Jack Hardy with harp, disguised, R.*]

Jack. Mein herr, ze icle moosic spelia.

Prof. Italian.

JACK. Mein Ich by sweitzer zal—icle seven esenger spieler de watch on de Rhein.

PROF. I cannot say that I perfectly agree with you, mixey sarvey.

JACK. Shall I play you some little music on my harp, mein lieber Herr Gillypod?

PROF. Oh, you know me!

JACK. Yes. [*Whispers in his ear*]

PROF. Goodness gracious! You don't say so! [*Enter Betty with broom*]

BETTY. Here, you get out of this!

PROF. Stop, Betty! This man wants to see Mrs. Colville.

BETTY. My missus won't see him.

PROF. Betty, a word in your ear. [*Whispers*]

BETTY. What, now?

JACK. Yes, now! [*Exit L. All exit L.*]

CLOSE IN

SCENE 3: *Same as Scene 1. Beatrice at R. table, Florence in front of her, Violet, Matthew and Annie at table L. Mrs. Colville R. of R. table. Mrs. Dalrymple and Dexter up C.*

DEX. Mrs. Dalrymple, I've been at home and nothing seems to go right. I tried on my new spring suit, and it don't seem to set right. I can't even drive my horses, so I've come back to say I've changed my mind.

MRS. D. Mr. Dexter, there was quite a mistake in my communication to you. You were not the person for whom it was intended.

DEX. What! Then she don't love me?

MRS. D. No!

DEX. And she loves another?

MRS. D. Yes.

DEX. And does he know?

MRS. D. He knows everything.

DEX. [*Crosses to L. corner*] Oh, what an ass I've been! A broken heart beats beneath this new coat. All the world is blottened. [*Professor Gillypod and Colonel Elevator enter C.D.*]

MRS. D. Friends, I am proud to announce to you the marriage of my son and Mrs. Manheim. [*Colonel Elevator faints in Professor Gillypod's arms*]

VIO. I'm so happy.

ELIG. Walter, my dear boy, I congratulate you!

FIO. Stay, madam! Is your son acquainted with the past life of Madam Manheim?

MRS. D. Yes, sir, he is.

FIO. But there are those here who are not.

WALT. Be careful, sir. This lady is my affianced wife!

FIO. Her name is not Mrs. Manheim, she is Miss Anybody. She was never married. Her child is—

WALT. Villain, stop where you are or I shall choke the words down your throat! [*Walter and Fioretti start for each other, but are held by other gentlemen*]

EVERYBODY. Gentlemen! Gentlemen!

FIO. We are prevented, but we shall meet again.

WALT. As you please, sir! [*Enter Betty C.D.*]

BETTY. Please, m'am, there is a gentleman at the door who wants to see you. [*Professor Gillypod takes a camp stool and sits D.R.*]

MRS. C. If it's about board, tell him—[*Enter Jack Hardy*]

JACK. No, ma'am, it's not about board. My name is Hardy. Jack Hardy, a detective from New York. I've spied this house for a party. Now, don't say she isn't here, for I know she is. I'm looking for a party going by the name of Mrs. Beatrice Manheim.

WALT. The lady is here, sir.

JACK. Glad to know you, ma'am. Knowed you were here. Can I speak to you for a moment?

WALT. Certainly, speak out! This lady is my affianced wife. I desire all to know your purport.

JACK. Oh, it's no trouble, sir. Oh, no! If there had been any, I wouldn't have given myself away as a detective from New York. Party going by the name of Mrs. Beatrice Manheim, I am commissioned by the surrogate of New York to inform you that passing on the effects and estate of the late William Fioretti, your—

BEA. The father of my child.

JACK. That's it, ma'am. He finds the marriage all right and regular and that you are entitled to right of name, right of dowry, your child coming in for the residue.

FIO. But she was never married! The ceremony—

JACK. Not just the right thing, eh? You're right. He's right, ma'am. He's right, ladies and gentlemen. She was deceived by a mock marriage.

EVERYBODY. A sham marriage!

JACK. But in the State of New York, when a party lives together and calls her wife—bless you these two lived together for two years as man and wife. In the eyes of the law she is his wife, and the children are legitimate.

BEA. [*Kisses Florence*] Thank Heaven!

JACK. And furthermore, if the man dies without a will, the woman is entitled to right of name, to right of dowry and the children, if there be any, come in for the residue. And so I tell you, Mrs. William Fioretti is going by the name of Manheim; and so I tell you all, ladies and gents.

PROF. Very good story and very well told.

FIO. But ze will must be contest by law. I tell you the marriage was illegal. I was a witness to ze mockery. Ze certificate was signed by a false name.

JACK. And who are you?

FIO. Guiseppe Fioretti, brother to William and sole heir to ze estate.

JACK. Well, I'm in luck. Fioretti, my boy, we have been piping the Grand Pacific for you. [*Takes out paper*] Here I have a requisition from the governor of New York for you, or the possession of your body. Crime: participating in a sham marriage. So, Fioretti, is it to be the gentlemanly thing, or shall we wear these? [*Shows handcuffs*]

FIO. You damn scoundrel, you dare touch me! [*He starts. Jack Hardy draws pistol. Fioretti backs up stage, Jack Hardy after him*]

JACK. Take care, my boy, or I shall have to pop you! I beg pardon, ladies and gents, but business is business!

COL. Make no mistake.

PROF. There goes my ballast.

CURTAIN

America's Lost Plays

Lightning Source UK Ltd.
Milton Keynes UK
UKHW041834131019
351534UK00001B/119/P